A GUIDE TO

THE WORLD'S GREATEST BUILDINGS

Masterpieces of Architecture & Engineering

A GUIDE TO
THE WORLD'S GREATEST BUILDINGS

Masterpieces of Architecture & Engineering

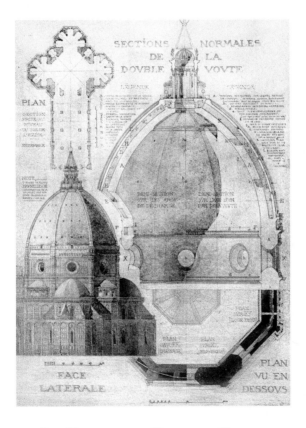

HENRY J. COWAN, RUTH GREENSTEIN,
BRONWYN HANNA, JOHN HASKELL,
TREVOR HOWELLS, DEBORAH MALOR, JOHN PHILLIPS,
THOMAS A. RANIERI, MARK STILES,
BRONWYN SWEENEY

CONSULTANT EDITOR
TREVOR HOWELLS

FOG CITY PRESS

Published by Fog City Press
814 Montgomery Street
San Francisco, CA 94133 USA

Copyright 1996 ' US Weldon Owen Inc.
Copyright 1996 ' Weldon Owen Pty Limited
Revised edition 2007

GROUP CHIEF EXECUTIVE OFFICER John Owen
CHIEF EXECUTIVE OFFICER Terry Newell
PUBLISHER Sheena Coupe
CREATIVE DIRECTOR Sue Burk
PRODUCTION DIRECTOR Chris Hemesath
SALES MANAGER Emily Jahn
VICE PRESIDENT INTERNATIONAL SALES Stuart Laurence
ADMINISTRATOR INTERNATIONAL SALES Kristine Ravn

PROJECT EDITORS Janet Healey
DESIGNERS: Clare Forte, Hilda Mendham
JACKET DESIGN Kelly Booth
PICTURE RESEARCH Joanna Collard

ISBN: 978-1-877019-45-6

Printed by Kyodo Nation Printing Services Co., Ltd.
Printed in Thailand

A Weldon Owen Production

Light, God's eldest daughter, is a principal beauty in a building.

The Holy State and the Profane State: Of Building
THOMAS FULLER (1608-1661), English cleric and writer

CONTENTS

F O R E W O R D

Of all the arts, none is more fundamental to the way we live than architecture. It is a mirror of our own time and of times gone by, a diary written in mud and timber, in brick and stone, in iron and steel, in concrete and glass. Our homes, our public buildings, and our cities reflect what we are, what we once were—and what we hope to become. Winston Churchill acknowledged their power when he reminded us that we shape our buildings and then they shape us.

Great buildings and structures are much more than powerful works of architecture and engineering: They capture the *Zeitgeist*—the spirit of their time. The unchanging structure of the Egypt of the pharoahs is present in the timeless simplicity of the pyramids; the exuberant energy of the Jazz Age erupts from the shimmering pinnacle of the Chrysler Building.

Who can gaze at the Parthenon as it watches over Athens, golden in the light of the rising sun or silver in the moonlight, and not be awed by the genius of the ancient Greeks for proportion? Who does not marvel at the patient hands that year by year refashion the sculptured surface of the Djenné Mosque? Who can imagine the Bear Run waterfall without Lloyd Wright's Fallingwater floating above it? Who can glimpse Sydney's Opera House from harbor or foreshore and not be dazzled by those seemingly weightless roofs billowing like immense sails?

You do not need to be an architect to experience the creative genius of a building. This book describes for the nonspecialist a hundred of the world's greatest structures and the technological advances in construction methods and materials that made them possible, in the context of the lives and times of those who built them.

TREVOR HOWELLS
Consultant Editor

A Synthesis of Form and Function

Buildings are where we live and work and spend much of our leisure time; of all the arts, it is architecture that forms the closest bond between us and our environment.

THE WAY THEY LIVED THEN
An artist's impression of a typical dwelling house in the ancient Bronze Age city of Çatalhöyük in Anatolia (modern-day Turkey).

Architecture began as a response to the need to seek shelter from the elements and from wild beasts. The earliest shelters were not buildings but caves—but even here the occupants claimed their territory: 40,000 years ago the Australian Aborigines decorated the interiors of their cave-dwellings with the oldest known expressions of art, and over 20,000 years later the people of Lascaux in present-day France ornamented their cave walls with amazingly sophisticated representations of their environment. Building techniques emerged many years later still, as a nomadic hunter–gatherer lifestyle gave way to a settled way of life based on agriculture.

MAKING THE MOST OF THINGS

Until as recently as 1850, structural methods were essentially determined by the limits of building technology,

THE MYSTERIES OF POWER *Huge statues of the pharoah Ramesses II in Abu Simbel repelled invaders (above right). The Druidic monoliths of Stonehenge still defy interpretation (right).*

the availability of materials, and regional conditions. In forested areas builders used timber; in rocky landscapes they used stone. Sometimes early builders cut directly into the solid rock of cliff faces, as in the 13th century BC temple of Ramesses at Abu Simbel in Egypt and the 1st century AD treasury at Petra in Jordan. In places where there was neither timber nor rock, human ingenuity devised mud brick—molded blocks of sun-baked earth, the oldest manufactured building material that is still widely used today. The roofs of Çatalhöyük, a Bronze Age settlement in Turkey from about 7000 BC, are of mud brick, as is the core of the Ziggurat at Ur (c. 2000 BC). And in our times the Great Mosque at Djenné in West Africa is the world's largest mud brick building.

TWO BASIC TECHNIQUES

Post-and-beam, the earliest structural method, is still

widely used today. A horizontal beam carries the weight of the floor above it and is supported by vertical posts. The Palace at Knossos (16th century BC) has masonry walls serving as posts, and timber beams; about 3,000 years later, China's Forbidden City, Japan's Castle of the White Heron, and Shakespeare's Globe Theatre in London employed timber posts and beams. Where permanence was important, early builders preferred stone. The elements could be rough-hewn and unornamented, like those of Stonehenge (c. 2700 BC), or perfectly proportioned and exquisitely carved, like those of the Parthenon, built over 2,000 years later.

But stone beams could not provide large spans between supports, which severely limited the enclosure of space, so the second important structural innovation was the arch, which can span considerable distances. Tapered blocks of stone, called voussoirs, are supported on a timber framework until the keystone is dropped into the crown of the arch. The keystone locks the structure into place and the formwork can be removed. In the 1st century BC and the 1st century AD the Romans used this technique to build the Pons Fabricius and the ceremonial Arch of Titus in Rome, and the aqueduct in France now known as the Pont du Gard.

Elaborations of the arch such as the vault (an extended arch) and the dome (an arch revolved) developed with the Roman invention of concrete at the height of the Roman Empire in the 1st and 2nd centuries AD. Clad in marble or other stone, concrete formed the structural core of buildings such the Colosseum; or it could be left exposed, as in the dome of the Pantheon.

After the fall of the Roman Empire the secret of concrete was lost and vaults were built with brick. In the 6th century, Byzantine architects extended the possibilities of dome construction with the invention of the pendentive—a triangular piece of masonry joining a four-piered square base to a circular dome. This brilliant innovation, which allowed greater freedom of plan and space, found its greatest expression in the church of Hagia Sophia in Istanbul. The exteriors of most Byzantine churches were quite plain, but the interiors glittered with gilt mosaics and colored marbles.

Early medieval buildings such as Krak des Chevaliers in Syria and the Tower of London, both built in the 11th century, were military in character with thick masonry walls pierced by small, defensible openings. Similar features characterize the walls and ceilings of Romanesque churches such as the 12th century cathedral of Santiago de Compostela in Spain.

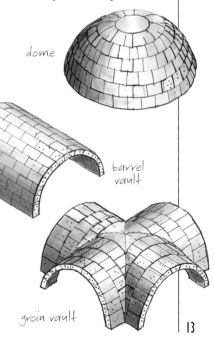

dome

barrel vault

groin vault

FLYING BUTTRESSES AND STAINED GLASS

The next structural break-through occurred in the French Gothic architecture of the 13th century with the development of the ribbed vault—a system of intersecting masonry vaults strengthened with projecting ribs (or arches). The masonry structure functioned as a stone skeleton and the pointed arch became the *Leitmotiv* of the Gothic style. The upper walls of the nave—which were ponderously heavy in Romanesque churches—could be almost entirely replaced by stained glass windows. What made this possible was the invention of the flying buttress, a free-standing flying arch springing from a buttressed pier to support the top of the external nave walls. The superlative 13th century cathedral of Chartres in France represents a perfect synthesis of all of the elements of Gothic architecture.

RENAISSANCE TO BAROQUE
The vast interior of St. Peter's Basilica (above) and the Baroque splendor of the Residenz at Würzburg (right).

HARMONY AND PROPORTION

The architects of the Italian Renaissance were more interested in geometric harmony than in structural innovation. Domes became important again; in the 15th century dome of Florence cathedral, Brunelleschi combined Roman construction techniques with Gothic ribbed vaulting. In the 16th century Andrea Palladio transformed Renaissance architecture when he crowned the Villa Capra at Vicenza with a central dome—the first use of a dome for a secular purpose since Roman times. Later Italian Renaissance architects borrowed from classical Roman architecture to rival the grandeur of imperial Rome: St. Peter's Basilica in Rome enclosed the most impressive spaces since the Roman basilicas and baths. Complementing these interior spaces were open squares like Michelangelo's magnificent Piazza del Campidoglio, usually featuring complex geometrical designs.

THE SPLENDOR OF THE BAROQUE

In the 17th and early 18th centuries the Counter-Reformation—the response of the Catholic Church to the Protestant Reformation of the 16th century—spawned the Baroque, a new style of religious architecture that broke many of the established rules. Sinuous, dynamic lines suggesting power and movement, like those Bernini employed in the sweeping colonnades of the Piazza di San Pietro that fronts St. Peter's Basilica

Gothic window traceries

introduced a new order in which axial arrangements and the manipulation of illusion, scale, and space overwhelmed human emotions. Inside these buildings, colored marbles, lapis lazuli, bronze, and gold extolled the glory of God and reasserted the prestige and authority of the Church.

In some countries, even the magnificence of the new Rome was surpassed: The Abbey of Melk and the Residenz at Würzburg display a perfect marriage of opulent painting, sculpture, and architecture. The Château de Versailles, built by France's "Sun King," Louis XIV, adapted the style to reflect his concept of divine kingship. Bernini's legacy extended even to Protestant England in the elegant sweep of Georgian townhouses that graces Bath's Royal Crescent.

THE NEW CLASSICISM

In the late 18th and early 19th centuries the inevitable revolt against the excesses of the Baroque gave birth to Neo-classicism—a return to the pure sources of antiquity. Thomas Jefferson's white-painted stucco and red brick University of Virginia drew on the architectural style of Republican Rome and the Italian Renaissance to create an architecture that would be fit for the new American republic. Washington's Capitol, surmounted by a baroque dome based on that of St. Peter's Basilica, is Imperial Roman in scale.

THE AGE OF IRON AND STEEL

The Industrial Revolution, which began in England in the late 18th century, transformed structural methods with the discovery of cost-effective technologies for manufacturing iron and steel—and, equally importantly, of transporting them over long distances. The first major cast iron structure in the world, the Iron Bridge at Coalbrookdale in England, was built in the form of a traditional masonry arch, like the Rialto Bridge in Venice—but it was constructed of cast iron. The 19th century saw the potential of iron and steel: The Forth Bridge achieved huge spans with horizontal steel trusses; the Eiffel Tower and the Statue of Liberty reached for the sky on vertical

The art of building, or architecture, is the beginning of all the arts that lie outside the person; and in the end they unite.

The Dance of Life,
HAVELOCK ELLIS (1859–1939),
English physician and writer

TRIUMPHS OF TECHNOLOGY
The Forth Bridge in Scotland was built of steel to withstand the elements (above). At about the same time New York's iron-framed and copper-clad Statue of Liberty was erected (below).

trusses. The exceptional tensile strength of steel supports New York's Brooklyn Bridge and San Francisco's Golden Gate Bridge, and more recently, the roof of the Olympic Stadium in Munich.

NINETEENTH CENTURY ECLECTICISM

While 19th century engineers were pioneering structural innovations, architects were arguing over the use of historical styles. The "battle of the styles" was a contest between classicists and medievalists. Some architects championed one or the other, but most designed in both, as well as dabbling in other exotic styles. Nowhere was the conflict better illustrated than in London's Palace of Westminster, the seat of British government and the most celebrated monument of the Gothic Revival. It was an immensely influential building in which the leading classical architect of the day, Charles Barry, collaborated with

A. W. N. Pugin, the foremost medievalist. In Bavaria a vision of the age of chivalry reached sublime heights with the castle of King Ludwig II, Neuschwanstein. In the United States of America the newly rich commissioned mansions such as Biltmore House, a glorious concoction designed in the style of a 15th century French château but full of the most up-to-date conveniences. When functional needs and new technologies embraced the cult of the Gothic, delightful if a little absurd results were possible, as in London's quasi-medieval Tower Bridge.

The classical tradition was equally versatile. Richly overlaid with ornamentation, it could be theatrically dressed up to suit Garnier's Opera House in Paris, or the grandeur of the Roman Baths could be recreated in New York's Grand Central Station. Even an eclectic mix of styles—Hindoo, Mughal, Chinese, Neoclassical—could be made coherent, as John Nash managed to do in the Royal Pavilion at Brighton.

HARKING BACK TO THE PAST

Neuschwanstein nostalgically evoked the age of chivalry (above), and Britain's Palace of Westminster restated the identity of the medieval past (left).

In the late 19th century the movement called Art Nouveau emerged. A combination of sinuous and curving lines suggesting plant forms, all rendered in exquisite handcraft, the style has left such architectural icons as Horta's van Eetvelde House in Brussels and the Church of La Sagrada Familia in Barcelona, where Antoni Gaudí's genius fused Gothic, Art Nouveau, and Catalan themes into a harmonious whole.

ARCHITECTURE IN THE 20TH CENTURY

The great engineering achievements of the 19th century had little impact on architectural styles until the 20th century. But after World War I avant-garde thinkers rejected the traditions of the past and architects abandoned historically based styles—so much so that ornamentation became an esthetic crime! A new functional architecture emerged, composed of pure, geometric volumes and planar surfaces. Among the innovations were the employment of cantilevered steel-reinforced concrete, lyrically exploited by Frank Lloyd Wright at Fallingwater, and walls of glass, as in Ludwig Mies van der Rohe's ground-breaking Farnsworth House.

reinforced concrete

SCULPTURES IN CONCRETE

Architecture took on sculptural dimensions with Notre Dame du Haut (above), the Sydney Opera House (below), and Bilbao's Guggenheim Museum (right).

The skyscraper—that quintessentially American invention of the 1880s—was surprisingly slow to embrace European modernism. New York's Flatiron Building had a modern steel frame but was dressed in classically detailed stone. Chicago's Tribune Tower was ultra-modern in everything except its Gothic exterior. New York's inter-war Art Deco skyscrapers, the Chrysler Building and the Empire State Building, were clad in a zigzag geometry of stone. After World War II glass curtain-walling replaced stone cladding: I. M. Pei's pyramids at the Louvre in Paris form one of the 20th century's most eloquent uses of the glass curtain wall.

Toward the end of the 20th century, architects daringly experimented with exposing the structure and mechanical services of buildings, as in the Pompidou Center in Paris and the Hong Kong and Shanghai Bank, or simply kept building taller and taller, as in Kuala Lumpur's Petronas Towers and Taiwan's Taipei 101.

SCULPTURAL BUILDING

Concrete offered exciting new sculptural possibilities for architecture. Pre-cast elements were exploited to great effect in Moshe Safdie's Habitat buildings. In the 1950s Le Corbusier's Chapel of Notre Dame du Haut, Frank Lloyd Wright's spiraling Solomon Guggenheim Museum, and Jørn Utzon's Sydney Opera House relied on the unique plasticity of concrete. By the beginning of the 21st century the lyricism of sculptural architecture captured the human imagination more strongly than the triumphs of engineering and technology: Frank O. Gehry's metal-clad Guggenheim Museum in Bilbao has drawn the attention of the world as no building has done since the Sydney Opera House.

Chapter One
Places of Worship

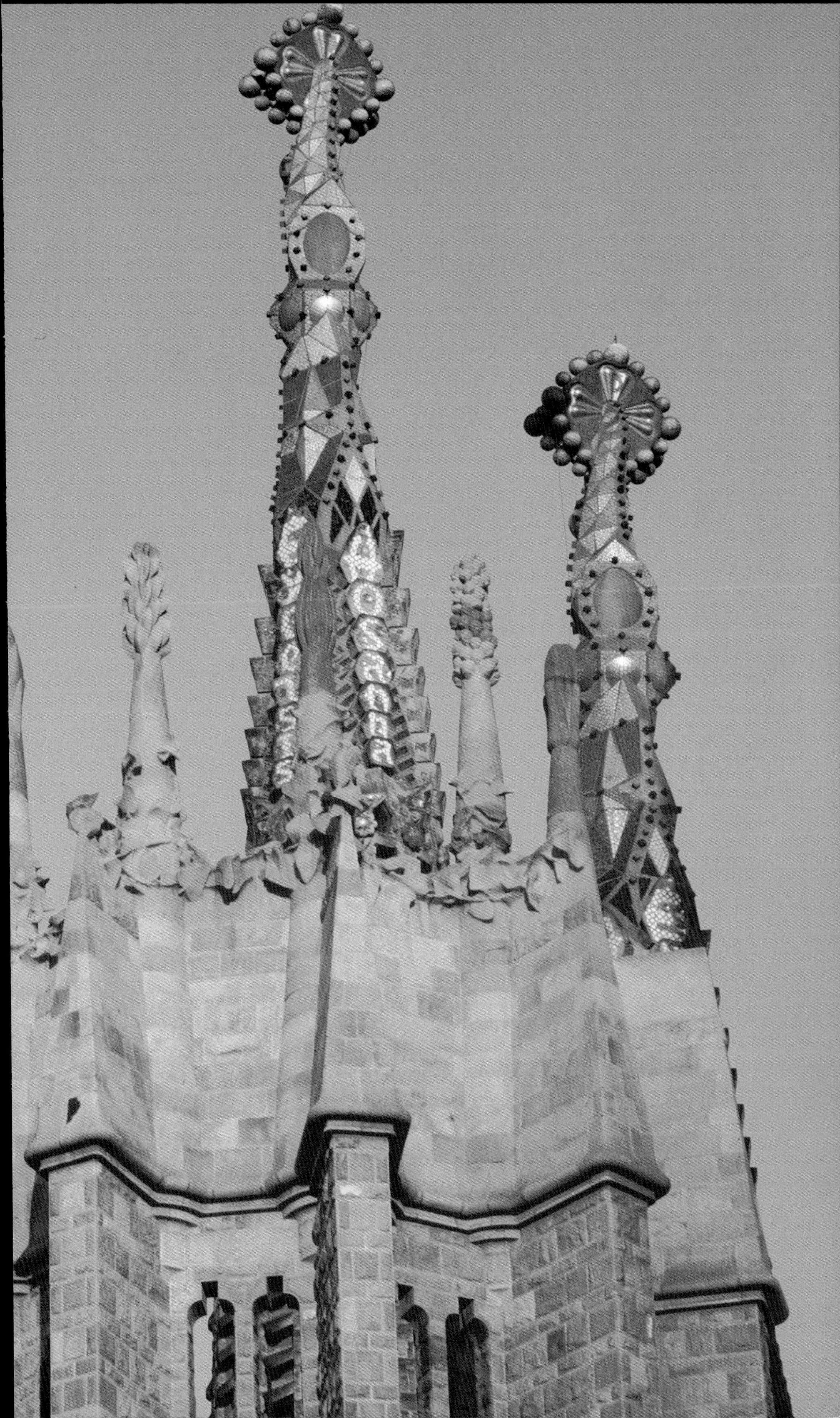

PLACES OF WORSHIP

Central to the spiritual life of every culture

throughout history, places of worship have also

provided some of the world's most sublime architecture.

Places of worship have been an integral part of human life for thousands of years. They exist not only for the gathering of a community to honor its ancestors, but—more importantly—to tell the story of a people and to enable them to approach the spiritual forces that they believe shape their destinies.

Lewis Mumford, the great 20th century American historian of cities, believed that "the city of the dead" came about before "the city of the living." According to Mumford's theory, the primitive nomadic peoples of the remote past ritualized the burials of their dead and returned from time to time to the graves of their ancestors. Eventually these sacred sites attracted more permanent settlements, and the conjunction of the living and the dead was crucial in defining the status and significance of a community.

In today's generally secular society, the role of religion is often limited to merely ritual observances, and most welfare functions are now the responsibility of the state, but this is a fairly new phenomenon, at least in the developed world. Before the comparatively recent separation of church and state, most societies perceived the world as a sacred realm that was subject to divine law and capable of

ABIDING INFLUENCES *For centuries, architects have been inspired by ancient Greek and Roman temples, such as the Parthenon (above) and Pantheon (right). Their harmonious proportions and pleasing esthetics have provided the model for many other famous buildings, both religious and secular.*

a response to prayer and petition. Consequently, it was religious institutions that shouldered much of society's welfare burden; they cared for the sick, the poor, and the destitute, and provided such education as was available.

DIFFERENT WAYS OF WORSHIP

The buildings chosen here to illustrate this theme show the diversity of approaches to the act of worship. In medieval European cathedrals like those of Chartres and Salisbury, great congregations gathered to affirm their shared belief, and sculpture and stained glass

functioned as the poor person's Bible, instructing the faithful. Eastern temples such as the Buddhist temple at Borobudur in Java, no less magnificent than their counterparts in the West, symbolized a more individual quest—the solitary path to enlightenment.

For Christian pilgrims the arduous and hazardous journey on foot from departure points all over western Europe to the reliquary of St. James the Apostle, in the Spanish city of Santiago de Compostela, was a microcosm of life's pilgrimage. The same sense of spiritual

TO THE GLORY OF GOD *Religion inspired great architectural feats such as the massive dome of Hagia Sophia (left) and magnificent medieval European churches like Salisbury Cathedral (below).*

pilgrimage applies to inspiring modern shrines such as Notre Dame du Haut in Ronchamp, built since World War II. The church of La Sagrada Familia in Barcelona was conceived as an expiatory temple, seeking atonement for the sins of the community. This is another form of religious obligation or penance, as with the pilgrim's journey, aspiring to reach the objective of a higher spiritual awareness. The Benedictine Abbey at Melk, however, clearly proclaims the temporal glory of the Church.

EXPRESSIONS OF FAITH

Every four years ancient Athens celebrated its great cult festival, its pilgrims treading the 15-mile (24-km) "Holy Road" from Eleusis, on the Saronic Gulf (taking part in the mystery rites that all true Athenians participated in) to the Parthenon, on the summit of the Acropolis. This scene is depicted in marble on the frieze that forms part of the Elgin Marbles in the British Museum. On the other hand, we know little of the form of worship that took place in the Pantheon in Rome; worship for the ancient Romans was a civic obligation, not a private meditation, and apart from the standard observances it is unlikely that the ordinary

worshiper would have had much involvement.

The great dome of the Pantheon has never been surpassed, not even by Michelangelo's dome for St. Peter's, but it provided inspiration for many architects of the Italian Renaissance, notably Brunelleschi in his quest to design the dome of Santa Maria del Fiore in Florence. However, the dome of Hagia Sophia in Istanbul is not only a superb technical achievement, but also a supreme expression of religious faith revealed in architecture. More than 1,000 years later, a similar conjunction of religious

THE EASTERN WAY *While worship in Europe generally took the form of a shared act, Asian temples such as Angkor Wat symbolized the individual quest for enlightenment.*

faith and inspired architecture would once again occur in St. Peter's Basilica in Rome, and particularly in Bernini's great Piazza di San Pietro that fronts the church. These and other such places of worship help both to reveal the inner "truths" of religion, and to confirm the faith.

Parthenon and Acropolis

Athens, Greece

The rock of the Acropolis, with its collection of magnificent classical monuments, rises above the city of Athens. This craggy limestone plateau was the site of one of the first settlements in Greece and was gradually transformed from a fortified citadel to the heart of the first city state. After the Delphic Oracle pronounced that it should be the domain of the gods only, its function became strictly religious. And so, during the 5th century BC, a wealthy and powerful Athens built the temples that are visible today as part of a public works program instigated by Pericles, the Athenian military and political leader.

A Monumental Site

Entry to the Acropolis is through the Propylaea, a monumental gateway of the Doric order begun in 437 BC but never completed. On a nearby

FAST FACTS

- DATE 5th century BC
- STYLES Doric and Ionic
- MATERIAL Marble
- ARCHITECTS Ictinus, Callicrates, and Pheidias
- Originally richly decorated in gold, red, and blue

Doric

Ionic

Corinthian

spur is the delightful small Ionic temple of Athene Nike. Beyond this, close to the Parthenon, is the Erechtheion, also Ionic in design and famous for its elegant Porch of the Caryatids. (A caryatid is a column in the form of a young woman.)

Supreme, however, is the Parthenon, the temple built in 447–431 BC and dedicated to the city's guardian goddess, Athene. This building replaced an earlier one that burned to the ground when the Persians looted Athens in 480 BC.

The new Parthenon was designed by Ictinus and Callicrates, and overseen by the sculptor Pheidias. Superbly constructed in Pentellic marble using the Doric order (the most austere and disciplined of the classical orders), it achieves that quintessentially classical Greek sense of harmony—the effect could well have been quite different when painted in its original gold, red, and blue. The temple also has some wonderful refinements developed to correct various optical distortions that might

Aerial view of the Acropolis, towering above Athens and dominated by the Parthenon (above). The three orders of Greek columns (right).

otherwise have marred this perfection. Straight columns look concave, so the columns of the Parthenon gently bulge outward in order to appear straight; as well, the outer columns lean inward by 2 ⅓ inches (6 cm) to counteract the illusion of falling outward.

RELIGIOUS RITES

The Parthenon was lavishly decorated with beautiful naturalistic friezes and sculptures, worked in marble by the sculptor Pheidias. The Panathenaic procession on the frieze depicted the four-yearly religious procession of the time. People would enter the city walls, cross the Agora below the Acropolis, and climb slowly until they reached the Parthenon's east front. There, sacrifices were offered in the open; worshipers were not permitted to enter the temple or the walled area where Pheidias's

huge cult statue of Athene Parthenos stood, covered in ivory and gold plate and decked out in bracelets, rings, and necklaces.

The Parthenon remained virtually unaltered for more than 2,000 years, despite being converted into a church and, during the Turkish occupation, a mosque. The Erechtheion was used as a harem. But in 1687, a shell from Venetian forces besieging the city hit a Turkish powder magazine stored inside. The explosion tore the Parthenon apart and destroyed much of the frieze. Despite reconstruction efforts, the damage is still evident. In 1799–1802 the British Lord Elgin removed a great many of the remaining marble carvings and statues, which were thought to be in danger of further destruction. He sold them to the British Museum, where they remain on display today.

The Erechtheion, with the beautiful Porch of the Caryatids (above). This early view of the Parthenon (right) shows the friezes and the statue of Athene in place.

Pantheon

Rome, Italy

Since ancient times, the Pantheon's sense of space and seeming simplicity of design have inspired awe in all those who stand under its great dome. Despite depredations and alterations over 2,000 years, it is among the most complete and best preserved of all the ancient Roman monuments.

Built by the Emperor Hadrian between AD 118 and c. 128, the Pantheon covered a temple erected by one of the Emperor Augustus's sons-in-law, general Marcus Agrippa, in 27 BC. Perhaps with a sense of history, Hadrian had Agrippa's name inscribed above the columns of the entrance portico,

FAST FACTS

■ DATE AD 118–c. 128

■ STYLE Imperial Roman

■ MATERIALS Concrete and brick

■ COMMISSIONED BY The Emperor Hadrian

■ The first pagan temple in Rome to be rededicated as a Christian church

vowing, with touching filial loyalty, to dedicate his own name to one monument only—that of his adoptive father, Trajan.

The exterior, fronted by a portico eight columns wide and three deep, barely hints at the expanse within. A central block contains the huge, bronze-covered doors, flanked by niches, leading into the immense rotunda. The dome is a half-sphere, its 144-foot (44.3-m) diameter precisely equal to its floor-to-summit height. The *oculus* ("open eye") at its center provides an unexpected view of Rome's changing skies, the principal source of light.

The dramatic scale of the Pantheon was made possible by two factors: the wealth of an empire at the height of its power, and expertise in constructing vaults in concrete, a revolutionary material developed by the Romans. The sunken panels, or coffers, create a pleasing geometric design in the dome, but they are also functional—they hollow out the concrete, reducing its dead weight as it bears down onto a wide surrounding wall of brick.

The eight-column portico of the Pantheon proclaims it to be a temple (above). Bronze doors and coffered ceiling (left).

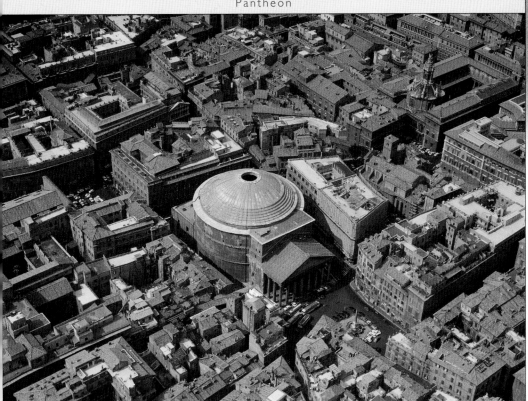

Aerial view (above), showing the colonnaded portico and the 30-foot (9.2 m) oculus, or "open eye," at the center of the dome—a source of natural light.

The wall contains a series of restraining arches, allowing for the alternating curved and squared recesses within, with their columns, cornices, and entablatures. The lack of obtrusive vaulting or arching creates a unified, pure space and a sense of architectural grandeur.

"Pantheon" means "all the gods," and the building was probably originally dedicated to the seven planetary deities. In 609, it became the first pagan temple in Rome to be rededicated as a Christian church. It was renamed the Church of Santa Maria ad Martyres, and cartloads of the remains of Christian martyrs and others were brought from the Roman catacombs and reburied below its floor.

DEPREDATIONS AND DESPOLIATIONS

Over the years, the building suffered various outrages. In 663, the Byzantine Emperor Constans II plundered the roof of its gilded bronze tiles. In medieval times, although considered a "marvel" and a symbol of the city, the Pantheon was used for many years as a fort. In the Renaissance, it became one of the most important examples of classical Roman architecture, but, despite its fame, in the 17th century Pope Urban VIII Barberini stripped the bronze from inside the portico to make Bernini's *baldacchino* in St. Peter's, giving rise to a famous taunt: "What the barbarians didn't do, the Barberini did."

AN EMPEROR'S LEGACY

Hadrian's Pantheon has inspired many later architects, including Brunelleschi, Bramante, Palladio, Bernini, Vanbrugh, and Jefferson. And it is the resting place of many noted Italians, including Raphael, who died in 1520.

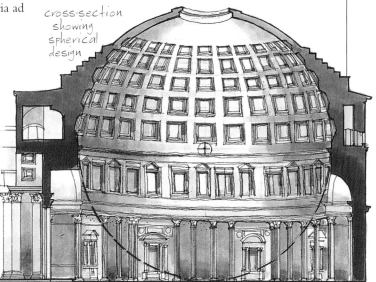

cross-section showing spherical design

Hagia Sophia

Istanbul, Turkey

When the original Hagia Sophia, the Church of the Holy Wisdom, was razed during riots in Constantinople in the 6th century AD, the Byzantine emperor Justinian took the opportunity to commission a replacement designed to impress. The new Hagia Sophia was one of the most lavish and expensive buildings of all time—and the largest enclosed space in the world for almost 1,000 years. Designed by Isidorus of Miletus and Anthemius of Tralles, it took more than 10,000 workmen just five years, from 532 to 537, to build. When Justinian entered the finished church for the first time, he exclaimed, "O Solomon, I have excelled thee!"

AN ELEGANT SOLUTION
The great triumph of the two architects and their Byzantine builders was their discovery of a technique for erecting a dome

FAST FACTS

■ DATE 532–537

■ STYLE Byzantine

■ MATERIALS Masonry, plaster, and mosaics (walls); lead (domes)

■ ARCHITECTS Isidorus of Miletus and Anthemius of Tralles

■ First use of dome on pendentives

107 feet (32.5 m) wide over a huge central square by using pendentives (curved triangles). They could thus dispense with supporting walls, adding half domes to the east and west of the central space to buttress the main dome. The result, in the words of Justinian's historian, was a dome "marvellous in its grace, but by reason of the seeming insecurity of its composition altogether terrifying. For it seems somehow to float in the air on no firm basis, but to be poised aloft to the peril of those inside..." Indeed, 20 years and several earthquakes later, the central dome did collapse, and Isidorus the Younger, a nephew of one of the original architects, oversaw the rebuilding; he reinforced the structure by adding heavy buttresses and a steeper dome which, much repaired, still survives.

With its dome overlaid in gold evoking Heaven and the

dome on pendentives

Hagia Sophia dominates the Istanbul skyline (above left). Disks bearing texts from the Koran hang below the dome (above). Mosaic in the south gallery, showing Christ enthroned (below).

square space below layered in colored marbles evoking Earth, the Church of the Holy Wisdom combined innovative architectural design with icons of theological symbolism. It became the focal point of religious life in Constantinople, and was the place where Byzantine emperors were crowned.

CHANGING FORTUNES

But the cost of its upkeep and the decline of the Byzantine empire took their toll. The building was ransacked during a number of invasions, most spectacularly by soldiers of the Fourth Crusade in 1204—they broke up the altar, looted the silver and gilt relics, and sat a prostitute on the throne of the patriarch. And when the Ottoman Turks stormed Constantinople in 1453 (and renamed the city Istanbul), their leader, Mehmet II, claimed Hagia Sophia for himself. It was converted into a mosque, four minarets were added, and it functioned thus until the 1930s, when Kemal Ataturk, the Turkish president of the day,

turned it into a museum. Today, Hagia Sophia's exterior of fading orange plaster walls, dull lead domes, and pale minarets gives little hint of the extraordinary space—with many of its original mosaics of glass and semi-precious stones now restored—that lies within.

SULEIMANYE CAMII

Perhaps the greatest tribute to Hagia Sophia is the fact that more than 1,000 years later the renowned Ottoman architect Mimar Sinan (c. 1489–1588) used its plan as the basis for his famous mosque, the Suleimanye Camii. It was built for Suleiman the Magnificent over seven years, from 1550 to 1557. Sinan, often referred to as the "Ottoman Michelangelo," used a very similar system to that of Hagia Sophia: two half domes, front and back, bolstering the main dome, together with a stair tower over each of the four main piers.

The mosque complex included a soup kitchen, a school, and wrestling grounds. Entry was through an arcaded courtyard with a delightful fountain at its center. In the enclosed garden behind the mosque are the mausoleums of Suleiman and his wife, Roxalane. Close by is the tomb of Sinan himself, on the site of his former house.

Temple at Borobudur

Java, Indonesia

The ruins of the great Buddhist temple at Borobudur, in central Java, take the form of a gigantic stone stupa. The temple is one of south-east Asia's best preserved monuments to Buddhist culture, but many details about it—such as the name of the ruler who commissioned it and why it was abandoned so soon after completion—are uncertain and highly speculative.

The structure lay deserted and partially buried in jungle for about 800 years, until 1815, when the British governor, Sir Thomas Stamford Raffles, sent a surveyor to inspect and draw it. Raffles visited it himself and mentioned the ruins in his 1817 *History of Java*, but still the temple remained mostly forgotten until the 1870s, when the Dutch began to take an interest and the Batavian Society gradually began clearing the monument. In 1886 Dutch archaeologist Jan Laurens Andries Brandes uncovered the hidden reliefs that show the karmic cycle of life, death, and rebirth.

FAST FACTS

- DATE 8th–9th centuries
- STYLE Mahayana Buddhist
- MATERIAL Volcanic stone
- COMMISSIONED BY Sailendra dynasty
- Borobudur was unknown to the West until it was "discovered" by Sir Stamford Raffles in the 19th century

As a result of this discovery, it was decided to restore the monument to its former glory.

In 1907–11 the site was cleared of trees and undergrowth and archaeologically investigated by Dr. Theodoor van Erp, under the auspices of the Dutch colonial government. Rain, unable to escape because of the build-up of debris, had waterlogged the foundations, and the first and fourth galleries had begun to subside. Subsidence continued until 1968, when UNESCO mounted its "Save Borobudur" appeal. The resulting $25 million restoration project lasted for a decade from 1973.

It is known that the temple was begun in the mid-700s and was later modified (794–824) by a powerful but unknown ruler of the Sailendra dynasty (who were possibly identified with "the Lords of the Mountains"). The Sailendra were devotees of Mahayana Buddhism, which had

Bell stupas on round terraces (above). Detail of sculpted Buddha (left).

Nearly 2 million cubic feet (55,000 cubic m) of stone was used in the temple's construction (above). Detail of carvings showing stories from the life of Buddha (right).

spread from India in the 5th century, but they thrived side by side with the Hindu Mataram on the plains of central Java for nearly 300 years. By the end of the 10th century, however, the temple at Borobudur had been abandoned; at around the same time the great Mataram monument, a nearby 9th century Hindu temple complex, was also deserted. Possibly these two inland agricultural dynasties both declined as the more outward-looking kingdoms of east Java became powerful.

Symbolizing the Spiritual

The site of the temple was carefully selected to lie surrounded by rivers and mountain ridges— most likely for their symbolic significance, as well as for practical protection. Its construction is estimated to have taken between 80 and 200 years, but no records remain of the obviously large, skilled workforce that was employed.

The complex—a stone-covered hill, or "holy mountain," representing the ascent to nirvana—is conceived in three broad sections, linked by four axial staircases. The base, essentially an indented square with sides of 464 feet (118 m), symbolizes the "world of form"—the earthly world of the senses—rising through four diminishing square terraces. Erotic scenes feature in the karmic cycle depicted on the

base. The parapets above are decorated with continuous carved reliefs depicting the life and teachings of the Buddha, interspersed with open niches housing seated Buddhas.

The middle section comprises three circular terraces. These symbolize the "world of formlessness" (the heavens); the lowest terrace is somewhat distorted, but the circular form is successively perfected in the higher levels. More statues of seated Buddhas smile serenely from a series of perforated, bell-shaped stupas. Finally, at the summit, a single tall, hollow stupa signifies eventual nirvana.

The temple at Borobudur can be interpreted as an immense diagrammatic representation of the path of the true believer in the search for enlightenment. Its profound beauty continues to attract visitors of many faiths.

29

Temple of the Magician

Uxmal, Mexico

The heartland of Mayan civilization was the Yucatán Peninsula in south-east Mexico—a great expanse of level, jungle-covered country edged by the rolling Puuc hills, where some of the most spectacular Mayan sites, such as Chichen Itza, Sayil, and Labna, are to be found. For many, however, the ruins of the ancient city at Uxmal are the finest, for both their architectural interest and the scenic beauty of their setting.

FAST FACTS
- DATE c. 9th century
- STYLE Mayan
- MATERIAL Sandstone
- BUILDERS The Maya
- The temple's precisely cut stonework was fashioned without the use of metal tools

A CULTURE AHEAD OF ITS TIME

The Maya were the most advanced and cultured of the pre-Hispanic Meso–American peoples, having developed by the beginning of the Christian era an extensive knowledge of astronomy—the accuracy of their celestial observations remained unmatched for 1,000 years. They formulated a complex system of mathematics and were the first to adopt the use of the "zero" in their calculations. They built some of the most architecturally accomplished structures in central America, yet they seem to have begun working in stone only in the 4th century AD and never developed metal tools to move, work, or carve it—their stoneworking tools were made of flint or obsidian. Despite this, their stonemasons cut, polished, and fitted stones together so tightly that a knife blade will not slide between them even today.

The Maya were the only pre-Columbian American culture to invent the corbeled arch, in which each stone slightly overhangs the one below, thus bridging a space too wide to be spanned by a post-and-lintel structure. They used these arches to span doorways and to form vaulted chambers. More than two millennia earlier the Mycenaeans were the first to use corbeling in the beehive domes of their important tombs; centuries later the Khmer people used corbeled arches at Angkor Wat.

MAYAN MYSTERIES

Many mysteries still surround the Maya, our lack of knowledge being largely the result of the systematic campaign waged by Spanish missionaries to eradicate what they considered an idolatrous and pagan culture. The Spanish conquistadores landed on the Yucatán Peninsula early in 1517. Within only a few years, much of the Mayan civilization and its population had been destroyed, as much by introduced European diseases such as smallpox as by the sword. Zealous friars and priests burned

The Uxmal site (left). A detail of the Chaac mask shows how closely the stone blocks fit together (above). Two sides of the pyramid have steep stairs, and a row of carved masks of Chaac, the god of rain, lines both sides of the staircase (right).

so many records and artifacts that only three codices of Mayan written texts survive today.

Nonetheless, the archaeological quest for the Mayan civilization continues apace, and much is being added, year by year, to our current knowledge of the Maya. Uxmal provides some of the finest examples of Mayan structures, chief among which is the so-called Temple (or Pyramid) of the Magician, a lofty structure almost 133 feet (40 m) high, commenced sometime in the 9th century. Its name commemorates the popular myth that a dwarf who had magical powers built the pyramid in one single night. In reality, however, its construction extended over several centuries, and the structure visible today was built over a series of earlier temples, each enclosing the remains of its predecessor.

For the Maya, as for other pre-Hispanic peoples in Mexico, the pyramid symbolized the holy mountain, but its form seems particularly appropriate in the Yucatán Peninsula, punctuating its vast expanse of flat terrain. Unlike the squared geometry of most Mayan temples, however (for example, the 9th century Temple of Kukulkan at Chichen Itza), the Temple of the Magician has an oval floor plan. Its curved sides are built in smooth stone and flank the dizzily steep steps on either side leading up to the twin temple structures—stone replicas of Mayan thatched huts—at its summit. Near the top, on the west side, is a doorway into the previous temple. The doorway is decorated with masks of the Mayan rain-god Chaac, with similar decorative masks around the base of the structure. Archaeologists have uncovered evidence that the whole structure originally was plastered, then painted a red-pink color with highly colored decorative details, but today its remains have returned to their natural honey-colored sandstone.

Chartres Cathedral

Chartres, France

Chartres Cathedral is one of the finest examples of French Gothic architecture in a country renowned for its great Gothic churches. It also has a stylistic unity that was unusual for a time when great churches could take centuries and many architects to build. Chartres' construction, however, was largely completed in about a quarter of a century, thanks to one of the great communal efforts of medieval Europe.

FAST FACTS

- DATE 1195–1220
- STYLE French High Gothic
- MATERIALS Stone and stained glass
- BUILDERS The citizens, merchants, and artisans of Chartres
- A fine example of French Gothic architecture

A MONUMENT TO MARY

When the fifth church on the site burned down in 1194, rebuilding began immediately. The earlier Romanesque cathedral, dedicated to the Virgin Mary, *Notre Dame*, claimed as its most treasured relic the "Veil of the Virgin." The Veil had survived the fire unscathed, and this was believed to be due to divine intercession by the Virgin. The rebuilding became a fervent civic enterprise undertaken by the citizens, merchants, and artisans of Chartres alike, with lavish gifts from the French king and nobles, all spurred on by their devotion to the Virgin. Apart from the Veil, only the lower part of the west front and the bases of the west towers remained after the fire, and these were incorporated in the new cathedral, designed in the High Gothic style. By 1220, the cathedral was virtually complete, although its consecration did not take place until 1260.

The wonderful geometry of Chartres Cathedral remained essentially intact until the northern spire of the west front collapsed in 1506. It was replaced by one in the Flamboyant idiom, giving the cathedral its frontal asymmetry.

Chartres Cathedral and environs from the air (above). Detail of the rose window in the south transept (right).

GOTHIC GLORIES

Chartres exemplifies the typical features of French Gothic: twin west towers but no central tower over the crossing, a single transept, a curved east end with radiating chapels, and the structural daring of external flying buttresses. Rose windows are another French feature, the rose being a symbol of the Virgin, and those at Chartres are exceptionally beautiful. So, too, is the figured stained glass around the walls, much of which dates from the 12th and 13th centuries. When the sun shines through this array of glass, the experience of standing amidst its famous cool blue light has been likened to standing inside a sapphire.

The cathedral is also graced with a wealth of sculpture, from the stone figures adorning the west front and the north and south porches to the ornate woodwork of the Renaissance choir. And on the floor of the nave, usually hidden by rows of chairs, is a 13th century floor maze, its 660-foot (200-m) long meditation path contained in a diameter of 42½ feet (13 m)—the same size as the rose window above the main door. All this inspired the historian Henry Adams to write, "Chartres expressed … an emotion, the deepest man ever felt."

Detail of external flying buttresses (above). Salisbury Cathedral, England (right), a fine example of English Gothic architecture.

SALISBURY CATHEDRAL

There were many links between England and France during the period of great Gothic construction, the essence of which was an airy combination of flying buttresses, pointed arches, and ribbed vaults. Much of the culture was common to both countries, too, yet there were characteristic differences.

Salisbury Cathedral, also dedicated to the Virgin Mary, is as representative of English Gothic cathedrals as Chartres is of French and, like Chartres, it was built in one sustained campaign. Begun in 1220, it was largely completed by 1260. Its central tower and spire—at 406 feet (123 m), the world's tallest for many centuries—was added between 1330 and 1350. With or without the spire, the crossing tower was typical of English Gothic, as were the double transepts, the square east end, an emphasis on length inside, the avoidance of external flying buttresses, and a preference for tall, thin "lancet" windows.

Salisbury Cathedral has a calm, almost austere quality and, with its cloister and chapter house inside the large walled close, set beside the River Avon, makes an idyllic picture, made famous by the great English painters John Constable and J. M. W. Turner.

33

Angkor Wat

Angkor, Cambodia

In the great city of Angkor, which was built by the Khmer kings of north-west Cambodia between the 9th and 15th centuries, lies the monumental Hindu temple complex known as Angkor Wat. The city of Angkor, stretching 31 miles (50 km) over the Cambodian plain, was both an administrative center for the powerful Khmer kingdom and, through the artistic and engineering feats of its design and construction, a symbolic representation of the Hindu universe—a dwelling place of monarchs believed to be divine.

FAST FACTS

- DATE 12th century
- STYLE Khmer Hindu
- MATERIAL Stone
- COMMISSIONED BY Khmer rulers
- Originally Hindu, the temple became a pilgrimage destination for both Buddhists and Hindus

The temple complex also replicated this universe, being oriented around a central structure that represented the Hindu concept of the holy Mount Meru, the home of the gods, lying at the axis of the Hindu cosmos. Its outer walls symbolized the mountains that were thought to mark the edge of the cosmos, and were encircled by a wide moat that signified the oceans beyond. Angkor's system of artificial moats, canals, and reservoirs owed their existence to this metaphysical concept, but they also had a very practical application: They harnessed the rivers' seasonal water supply, providing irrigation for vast tracts of rice padis, and so were the basis of the kingdom's agricultural prosperity and power.

GODS AND KINGS

Each Khmer king, believing that he was an incarnation of a Hindu god, built a temple complex to glorify his patron deity—and himself. The first rulers started in a small way, but later kings struggled to outdo their

A moat 4 miles (6.4 km) long and 600 feet (180 m) wide protects the wat (above). Tree roots covering temple (left).

Aerial view showing the layout of the temple (above). Detail of bas-reliefs illustrating deeds of the gods (right).

predecessors with the size and magnificence of their temples, culminating in the majestic Angkor Wat. Built in the early 12th century, this is the greatest and most famous of the Hindu temple complexes of the region. Dedicated to Vishnu, one of the three major Hindu gods, it was also intended as the tomb of its builder, Suryavarman II, and is oriented toward the west—to which the dead were believed to depart—rather than the east, as was customary.

The wat occupies almost a square mile (about 2.6 sq km) and is contained within an immense external cloister. A stone causeway, with balustrades carved as the serpent of Hindu mythology, leads over a moat to the massive entrance portal and then into the enclosure of the temple proper. This rises in three levels, each tier punctuated by corner towers linked by covered porticos and steep steps up to the pavilions and, eventually, the central tower. Decorative motifs are carved into the sandstone and volcanic rock throughout, and statues grace the various courtyards and terraces.

But it is around the internal walls of the lowest open gallery that the sculptural highlight of Angkor Wat is to be found—more than a mile (1.6 km) of delicately carved, larger-than-life bas-reliefs depicting the deeds of the gods and Suryavarman II in wonderfully vital style.

RESTORATION
Within 300 years of being built, the city of Angkor had been abandoned to the encroaching jungle after being overrun by the Thais in the 15th century—except for Angkor Wat. Inhabited and preserved by Buddhist monks, it had become an important pilgrimage site, visited by both Buddhists and Hindus from throughout south-east Asia. To Europeans, however, it remained a lost world, hidden in near-impenetrable jungle, for almost 400 years.

Then, in the 1860s, the colonial French "discovered" the site and began an important reconstruction program. International efforts continue—after further damage caused by war, neglect, and, worst of all, plunder of the carvings—to try to preserve the remains of this once magnificent city. The temple complexes of Angkor are among the supreme architectural achievements of their time, as Angkor Wat, the city's crowning work, attests: It is the equal of any of the great medieval cathedrals of Europe that were being built at the same time.

Santa Maria del Fiore

Florence, Italy

If there is an abiding image of Florence, it is that of Il Duomo—the magnificent ribbed dome of the cathedral of Santa Maria del Fiore, perched atop the fabulously patterned red, white, and green marble exterior, and rising above the cityscape of terracotta roofs. This cathedral was the result of the city's efforts to outdo its great rivals, Siena and Pisa. By the end of the 13th century, Florence was the most powerful, politically and economically, of the three cities, but its inferior cathedral failed to reflect this. And so the city council ordered the architect Arnolfo di Cambio "to make a design … in a style of magnificence which neither the industry nor the power of man can surpass."

In response to such a brief, Arnolfo designed a massive vaulted basilica in the High Gothic style with an octagonal crossing. This was an unusual feature given the predominance of the square crossing at the time, and one that, at 140 feet (42 m) wide, would require a huge dome that would put the cathedrals of Siena and Pisa in their respective places! Such a dome posed considerable structural difficulties: In fact, at the time, no one knew quite how it could be done, though there was an earlier and much smaller prototype immediately outside the cathedral—the famous eight-sided Romanesque baptistery (built 1128–50).

Despite this potential problem, construction work began in 1296. It was to continue,

---

FAST FACTS

- **DATE** 1296–1461
- **STYLE** High Gothic
- **MATERIALS** Marble, stone, and brick
- **ARCHITECTS** di Cambio, Talenti, Brunelleschi, and Ghiberti
- The supreme architectural achievement of the Early Renaissance

---

intermittently, for well over 100 years, amid a succession of architects, alterations to plans, and controversies. Arnolfo's design was followed approximately, although the façade he built was demolished and replaced by Francesco Talenti's Gothic front. In 1334 a campanile (bell tower), designed by the famous painter Giotto, was added. By 1418 the nave and the tribunes were completed, but there was still no solution to the problem of the dome. Indeed, the situation was even worse because the cathedral and the octagonal crossing had been enlarged, and walls around the crossing had been added to form a "drum," which reached almost 180 feet (55 m) above the ground.

THE CROWNING GLORY

The Florentines' inability to complete their cathedral was a constant source of civic embarrassment. Eventually, the authorities launched an open competition. The concept designed by Filippo Brunelleschi, aided by Lorenzo Ghiberti, was selected from several submissions, and construction began in 1420. Both were sculptors, but they devised

Il Duomo—the dome of Santa Maria del Fiore—and the skyline of Florence (bottom left). Detail of a Luca Della Robbia sculpture in the Duomo Museum (far right).

a technically innovative scheme that did not require the usual forest of timber scaffolding (which would not have worked at such a height and span), and instead built the dome in a series of self-supporting concentric rings.

Brunelleschi had earlier visited Rome and there studied and been influenced by the construction techniques evident in ancient Roman ruins, particularly the Pantheon.

He eventually opted for a pointed, Gothic-type dome rather than the round, Pantheon-like one that he would have preferred, because a pointed dome would direct its weight downward onto the supporting walls. It had a series of main and subsidiary ribs, in-filled with brick laid in a "herringbone" pattern, and an inner and outer shell (with steps in between that can still be climbed), to reduce its weight as much as possible. The ribs rose to meet the open ring at the summit of the dome. The ring was later covered by the lantern, the final work of Brunelleschi, finished in 1461 after his death.

At last, on March 25, 1436, Pope Eugenius IV consecrated the cathedral, thus marking the completion of the building's crowning glory—although the cathedral's main façade, the west front, was not finished until more than 440 years later, in 1887. Inside is a vast stone space, surprisingly bare. This is in marked contrast to the spectacle outside, where Brunelleschi achieved for Florence an abiding image of its cultural supremacy.

The dome's ribbed construction solved the problem of how to span such a massive space. The weight of the structure is reduced by the use of an inner and outer shell, shown in this cutaway view.

37

Basilica of St. Peter

Rome, Italy

St. Peter's Basilica in Rome is the spiritual home of the Catholic Church, its principal shrine, and the largest of its cathedrals—to prove it, there are bronze plaques set in the marble floor, showing size comparisons with other cathedrals. St. Peter's is built on the site venerated since the 1st century AD as the burial place of the Apostle Peter. A lavish church was built there by the Emperor Constantine in the 4th century AD, once Christianity was no longer forbidden in ancient Rome. This building

FAST FACTS

■ DATE 1506–1667

■ STYLES High Renaissance and Baroque

■ MATERIALS Stone and marble

■ COMMISSIONED BY Pope Julius II

■ In July 1626, 120 years after it was commissioned, St. Peter's was consecrated by Pope Urban VIII

lasted for almost 1,200 years, but with its gradual decay and the coming of the Renaissance, the Popes wanted a new building, one that would better suit their times—and that would rival the majesty and grandeur of ancient Rome.

Pope Julius II commissioned the great Milanese architect Donato Bramante to undertake the new St. Peter's and the adjacent Vatican Palace in the early 16th century, and Bramante's design certainly matched the grand aspirations of the Pope. It set a grand new scale for urban architecture, conceiving of a structure large enough to visually dominate Rome. The new church was to be built on a Greek cross plan (a cross with four arms of equal length) covered by an immense Pantheon-inspired dome, with four minor domes at the sides. It was one of the most ambitious building projects of the 16th century, and its construction, lasting from 1506 to 1626, was to involve many of the major architects of the High Renaissance and Baroque stylistic periods.

Bramante had largely completed the Vatican Palace and begun work on the new St. Peter's by the time he died in 1514, shortly after Pope

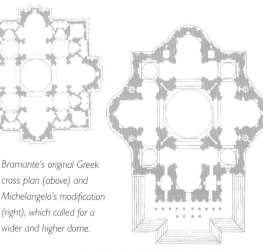

Bramante's original Greek cross plan (above) and Michelangelo's modification (right), which called for a wider and higher dome.

Views of St. Peter's (left and above). The Emperor Caligula brought the central obelisk to Rome from Egypt and erected it in Nero's Circus nearby. Detail of the dome (right).

Julius II. Raphael took over, to be succeeded on his death in 1520 by Baldassare Peruzzi, who was followed in turn by Antonio da Sangallo. The building of the new cathedral within the partly demolished structure of the Constantinian basilica proceeded slowly, while Bramante's original idea of a Greek cross plan was exchanged for a Latin cross plan with an extended nave, heavily embellished by various side chapels and monuments.

A CHANGE OF PLAN

It was not until Michelangelo, then 72 years old, was appointed chief architect in 1546 that the Greek cross plan was reinstated, albeit in a modified form. Michelangelo died in 1564 and the monumental dome, with its slightly pointed profile, was finished between 1586 and 1593 by Giacomo della Porta and Domenico Fontana.

That, however, was not the end of the story. Because the centralized Greek cross plan did not complement the rituals of the Church and did not allow for large congregations, the nave was extended by Carlo Maderno between 1607 and 1612. Thus St. Peter's does, ultimately, form a Latin cross. Unfortunately, the extended nave and porticoed façade obscure the view of the dome from the Piazza di San Pietro—the vast square designed by Gianlorenzo Bernini

from 1656 to 1667. Surrounded by colonnades topped with 140 statues of the saints, the square seems to embrace the approaching faithful.

The interior of the church displays the work of Bernini and the influence of the Baroque era. The centerpiece is Bernini's extraordinary *baldacchino* (canopy), created from bronze stripped from the Pantheon, beneath which only the Pope may celebrate Mass. Near the entrance stands the *Pietà*, a masterpiece sculpted by the young Michelangelo of Mary holding the dead Jesus. It is now behind glass after a hammer attack by a religious fanatic in 1972.

But it is the work of an older Michelangelo, and of some of the greatest artists and architects of the 16th and 17th centuries, that gives St. Peter's the imposing grandeur for which this world center of Catholicism is renowned.

39

Abbey of Melk

Melk, Austria

The site of the Abbey of Melk, on a rocky granite outcrop overlooking the River Danube in Austria, makes it one of the most dramatic religious buildings in Europe. And with its creamy stone silhouette of a central dome framed by sculpted saints and twin towers, the abbey also qualifies as one of the most imposing and spectacular manifestations of the Austrian Baroque style.

The site was originally chosen as a strongly defensible location for the monastery that was first built there in 985, when Melk was a border fortress. The Benedictines took control of

FAST FACTS

■ DATE 1702–40
■ STYLE Austrian Baroque
■ MATERIALS Stone and stucco
■ ARCHITECT Jakob Prandtauer
■ First chosen as a Christian border fortress, the site was taken over by the Benedictines in the 11th century

the monastery about a century later and began to make it into one of the largest medieval abbeys in the region. But the structure visible today essentially dates from 1702 to 1740, when the earlier buildings, which by then were quite dilapidated, were almost entirely rebuilt by Jakob Prandtauer (1660–1726), whose great scheme was completed after his death by his cousin, Josef Munggenast.

Prandtauer was a master mason and sculptor from the Tyrol who had never journeyed outside Austria. But Baroque architecture, with its complex oval geometries, sinuous curves, and elaborate façades, had traveled from Italy, where it originated, to Austria in the 17th century. Once there, it acquired a particular local flavor. Its exuberance reflected a renewed sense of national confidence, following upon Austria's decisive victory over the Ottoman Turks in 1683. Prandtauer's Abbey at Melk came from this period of intense creative energy, enthusiasm, and artistic patronage.

Dominating this stretch of the River Danube (above), the abbey features magnificent examples of Baroque architecture, such as this highly ornamental spiral staircase (left).

The interior of the abbey church, looking toward the altar (above). Lively frescoes decorate the ceiling of the library and the surrounds of the archway leading to it (right).

BENEDICTINE TO BAROQUE

The abbey still has some of the fortifications of the 12th century Benedictine foundation, most notably the external bastions on either side of the gatehouse, the main entrance, which is on the eastern side (at the back if it is approached from the Danube). But once within, the 18th century reconstruction is apparent in all its splendor: It includes monastic quarters, a school, and other ancillary buildings, and stretches well over 990 feet (300 m) in length. An east–west axis leads from the entrance into the forecourt, through a second portal and into the Abbot's Courtyard, which is adorned with a large fountain. Here, in the center of the complex, lies the vast abbey church, its domed cupola rising to a height of 210 feet (64 m), its long nave lined with small chapels and set below undulating cornices, galleries, and arcades with their interplay of rich ceiling frescoes and concentrations of light.

All this great splendor culminates with the Kolomani Courtyard at the western end of the abbey—the end visible from the river. And it was exactly the possibilities provided by this beautiful vantage point that Prandtauer realized with such dramatic effect in his layout of the buildings. The twin towers of the west front of the abbey are framed between two side wings.

On one side is the Imperial or Marble Hall, a grandly decorated room designed for receiving the emperor. On the other side, the equally grand library, with more than 70,000 books and a ceiling full of cherubs fluttering about Hercules, is a testament to the Benedictine tradition of learning. A semicircle of buildings with a central arched balcony links the side wings and completes the whole vast composition for the viewer who approaches along the Danube. The arched balcony provides a viewing platform over the river, the town of Melk, and the vineyards and fertile valleys beyond. Thus the Abbey of Melk is not only a delightfully exuberant building, but also a masterpiece of architectural design that is the perfect complement to its dramatic rocky setting.

41

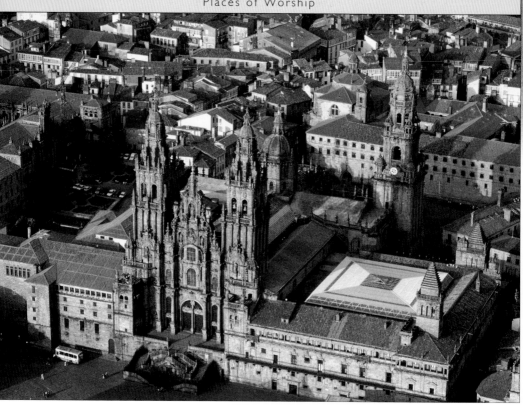

Santiago de Compostela
Santiago de Compostela, Spain

After Jerusalem and Rome, Santiago de Compostela, in the north-western corner of Spain, was the most popular shrine of Christian pilgrimage during the early Middle Ages. For in this pre-served medieval city, in the tomb beneath the high altar of the cathedral, are said to lie the remains of the apostle St. James (Sant Iago in Spanish), who was beheaded in Jerusalem in AD 44. According to legend, his body was placed on a ship without sails or crew and miraculously arrived in north-west Spain in what is now Galicia, where it was buried and somehow forgotten, only to be rediscovered in 810 in the remote town of Compostela. Several earlier churches were built on what quickly became a pilgrimage shrine. But after the Muslim vizier al-Mansur sacked the town in 977, work started on a splendid Roman-esque cathedral designed to house the relics of the saint.

FAST FACTS

■ DATE 1077–1747
■ STYLES French Romanesque and Spanish Baroque
■ MATERIAL Golden granite
■ One of the most famous of medieval shrines; still visited by thousands of pilgrims

Aerial view of the cathedral and town (above). The entrance to the cathedral is through the Portico de la Gloria, the original west front (left).

THE PILGRIMAGE

Christians of the time believed that visiting a sacred site would ensure a place in heaven. And so from all over Europe, pilgrims con-verged on the little town, following various routes through France, over the Pyrénées, and across northern Spain. From Francis of Assisi to King Fernando and Queen Isabella and, perhaps most famously, Chaucer's Wife of Bath, they traveled on horseback or foot, carrying their packs, staffs, and scallop shells—the emblem of the saint—and stopping at the monasteries, hospices, and small villages that mushroomed along the road. The journey could take up to a year, across hot, dusty plains and snow-covered mountains, and was fraught with danger. At its height in the 11th and 12th centuries, more than half a million pilgrims

arrived in Santiago every year (this was at a time when most people never traveled further than the next village). Even today, thousands of pilgrims still make the journey—many of them on foot.

Detail of bas relief sculpture on the exterior of the cathedral (above). The Botafumiero, a large silver censer that can be made to swing from one end of the transept to the other (left).

ROMANESQUE SPLENDOR

From the last hill before the city, the cathedral is clearly visible, its striking golden granite towers, spires, and turrets piercing the skyline. The surrounding old medieval town is full of narrow winding streets, arcades, squares, and statues, all created from the same honey-colored, lichen-covered stone.

Its twin bell towers and west front, a fine example of Spanish Baroque added in 1747 by Fernando de Casas y Novoa, loom over the vast Plaza del Obradoiro. A double stairway leads up to the main entrance, where, beyond the Baroque façade, lies the original cathedral. Built in about 1077–1122, it is a completely Romanesque structure of round-headed arches and massive masonry. Entrance is through the original west front, the Portico de la Gloria, a masterpiece of Romanesque sculpture. Added between 1166 and 1188 under the supervision of the sculptor Mateo, the portico shows exquisitely realized figures of Christ and the Apostles—with Saint James below Christ—

musicians, and even its creator, Mateo, crouching at the base of the central pillar.

Typically French Romanesque in plan— the workmen who built it were supervised by Frenchmen—the cathedral has a central nave and side aisles that flow into the transepts. A curved east end enables pilgrims to attain their goal, walking around the ornate reliquary of the saint behind the high altar.

Much of the exterior of the original building has been concealed by additions and renovations, but the Portico de las Platerias, dating from 1117, in the south transept affords an excellent glimpse of how it must have once looked. And it is within the transept after midday mass on most days that an immense silver censer, the *Botafumiero*, is hooked up to a complex system of pulleys and set swinging by eight priests, until the censer moves in an 83–100-foot (25–30-m) arc, almost reaching the cathedral's vault. The present censer dates from the mid-19th century; the original was carried off by Napoleon's troops during their Spanish campaign in the early 1800s.

La Sagrada Familia

Barcelona, Spain

Barcelona, the capital of Catalonia in Spain, is a city popularly symbolized by one famous building—the church of La Sagrada Familia (the Holy Family). This extraordinary architectural creation is the vision of the Catalan architect Antoni Gaudí. Superficially, it looks like a fantastic medieval cathedral, with the towering scale of its spires and steeples and great entrance portals, while its integration of sculpture and structure suggests something of the Spanish Baroque. And yet the sheer bravura of its fantastically curving shapes and fluidly twisting forms, often incorporating contrasting colored elements, makes La Sagrada Familia seem utterly modern, recalling as it does the work of other famous Catalan artists such as Joan Miró and Pablo Picasso.

A STATEMENT OF FAITH

The design and building of La Sagrada Familia occupied the major part of Gaudí's life, but he did not initiate the project and was introduced to it only when the architect originally commissioned, Francesc de Paula del Villar (who had produced an orthodox Neo-Gothic design), resigned in 1882, after work had begun on the crypt. Gaudí was 31 years old, a qualified architect with several interesting buildings to his credit, but from then on he devoted himself almost entirely to the project. He was a devout Catholic, and the construction of the church became for him a profound act of faith.

The inspiration for the building—conceived as a church of atonement for Barcelona's increasingly revolutionary ideas and known originally as the Expiatory Temple of the Holy Family—came from a prominent Catholic bookseller and businessman, Josep Bocabella, who was a friend of Gaudí's. It was to be funded entirely by donations, and when Gaudí began work he confidently expected to complete it before the end of the century. However, World War I intervened, and funds dwindled. Yet Gaudí labored on with every aspect of the building, like a latter-day medieval master mason. Eventually he lived in a hut on the site, a virtual recluse; when, in 1926, he was accidentally killed by a tramcar, the city authorities at first thought he was a vagrant.

> **FAST FACTS**
> - DATE 1884–present
> - STYLES Catalan Art Nouveau and Gothic Revival
> - MATERIALS Stone and ceramics
> - ARCHITECT Antoni Gaudí
> - Sculptures on the façade suggest the unity of natural and spiritual worlds

A detail from one of the towers (above). The Passion façade at the west entrance (left) is more somber and angular than the joyous Nativity entrance. A statue of the crucified Christ dominates the central door.

AN UNFINISHED MASTERPIECE

Gaudí's concept was of a basically traditional Latin cross plan, with wide transepts and seven radiating chapels grouped around the high altar at the eastern end. Over this plan, he envisaged a tall central tower, almost 594 feet (180 m) high, symbolizing Christ, surrounded by three groups of four lesser spires, each 297 feet (90 m) high, representing the 12 apostles; lights from the 12 spires would illuminate the central tower symbolizing Christ as "the Light of the World."

Gaudí worked first on the east entrance, the Nativity transept. Many of the transept's stalactite-like gables, symbolic sculptures, and astonishingly tall, openwork towers topped with ceramic-encrusted "pompom" finials were completed before his death. Sculptures of about 100 plants and a similar number of animal species decorate the façade. Three doors are dedicated to Faith, Hope, and Charity. The towers begin in the shape of a square and, as they rise, become circular.

Work ceased until the 1950s, when it was resumed amid much controversy, since most of Gaudí's plans and models had been destroyed in 1937 during the Spanish Civil War. However, it was known that his design envisaged the west entrance as depicting the Passion, a bleak entrance that would balance the joy of the Nativity entrance. This façade was completed only in the last decade of the 20th century, with the help of artists and technicians from all over the world. Work continues slowly on the nave, and it is a tribute to Gaudí's inspired and inspiring vision that the realization of La Sagrada Familia—which has been called a "Bible in stone" because of the religious symbols woven into its fabric—is still the goal of so many creative artists.

The intricate, hollow towers of La Sagrada Familia soar high above Barcelona.

45

Unity Temple

Chicago, United States of America

When the original Unity Church in Oak Park, Chicago, burned to the ground in 1905 after being struck by lightning, the congregation decided to commission one of its members, Frank Lloyd Wright, an architect with a burgeoning reputation for innovative ideas, to design the replacement. The new church, Unity Temple, was to amaze and ultimately please its congregation: With its squat, horizontal concrete mass lined with squarish columns, and its recessed windows set high under its overhanging roof, it was like no church seen before.

The site selected for the new church was a very busy corner, which precluded the main entrance from opening onto the major street. A further constraint was its

FAST FACTS
- DATE 1904–08
- STYLE Modern
- MATERIALS Reinforced concrete, stained glass, and timber
- ARCHITECT Frank Lloyd Wright
- One of the first buildings to be constructed of reinforced concrete

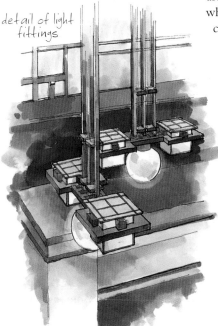

detail of light fittings

location among other public buildings, including churches, for which cost had not been the constraining factor that it was for the Unitarians: The budget for the new temple was a mere $45,000 (including the price of the land). Wright turned this economic imperative into an artistic asset by building the whole structure in reinforced concrete, making it one of the first buildings in the world to be built in this material. (The exterior was covered in render in the 1960s.)

But Lloyd Wright's use of reinforced concrete throughout was not determined solely by economic factors. It also reflected the architect's principles of unity and integrity: He believed that a building should be a fusion of space, material, and experience, "built in character out of the same material."

46

Frank Lloyd Wright (right) photographed c. 1938. The detailing in the interior of Unity Temple (above) is in marked contrast to the austere exterior.

A UNIFIED DESIGN

Unity Temple is entered from a side street, up a set of stairs behind a low wall, with the message "For the worship of God—and the service of man" inscribed in bronze letters above its doors. The broad entrance hall acts as a link between the two parts of the church: the more-or-less square temple, the main place of worship; and the rectangular Unity House, a hall for social functions (Wright called this "the good-time place").

A dimly lit cloister, rather than abutting the church as in medieval times, runs below the entire building. It skirts the temple, the floor of which is 4 feet (1.2 m) above the cloister. An opening between the temple floor and the cloister ceiling allows worshipers to look up into the temple without being seen—and so to enter the building without disturbing the congregation and pastor.

The extraordinary interior, so different from the severe exterior, is an intimate, open space with a centralized floor plan of a square and cruciform interlocked. Every surface is carefully proportioned, with layered squares and rectangles that seem to float as planes of pastel concrete, lined and given depth by rich wooden trim boards and strips. All this is flooded in a golden amber light from above, which is filtered through a grid of 25 stained-glass skylights arranged in a complex pinwheel pattern.

AN EXPRESSION OF GOD ON EARTH

Building work on Unity Temple began in 1906 and was completed—and the first service held—in October 1908 (although the temple was not dedicated until almost a year later). The pastor, Dr. Rodney Johonnot, wrote of Wright's design: "Without tower or spire ... by its form it expresses the thought ... that God should not be sought in the sky, but on earth among the children of men."

It is this quality, and the fact that Unity Temple owes so little to traditional Western ecclesiastical architecture, that make it such an outstanding and original work, one that gives expression not only to Frank Lloyd Wright's architectural principles but also to his religious beliefs and to his ideas about what a place of worship should be.

Great Mosque of Djenné

Mali, West Africa

The Great Mosque of Djenné, in Mali, is an astonishing sight—it is a smooth, earthen structure the color of the savanna landscape that surrounds it, with cone-shaped turrets and protruding sticks, standing on a raised platform 807 feet square (75 sq m). The sense of the extraordinary is further heightened by the knowledge that the mosque is constructed entirely of sun-baked earth; indeed, it is believed to be the world's largest mud brick building.

Not surprisingly, given its central role in the religious life of the city, the mosque occupies a prominent position amid the mud brick and thatched houses of Djenné.

Scaffolding made of palm sticks is embedded in the walls.

FAST FACTS

■ DATE 1909

■ STYLES Islamic/Sudano–Sahelian

■ MATERIAL Mud brick

■ Each year the smooth, sculptured surface of the mosque is washed away by the annual rains and has to be renewed with mud plaster

Djenné, one of West Africa's oldest urban settlements, lies on a small hill on the upper reaches of the Niger River delta. (When there is flooding in the rainy season, the benefits of the mosque's raised platform become apparent—even the highest of flood waters cannot reach it.) Linked by the river with the city of Timbuktu, 220 miles (350 km) away on the edge of the Sahara, and situated at the head of trade routes to various gold mines, the city was an ancient trading center on the long trans-Saharan route, and at the same time it became a renowned center of Muslim scholarship.

AN INGENIOUS DESIGN

A mosque was probably first built here some time in the 1300s and survived until about 1830, when it was almost completely demolished by the Fulani leader Shehu Ahmadu Lobbo. A conjectural restoration of the original in 1896 was in turn replaced in 1909 by the present, slightly different mosque, which combines the Islamic structure of a walled enclosure containing a covered area at the eastern end with indigenous West African structures of conical ancestral pillars and shrines.

An aerial view shows the mosque's massive raised platform behind the magnificent eastern façade (above). Worshipers exit amid the mud pillars outside the building (below).

In this distinctive Sudano–Sahelian architecture, rectangular mud bricks of sun-baked earth, known locally as *ferey,* are the basic building material. They form the structure, which is then entirely covered with mud plaster. The recoating of the mosque with a fresh coat of mud is an annual ritual that is made necessary by the rainy season. Flattened hands—rather than trowels—were the traditional means of obtaining its smooth, rounded, almost sculptural surfaces. In dramatic contrast are the bundles of palm sticks that bristle and jut from these surfaces. They are part of the mosque's structural system, and they also function as permanent scaffolding during the constant renewal of the building.

Like all mosques, the Great Mosque of Djenné faces Mecca. The eastern façade—the *quibla,* or prayer wall—is supported by three large, rectangular minarets and overlooks the site of a busy market held every Monday. On the left is a walled enclosure containing a communal grave intended for the burial of important leaders; this is part of the original 14th century building. The main entrance is on the southern side, reached by a stairway lined with elaborate mud protuberances; the northern side is perhaps even more ornately decorated with pillars and rounded pinnacles.

Inside, the huge covered prayer hall contains a forest of 90 wooden columns that support the roof; this and the very few window openings make the interior of the mosque dark. Arches extend from pillars 45 feet (15 m) high to form a series of shadowy covered walkways around the large internal courtyard, which may also be used as an open-air prayer hall.

A staircase in the central minaret leads up to a platform on the roof, from which the *imam* can summon the faithful to prayer—to this extraordinary mosque with its eerily beautiful silhouette, its tactile surfaces, and its monumental scale, that has been created out of such a seemingly fragile material as sun-baked mud.

Notre Dame du Haut

Ronchamp, France

On a wooded hill above Ronchamp, a village in the Vosges Mountains of eastern France, stands one of the most influential and radically innovative buildings of the 20th century: the pilgrimage chapel of Notre Dame du Haut. It was designed by one of the century's great artists, the Swiss architect Le Corbusier (born Charles Edouard Jeanneret, 1887–1965), a man who consistently claimed to be non-religious. But with this unique building, he was to create, intuitively, a poem written in concrete, stone, and glass, a place, as he described it, "of silence, of prayer, of peace, of spiritual joy."

The previous chapel on the hill, long revered as sacred, had been destroyed by artillery fire during World War II, and Le Corbusier was asked to design its replacement in 1950—a new chapel, built as inexpensively as possible and

using the stone remaining from the previous building, that would harmonize with the site and the surrounding landscape. Le Corbusier was known for his rational, scientific, and highly personal style, influenced by the machine esthetic. His prewar buildings, with their unadorned geometric shapes rendered in slabs of reinforced concrete and plate glass, reflect his famous dictum that "a house is a machine for living in." When, in 1955, the new chapel at Ronchamp was finished and dedicated, many thought he

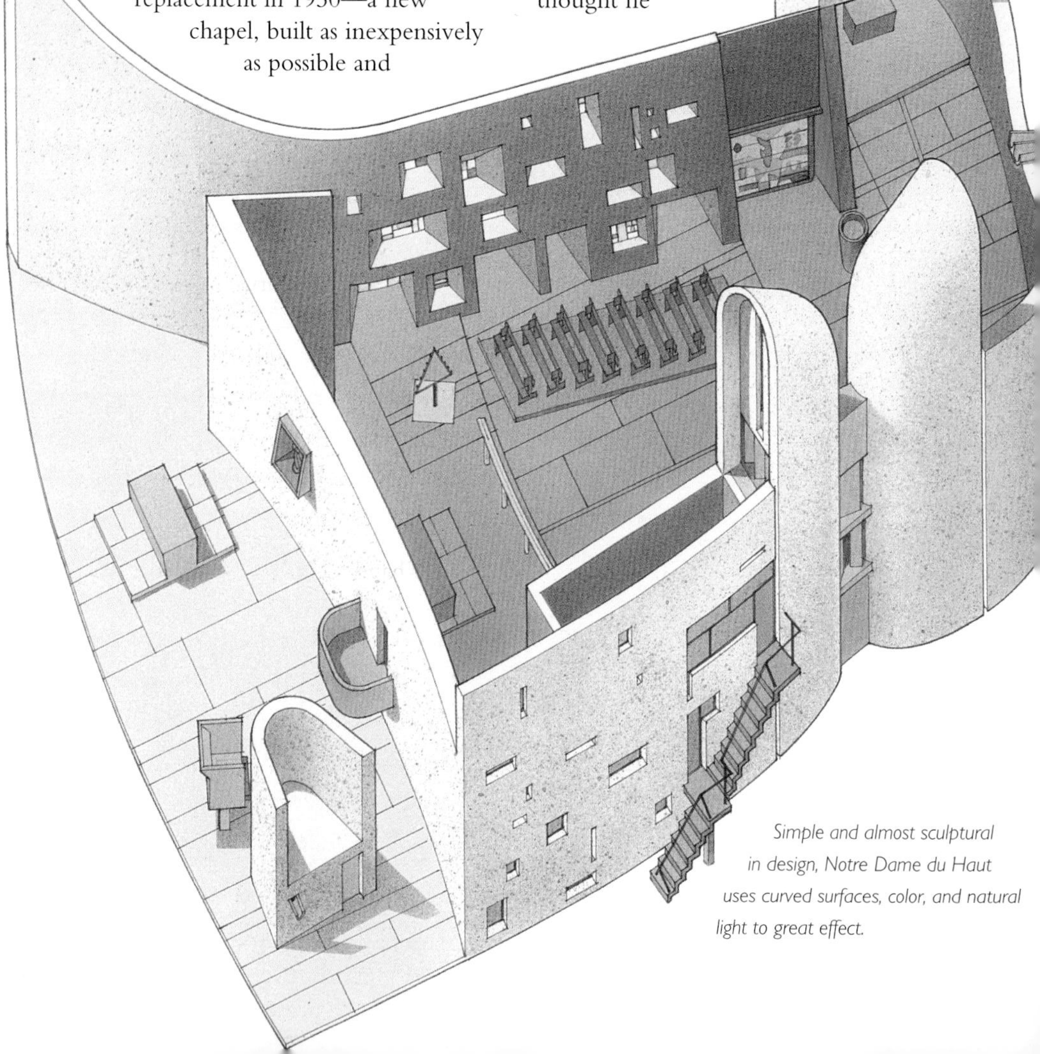

> **FAST FACTS**
> ■ DATE 1950–55
> ■ STYLE Expressionist
> ■ MATERIALS Concrete, stone, and glass
> ■ ARCHITECT Le Corbusier
> ■ Recycles stone used in the original building, destroyed during World War II

Simple and almost sculptural in design, Notre Dame du Haut uses curved surfaces, color, and natural light to great effect.

had abandoned his old rational, scientific tenets for an irrational freedom. Little did they realize that he had in fact applied his famous "Modulor" (a mathematical system of proportion) and a refining of his earlier ideas to this free-curving, almost sculptural masterpiece.

Le Corbusier's chapel stands serenely in the French countryside (above). A detail from one of the stained glass windows (left), which were designed and painted by the architect (below).

SMALL BUT STRIKING

To walk around the chapel is to see it unfold in a new and different shape with each vantage point—it certainly looks like a departure from Le Corbusier's earlier work. It is not large, but because of its siting and striking design, it creates a monumental presence, enhanced by the great curving roof that sweeps up to a prowlike point. The use of reinforced concrete, so beloved by this architect, is given a new dimension of apparent lightness as the upturned shell of the roof hovers about a foot (30 cm) above the tapering, whitewashed walls. It is supported on columns concealed from view, and the glass strip between it and the walls sheds a brilliant band of natural light (another favorite element) inside the chapel. The overhang of the roof also provides a canopy for an external altar and pulpit.

The walls of Notre Dame du Haut appear "absurdly thick" (in Le Corbusier's own words); they are built double with a wide cavity, reusing much of the stone of the old chapel. The curving walls of two small side chapels become the "door posts" of the main entrance, while those embracing another chapel rise up in a seamless curve to form a bell tower and additional source of light. The main eastern wall is pierced by small external windows, which splay wide open inside and, illuminated by colored glass designed and painted by Le Corbusier himself, pattern the dipping floor inside the main chapel with glowing pools of ethereal reds, blues, and greens.

The prevailing idiom is one of hand-crafted simplicity. And, as befits a sacred space, the chapel has inspired many—although not all those who visit do so for religious reasons. For like Michelangelo during the Renaissance, Le Corbusier, with Notre Dame du Haut, charted a new course for modern religious architecture.

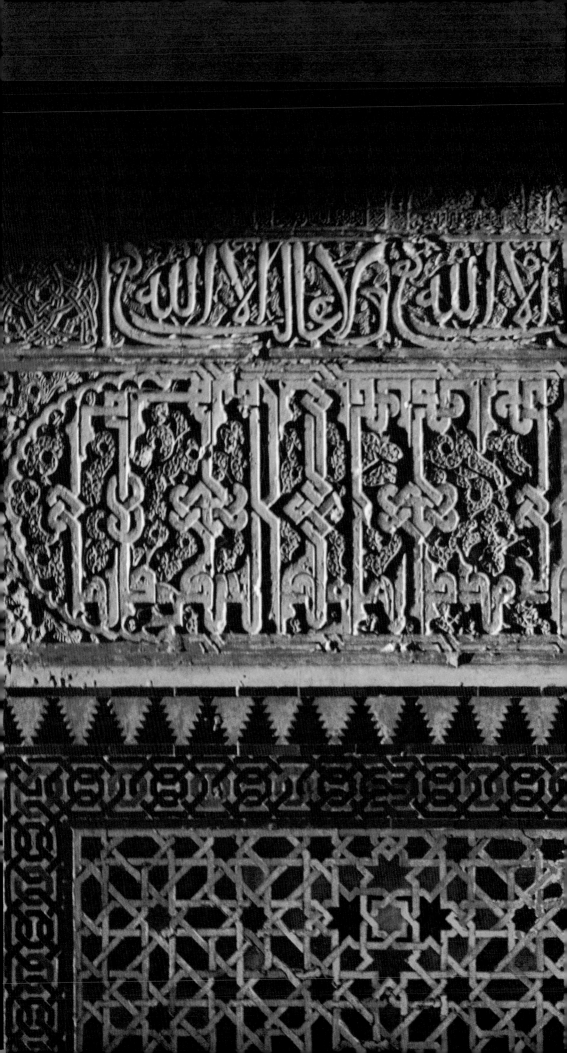

CASTLES, PALACES, AND FORTS

Whether built primarily for defense or for show, castles, palaces, and forts have always expressed the power and wealth of their owners.

Nowadays we think of castles, palaces, and forts as synonymous, but these buildings originally had separate functions. The word "palace" is derived from the Latin *palatium*, which was the name of the hill in Rome where the Emperor Domitian built his private residence at the end of the 1st century AD. Its official name was Domus Augustana, but it soon became known as the Palatium after the hill itself. Architectural splendor went hand-in-hand here with connotations of power and authority; hence the emergence in later centuries of the tradition of giving the name "palatium" to any substantial dwelling occupied by a ruler or a group of rulers. Hadrian's Villa at Tivoli is an early case in point.

WALLED OFF *The Great Wall of China takes the idea of the fortress to extremes, fortifying an entire country.*

"Castle" is derived from the Latin *castrum*, and its diminutive form *castellum*, originally meaning a Roman military camp, but later, by the middle of the 11th century, a fortified residence occupied by a king or baron. It is the residential aspect of the castle and the exclusiveness of its ownership that distinguishes it from other types of fortress. When the need for fortified residences no longer exists or when a central authority is strong enough to curtail their construction, as in France and England during the

HOLDING FAST *The scarred walls of the Crusaders' castle Krak des Chevaliers testify to the many attacks it has withstood.*

16th century, the history of the castle as a viable institution is over and the great house or palace, unfortified, replaces it as the characteristic residence of the ruling class.

However, this distinction between palaces and castles is not always so readily apparent. For example, in countries where relative peace has been achieved after a period of military or civil strife, palaces are likely to retain some of the defenses associated with castles. Conversely, castles that are still used as residences long after their military importance has ceased may be converted into palaces. Most major civilizations since the third millennium BC have built palaces, but in ways

STRENGTH AND BEAUTY *The Alhambra exemplifies the fortress-turned-palace. It is both heavily fortified (left) and exquisitely decorated, as shown in the pillars of the Court of the Lions (below).*

that are so diverse in planning, construction, and decoration as to defy easy classification. From a purely formal point of view, however, it is possible to detect two main lines of development: the first rooted in the pavilion-like palaces of the Eastern world, the second in the block-like palaces of the Western world.

CHANGING INTERPRETATIONS

At certain times and in certain places these two lines of development have overlapped or coalesced, but most historians would agree that whereas in the East the tendency has been to favor delicacy of scale over overt monumentality, in the West the reverse has been true. While it is known that certain palaces in the East were built without the protection of an outer defensive wall, they are comparatively rare. But in the West, from the 16th century onward, the unfortified palace rapidly became the rule rather than the exception. The 18th century Baroque Residenz at Würzburg is an archetypal example of this style.

A MODERN CASTLE *The vastness, grandeur, and opulence of San Simeon, the estate of media magnate William Randolph Hearst (right center), make it the modern equivalent of the castle.*

Meanwhile, the meaning of the term "castle" and its French equivalent, "château," had been broadened to include any country house of social distinction, whether it was fortified or not. Later, the 18th century saw the rise of various architectural revivalist movements, and with them the not uncommon practice of designing great houses in the image of a medieval castle, complete with sham battlements and towers. In Britain such houses were said to be in the "castellated" or "Baronial" style, in France in the "Troubadour" style. By the end of the 19th century this craze for imitating, however arbitrarily, the military and domestic architecture of the Middle Ages had run its course, though not before producing such buildings as Ludwig II's fairytale castle of Neuschwanstein in Germany.

Nowadays, we tend to use the words "castle" and "palace" as metaphors for grandeur, opulence, luxuriousness of appointments, and defensive capability. William Randolph Hearst's San Simeon estate in California possesses all of these qualities—hence the durability of that other name that was bestowed on it by visitors in the 1920s: Hearst Castle.

Palace of Knossos

Knossos, Crete

Since the excavation and restoration of its remains by archaeologist Arthur Evans, the Palace of Knossos on the island of Crete in the Mediterranean continues to astonish by the cleverness of its design and the artistic brilliance of its decoration and detailing.

Evans discovered the fabled palace by pursuing clues from the legend of Minos, king of Crete. King Minos sacrificed Athenian youths to the Minotaur (half-bull, half-man), which was confined to an enormous labyrinth. Finally, the Greek hero Theseus

FAST FACTS

■ DATE 1700–1380 BC

■ STYLE Minoan (Bronze Age)

■ MATERIALS Stone, rubble, mud brick, and timber

■ COMMISSIONED BY Rulers of Crete

■ Sanitary conditions were superior to those of many 19th century cities

killed the Minotaur and, aided by the king's daughter Ariadne, escaped from the labyrinth. Built against a hill and buried under tumuli (mounds of earth), the palace that Evans uncovered in 1900 is indeed labyrinthine. In a further link to the legend, images of bulls adorn its walls.

The palace is proof of the thriving Minoan culture of the time. Believed to have been built between 1700 and 1380 BC, it is planned on a vast scale around a rectangular paved court that was a focal point of palace life, the scene of ceremonial and theatrical events; whether these included the bull games depicted on the palace's murals is disputed. The mostly flat roofs were supported by walls constructed of stone blocks, rubble, and mud brick, often reinforced with half-timbering. The interiors were plastered and painted with abstract and figurative designs in glowing colors, restored by Evans in the early 20th century. Wooden columns figure prominently, their shafts tapering downward in a reversal of the pattern adopted in later Greek architecture.

Part of Evans' reconstruction (above) and a detail of the columns topped by stone slabs (left).

SOPHISTICATED SYSTEMS

The palace was extraordinarily sophisticated. It was plumbed and drained through a system of terracotta pipes; light wells admitted light and air to the lower stories; valuables, and comestibles such as wine, grains, honey, and oil, were kept in *pithoi* (jars) in a great bank of store rooms.

Between the store rooms and the central court are the remains of several cult rooms. The Throne Room contains a worn stone throne—thought to be the oldest in Europe—symbolically guarded by two griffins painted on the wall behind it. It was probably occupied by a priestess or a queen rather than by a king, whose own throne was presumably set up in a chamber of the now destroyed floor above.

The royal apartments, which adjoin the eastern side of the central court, originally rose to a height of four stories, built into the side of the hill that fell away beneath. The grand stairway rises from the court and links the stories. It is illuminated by a light well and is bordered on one side by a colonnade. The main reception rooms are in the basement; the largest of these is the Hall of the Double Axes, named for the design carved on the walls of the light well at the western end: It may be this design (*labrys* in Greek) that gave its name to the labyrinth of the Minotaur. Close by is the Queen's Hall, illuminated by another light well and containing the famous dolphin fresco.

The Queen's Hall (above) typifies the structural and decorative style of the palace. A detail from the dolphin frieze (left). The Throne Room with its griffin frescoes (below).

THE BEGINNING OF THE END

Minoan palaces had no defensive walls, suggesting the confidence of the Minoans in the strength of their navy. But at the beginning of the 14th century BC, the Mycenaeans from mainland Greece invaded the island. It is not known whether they were victorious, but 150 years later the palace was in ruins. The invaders may have wrecked it, or perhaps it was the after-effects of the massive volcanic eruption of Santoríni, 100 miles (160 km) to the north.

Citadel of Mycenae

Mycenae, Greece

In his epic poems the *Iliad* and the *Odyssey*, Homer described Mycenae, the legendary mountain stronghold of King Agamemnon, as "a strong-founded citadel rich in gold." According to both Homer and Aeschylus's *Oresteia*, Mycenae was a site of bloody revenge, of mortals cursed by the gods. Agamemnon led the Greek army in the Trojan Wars, but only after agreeing to the sacrifice of his daughter Iphigenia to obtain favorable winds so that his warships could sail. Upon his victorious return, he was murdered in his bath by his wife, Clytemnestra, and her lover, Aegisthus. They in turn met violent ends at the hands of Orestes, Agamemnon's son.

MYTH AND REALITY

Of all the Greek archaeological sites that are redolent of a mythic past, Mycenae best fits the Greek legend, especially if it is understood as a merging of stories from various periods. The

FAST FACTS

- **DATE** 14th–12th centuries BC
- **STYLE** Mycenaean
- **MATERIAL** Stone
- The legendary palace and fortress of Agamemnon and Clytemnestra, whose family history was the basis of the great literature of ancient Greece

Mycenaeans were a warlike race who lived on the open plains of mainland Greece. They fortified their buildings with massive stone walls faced with huge boulders, each several tons in weight, roughly shaped, and bonded with clay. The Greeks of a later period were so amazed at this display of seemingly superhuman strength that they thought it was the work of mythical one-eyed giants, the Cyclops. The term "Cyclopean" has thus come to describe this kind of gargantuan masonry.

Mycenae stands on a rocky hill above the Argive Plain, from which it controlled the main road between Corinth and Argos. Its defensive walls and most of the structures within were built between about 1380 and 1190 BC, though the site was a center of power as early as the 16th century BC. The citadel now lies in ruins, but enough survives to bear dramatic witness to the architectural achievements of the Mycenaean culture.

The famously imposing Lion Gate was the main ceremonial entrance to the citadel, where the elite lived—most of the town lay outside.

The ruins of the royal cemetery (left). Outside and below the mountain fortress is the so-called Treasury of Atreus (right), the finest example of a Mycenaean stone "beehive" tomb.

To enhance the gate's grandeur, the masonry around it was much more highly finished than that of the other walls, and a magnificent sculpted relief was installed above the gate, depicting two muscular lions, now headless, flanking a column.

A gold death mask believed by Schliemann to be that of Agamemnon (left). The Lion Gate at the entrance to the citadel (below).

INSIDE THE CITADEL

Just inside the citadel is a royal cemetery marked by a circular wall. In these tombs the German archaeologist Heinrich Schliemann unearthed one of the richest archaeological finds ever—finely wrought bronze daggers, bowls, and wine cups, tiaras and necklaces of filigreed gold, and a magnificent gold death mask. Schliemann cried, "I have gazed upon the face of Agamemnon." Although further study revealed that the graves dated from 300 years before the Trojan Wars, they are testament to the wealth and power of Mycenaean civilization.

From the cemetery, a chariot ramp or set of stairs leads to the Royal Palace near the top of the hill, the outlines of which are still visible. It centers around a court that leads to the *megaron*, a grand reception room with a traditional circular hearth and walls that were once covered in gaily painted frescoes.

A throne room and many smaller rooms completed the palace. To the east is the House of the Columns, a stately building with columns around three sides of its open courtyard, and the base of a stairway that once led to an upper story.

A secret cistern lies near the eastern end of the ramparts, its steps spiraling down to a deep underground spring. It was built in the 12th century BC to help the citadel's occupants withstand siege, possibly from rival Mycenaean kingdoms or Dorian invaders from the north. By 1100 BC, the once thriving settlement had been abandoned.

Great Wall of China

Northern Frontier of China

Homes, towns, cities, military outposts, and national frontiers have been fortified against enemy invasion throughout human history—but never on a scale as vast as that undertaken along the northern frontier of China between the 3rd century BC and the 17th century AD.

FAST FACTS

■ DATE 217 BC–1644
■ STYLE Military fortification
■ MATERIALS Stone, brick, and earth
■ COMMISSIONED BY The Emperors of China
■ The Great Wall is the only human structure visible from space

WALLS UPON WALLS

There are, or were, four Great Walls of China, all intended to protect the country from the most aggressive of its adversaries—the nomadic peoples of Mongolia to the north. The first wall was built between 217 and 208 BC by the first emperor of China, Qin Shih Huang-ti.

Convicts and hundreds of thousands of peasants worked on the project under Qin's harsh scheme of labor conscription. This wall, approximately 1,800 miles (almost 3,000 km) long, ran from Shanhaiguan in the east to Yemenguan in the west and was punctuated by as many as 25,000 watchtowers.

The second Great Wall was founded in the early years of the 1st century BC by the Emperor Han Wu Di, who pushed the first wall westward for another 300 miles (500 km). The third Great Wall was also an extension, of similar length to the second wall but it ran in the opposite direction. Built between 1138 and 1198, it led from the old eastern terminus at Shanhaiguan and snaked its way north to Dandong on the Yalu River.

The best preserved and most formidable wall, and the one most commonly known as the Great Wall of China, is the fourth. Work on this essentially new structure started in 1368 during the reign of the first emperor of the Ming dynasty, Zhu Yuanzhang, and con-

A residential pavilion surmounting one of the towers of the fort of Jiayuguan in Gansu province (left).

The Great Wall snakes across inhospitable terrain (above). Detail showing a carving from the Jiayuguan fort, originally the base of a tower built in 1345 (below).

Mongolian Oirats broke through. Again, in 1664, the Manchus from the north-east crossed the wall and established themselves in Peking (now Beijing) as the ruling dynasty. From that moment the Great Wall fell into disuse, its military and strategic importance nullified by the Manchus' control of the territory on both sides of it.

One thing the Great Wall was never to lose, however, was its value as a national symbol memorializing the countless men and women who built it. Many of them died in the process, their bones interred—so it is said—in the very fabric of the wall.

tinued more or less unabated until the fall of the last Ming emperor in 1644. By this stage the wall, with its various offshoots, had reached an extraordinary length of about 4,000 miles (6,500 km).

There was a strenuously enforced policy of using local building materials and construction methods, so the eastern half of the wall is built of dressed stone or kiln-fired brick, while the western half is constructed of rammed earth or pisé, sometimes faced with sun-dried brick. The wall is reinforced by watchtowers, gateways, and forts; the fort of Jiayuguan at the western terminus is a particularly fine example.

THE END OF THE WALL
The Great Wall protected China from Mongol invasion for many years, but in 1449 the

Hadrian's Villa

Tivoli, Italy

When city life became too hectic, wealthy Romans could always escape to their version of the weekend retreat—a villa on their country estate. The Roman emperors set the standard; they spent vast amounts on fitting out their villas with libraries, gymnasiums, baths, pavilions, temples, promenades, statuary, pools, fountains, and formal and informal gardens—everything a discerning Roman might need to support a cultivated lifestyle.

But the Emperor Hadrian's celebrated villa near Tivoli, about 19 miles (30 km) east of Rome, was like no other. Not only was it the largest and probably the most sumptuous Roman villa ever built, spreading out across an undulating plateau for over half a mile (1 km), it also had a unique form and plan, the result of inventive design and technical virtuosity.

This figure of Mars is one of many statues lining the Canopus.

FAST FACTS

■ DATE AD 118–133
■ STYLE Imperial Roman
■ MATERIAL Stone, brick, and concrete
■ COMMISSIONED BY Emperor Hadrian
■ Many features were inspired by Egyptian and Greek structures

Built between AD 118 and 133, the villa is a collection of structures of extraordinary variety and complexity, all fitting into the natural contours of the landscape. Curvilinear architecture created dynamic combinations of concave and convex shapes, and undulating interior and exterior spaces. The curving motif appears again and again: The pavilion at the south-eastern end of the richly decorated Piazza d'Oro has a central chamber containing the remnants of a colonnade, which curves and counter-curves as it circumnavigates the interior. In buildings such as the Academy, the Small Baths, and the concentrically planned Island Retreat there is barely a straight line to be found anywhere.

The Island Retreat is one of the loveliest features of the entire villa. It was conceived by Hadrian as a central islet with a circular dwelling, enclosed by a reflective moat and surrounding portico. On the rare occasions that it was possible, he would completely isolate himself here, far removed from the demands of ruling the empire.

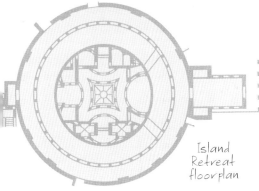

Island Retreat floorplan

The ruins of the Maritime Theater (above) show the curvilinear architecture that is characteristic of the villa as a whole.

A WEALTH OF TREASURES

Hadrian was a keen art collector, architect, and traveler, and his villa reflected his cultural interests. His collection of artworks filled the villa and its grounds. Pieces—or copies of pieces—from ancient Egypt, classical Greece, and contemporary Rome gave the villa the appearance of an open-air museum of antiquities. In addition, certain buildings were inspired by, or at least named for, some of the famous monuments that Hadrian saw on his travels. The Poikile, a massive, elongated courtyard with colonnades and a central pool, was named for a building in Athens. A temple in the Greek Doric style overlooks a Vale of Tempe, recalling a famous valley in Thessaly. But the villa's most evocative reminder of earlier civilizations is perhaps the Canopus—a long pool lined with columns and statuary, with a half-domed pavilion called the Serapeum at one end. It was named for the Sanctuary of Serapis at Canopus in Egypt, and Hadrian and his retinue used it as a summerhouse.

As well as the imperial suites (which are poorly preserved), there were buildings to accommodate staff, secretaries, advisors, friends, the Praetorian Guard (Hadrian's protectors), and those who sought an audience. Small wonder that the villa was described in later Roman texts as a *palatium* (a palace), and that today it still epitomizes the civilized yet vital and energetic world of ancient Rome.

Sunken passageways allowed the emperor's domestic staff to move quickly and unobtrusively around the villa.

Tower of London

London, England

In 1066 a Norman duke who is known to history as William the Conqueror won the Battle of Hastings and with it the English throne. But most of Saxon England still had to be brought under Norman control, so William mounted a succession of military campaigns and built fortified castles to consolidate his island kingdom. The castles were the keypoint of the conqueror's subjugation of England.

One of the most impressive of these was the White Tower—the core of the present Tower of London compound. Best known today as a grim, fearsome prison and a place of execution, the complex has also functioned as a palace, an armory, a mint, a menagerie—the famous ravens remain—

FAST FACTS

- DATE 1078–97
- STYLE Norman fortress
- MATERIALS Stone and timber
- COMMISSIONED BY William the Conqueror
- Dubbed "The White Tower" after it was whitewashed in 1240

and, more enduringly, as a safe deposit for the Crown Jewels.

William invited Gundulf, Bishop of Rochester, to design the Tower on the banks of the Thames, within the south-east angle of an old Roman town wall. Described as "very competent and skillful at building in stone," Gundulf also supervised the construction of the tower, which began in 1078. The great rectangular stone keep, the earliest of its kind in England and one of the largest ever built in Europe, was completed in the early 1090s, after William's death.

Measuring 118 feet by 107 feet (36 x 33 m), the tower rises to a height of 90 feet (almost 30 m); its four corner turrets are higher still. At its base, the walls are 15 feet (4.6 m) thick, thinning out in the upper sections to 11 feet (3.4 m). Numerous arrow slits once pierced these walls, but only a few survive; the rest were replaced in the late 17th century by the window openings of the great English architect Sir Christopher Wren, who also decreed that the whitewashing of the tower should cease.

The original entrance, on the southern side, was reached by a flight of wooden stairs that could be quickly dismantled in time of danger.

The impressive Tower of London (above). The fortified walls, showing an arrow slit (left).

The interior, organized on three levels, contained "all the essential accommodation of a royal residence." The King's apartments, with their fireplaces and garderobes, were on the upper two floors, and within quick and easy reach of the Chapel of St. John the Evangelist. This perfectly preserved Norman chapel is flanked on either side by a narrow aisle, with a gallery above, merging as one with the ambulatory and gallery at the eastern end; the interior is stone-vaulted throughout.

An aerial perspective showing the tower and its concentric fortifications (above). A view of the tower from a French manuscript of 1415 (left).

Princes"—12-year-old Edward V and his younger brother Richard, Duke of York. Finally, Edward I (1272–1307) carried out extensive work on the tower, including the moat surrounding the castle, and Traitor's Gate, the new river gate through St. Thomas's Tower, where prisoners came by boat before being tried at Westminster. Edward also instigated improvements to the castle's residential facilities.

CONTRIBUTIONS OF KINGS

After the reign of the Conqueror, it would be another 225 years before the tower assumed its familiar concentric configuration. William's son Rufus (William II, 1056–1100) built a wall around the tower in 1097; Richard I (1189–99) extended the defensive perimeter by constructing a new wall beyond William's. Henry III (1216–72) enlarged the enclosure yet again and established the alignment that now makes up the inner curtain. Most of the mural towers that punctuate this curtain are his additions as well, including the Garden Tower, which was later renamed the Bloody Tower after the alleged murder there in 1483 of the "Little

Later monarchs followed suit, including Henry VIII (1509–47), who built the Queen's House in the south-west angle of the inner enclosure, possibly for the use of his second wife, Anne Boleyn. Henry VIII also rebuilt the fire-damaged early 12th century chapel of St. Peter ad Vincula (St. Peter in Chains) to the north of the "Queen's House." The chapel tells a tragic story; according to one Elizabethan writer, under the pavement are the remains of "two dukes between two queens, to wit, the Duke of Somerset and the Duke of Northumberland, between Queen Anne and Queen Katherine, all four beheaded."

65

Krak des Chevaliers

Orontes Valley, Syria

Krak des Chevaliers, or Castle of the Knights, squats on a spur high above the Orontes Valley in Syria. Virtually impregnable and strategically positioned to defend the Homs Pass and surrounding rich agricultural lands, it was a vital outpost during the crusades of the 12th and 13th centuries, when the Christian armies of Europe tried to wrest control of Jerusalem, the Holy Land, and its pilgrimage routes from the Muslim rulers— and acquire land and wealth into the bargain.

FAST FACTS

- DATE *12th–13th centuries*
- STYLES *Romanesque and Gothic*
- BUILDERS *French crusaders*
- *First fortified in 1031 and garrisoned with Kurdish troops; at that time called Hisn al-Akrad, "the Fortress of the Kurds"*

French crusaders captured the already fortified site in 1099 and for a second time in 1110, and the Knights Hospitaller took control in 1144. This religious order of knights, originally founded to care for sick pilgrims, was by then also a wealthy military organization. The knights remodeled the castle and increased its fortifications, fashioning it into the jewel in their crown—a castle that was besieged unsuccessfully on 11 occasions during their 130-year tenure.

DOUBLE DEFENSE

Krak des Chevaliers is a concentric castle, made up of two lines of defense. The outer walls— with thickened bases to protect against enemy excavations, narrow chambers on the parapet from which stones could be dropped, and slotted openings for the archers—formed the first line. The inner walls, the second line, were strengthened by buttress towers and a talus (sloped wall) up to 80 feet (24.3 m) thick, almost as wide as it was tall, which gave

This early engraving shows the extraordinarily strong and complex fortifications for which the castle is renowned.

Krak des Chevaliers (above)—a fine example of medieval military architecture. The covered gallery (inset) features cross-ribbed vaulting.

excellent resistance against attack and the frequent earthquakes in the area.

Within the area enclosed by the reinforced upper towers lay the inner enclosure, or ward, the first part to be built. A small, irregularly shaped courtyard led to dormitories, store rooms, the apartments of the highest ranking knights, and the castle's chief architectural glories: a chapel and a great hall. The chapel is crowned by a pointed barrel vault with transverse arches, recalling earlier French Romanesque churches. In contrast, the great hall and covered gallery are in the Gothic style, with cross-ribbed vaults and elaborate carvings. This was the refectory, also used by the knights for meetings.

A CASTLE COMMUNITY

The castle was both a fortress and a community made up of the many men who defended it. During times of siege, the population would truly swell, to perhaps as many as 2,000 men. The knights were housed in the three upper towers. The men-at-arms and mercenaries, the bulk of the defenders, camped out in the outer enclosure. A windmill atop one tower milled corn; massive storehouses beneath the upper courtyard held provisions; drinking water came

from rainwater collected and piped into nine cisterns; and an aqueduct channeled water into an open reservoir (doubling as a moat) in the outer enclosure.

So impenetrable was Krak des Chevaliers that it was not until March 1271 that the Sultan of Egypt, Malik al-Zahir Baybars, captured the outer enclosure by breaching the south-west corner. But the more formidable inner enclosure stood fast. Baybars forged a letter, supposedly from the Grand Master of the Knights Hospitaller, ordering the knights to surrender. The ruse worked, and the garrison departed "to their own lands" under a safe conduct pass.

Baybars closed the breach in the outer wall with a circular tower inscribed with his name and a large rectangular tower was added by Sultan Qala'un (1280–90). The castle remained in use until 1932, when the village that occupied its interior was relocated. Today, it continues to overlook the valley, "the best preserved and most wholly admirable castle of the world," according to T. E. Lawrence, better known as Lawrence of Arabia.

Palace of the Alhambra

Granada, Spain

O n a hot, dry hilltop, with the harsh peaks of the Sierra Nevada looming behind it, stands the Alhambra, the palace-fortress of the Nasrid sultans, the last independent Moorish rulers of Spain. Viewed from the outside, its thick protective walls give no clue that inside lies a world of cool, airy courtyards and pavilions, trickling fountains, and lush gardens. For this is one of the most serenely sensual and beautiful buildings of Europe, a place where Moorish art and architecture reached their pinnacle.

THE RED FORTRESS

The complex was founded by the Nasrid prince Muhammad I, who built the citadel—called in Arabic *Qal'at al-Hamra*, "The Red Fortress"—which eventually contained the palace and a complete city, now ruined. Muhammad had established Granada as the capital of an independent Moorish kingdom in 1238 after being pushed out of northern Spain by the gradual Christian reconquest. By 1300, it was the only such kingdom left in Spain. It survived thus for 250 years.

The Moors and their last sultan, Boabdil, were finally expelled from Spain in 1492. Boabdil cried at his loss and was reproached by his mother: "Do not weep like a woman for what you could not defend like a

FAST FACTS

- DATE 1333–91
- STYLE Islamic
- MATERIALS Marble and ceramics
- COMMISSIONED BY Muhammad I of the Nasrid Muslim dynasty
- Represented the Muslim ideal of the earthly paradise

man." The building still stands. Dating mostly from the time of Yusuf I and Muhammad V (1333–91), much of it is exceptionally well preserved.

The palace unfolds through three separate sections linked by corridors. Each section, a series of rooms arranged around a courtyard, had a special function in Nasrid times. The first, the Mexuar, was where the sultan conducted public business, heard petitions, and received his ministers. Few passed beyond it and the small but beautifully articulated Cuarto Dorado, or Golden Court, which was possibly a waiting area for visitors.

The Court of the Myrtles, with its long pool of water and delicately columned arcades, led to

Austere serenity marks the Court of the Myrtles (left). A view from above shows the complex yet ordered system of corridors that links the public and private parts of the citadel (right).

Outside the fortress is the Courtyard of the Pavilions (right). Geometric designs reflect the Islamic concept of an ordered universe (inset).

the so called Hall of the Ambassadors. This, the largest room in the palace, was the throne room, as Arabic inscriptions on the walls, such as "I am the Heart of the Palace," attest. The vaulted wooden ceiling is inlaid with seven tiers of interlacing star-shaped patterns, in an allusion to the seven heavens mentioned in the Koran.

AN EARTHLY PARADISE

Beyond lies the most celebrated part of the palace: the Harem, the private retreat of the sultan and his family. It centers on the Court of the Lions, which takes its name from the 12 spouting lions that encircle the pedestal and basin of the central fountain. It is graced at its eastern and western ends by pavilions, and is divided by axial pathways into four gardens; during the Nasrid period the flower beds lay just below the paths, so that a stroller would have seen "a carpet woven with flowers instead of threads." It is surrounded on all sides by ornately carved arcades ornamented with more than 100 slender columns.

The palace floors are covered in cool marble, and its walls are encrusted with ceramic tiles and a delicate tracery of calligraphy or carved and painted stucco. In this quarter of the palace are 10 more fountains, all in interior spaces, some delivering their water into the four channels that run out into the center of the court. The design delineates a perfect world, invoking the universal idea of the four rivers of paradise and also the specifically Muslim idea of heaven as a place of "pavilions beneath which water flows."

Kronborg Castle

Elsinore, Denmark

The Castle of Kronborg, near Elsinore on the island of Zealand, stands on the end of a hook-shaped promontory that commands the narrowest part of the sound that separates Denmark and Sweden. Its founder, Eric of Pomerania, King of Denmark, built the first castle on the site in 1425 to enforce the toll that he was levying on foreign merchant vessels passing through the sound.

In 1558 King Christian II strengthened the castle's outer walls to withstand cannon fire. From 1574 to 1577, Frederik II, Christian's son, reconstructed the north and west wings in alternating bands of sandstone and red brick, prepared the south wing for the installation of a chapel, and built the main entrance to the present castle and the so-called Dark Gate.

A ROYAL RESIDENCE

Almost immediately, Frederik instigated a second rebuilding campaign, which was so ambitious that by 1585 the site held an almost entirely new castle. The design by Anthonis van Opbergen consists of four connecting wings, three stories high, enclosing a spacious rectangular courtyard; the attic above the wings

---

FAST FACTS

- DATE 1585–1699
- STYLE Danish Renaissance
- MATERIALS Stone and timber
- ARCHITECT Anthonis van Opbergen
- First a fortress, then a royal residence, then a military barracks, the castle is now a state museum

---

contains three more levels. Walls faced with sandstone support steeply pitched roofs covered with copper sheeting. Three of the four corner towers are topped by smaller towers, and a tall, many-tiered spire rises from the roof of the northern wing. The modernization of the castle emphasized its role as a royal residence rather than as a military strongpoint. Kronborg now looked like an elaborate palace, with its enlarged windows, "Dutch" gables, and crowning spire and towers, all detailed in the Renaissance style.

By the time the project was finished, the main lines of defense were no longer concentrated in the castle but in the surrounding walls and the pointed bastions, built of stone with an earthen core. Low in profile but very thick in section, these defenses were designed as gun platforms with an outer moat to keep the enemy at bay.

The royal apartments—including the Great Hall and the King's and Queen's chambers—were badly damaged by fire in 1629; they were repaired and redecorated under the auspices of King Christian IV after 1631. The chapel survived the blaze and remains very much as it was when consecrated in 1582.

In 1658 Kronborg Castle was besieged and captured by the Swedes, who before abandoning it the next year, stole some of its finest art works. In order to discourage further attacks, Christian V (1670–99) constructed a new outer line of walls, with bastions and a moat, on the landward side of the castle.

But Kronborg's life as a royal residence was almost over. In 1785 it was pressed into service as a military barracks, and after 1922 it became the property of the Danish state. Restored and refurbished between 1926 and 1929, it is now a museum.

THE PRINCE OF DENMARK

The site of Kronborg Castle is the setting for Shakespeare's *Hamlet*, though Shakespeare called the castle "Elsinore." The ghost of Hamlet's murdered father appears on the battlements to incite Hamlet (portrayed by actor Richard Burton, right) to vengeance, precipitating the tragedy of Hamlet's own death. But the castle that Shakespeare had in mind is not the elegant structure of today; rather it is a fortress on the brink of a massive cliff …

> That beetles o'er his base into the sea …
> The very place puts toys of desperation,
> Without more motive, into every brain
> That looks so many fathoms to the sea
> And hears it roar beneath.

The present design of Kronborg Castle (in Danish "A Royal Fortress") is largely that of the architect Anthonis van Opbergen, who was commissioned by King Frederik II of Denmark.

Castle of the White Heron

Himeji, Japan

The fortified castle at Himeji is one of the last great castles to be built in Japan and the most impressive of the few authentic surviving examples of Japan's fortified castles. The Japanese named it the Castle of the White Heron—an allusion to its high, white-plastered walls. Its main keep, magnificently articulated in the traditional Japanese style, with tier upon tier of roofs and gables, soars over the castle to overlook the town of Himeji and the surrounding country of Kansai province. But for all its

FAST FACTS

- **DATE** c. 1601–09
- **STYLE** Japanese fortified castle
- **MATERIALS** Masonry and wood
- **COMMISSIONED BY** Ikeda Terumasa
- Impressive though its fortifications were, the castle at Himeji was never called upon to defend itself

beauty, the castle is a brilliantly ingenious fortification—and, ironically, one that was never tested in battle.

A JAPANESE MODEL

In Japan, fortified castles as an identifiable building type came into their own in the second half of the 16th century, when they were used by the *daimyo*—feudal lords of Japan—as refuges in time of war and as centers from which to exert their authority over newly acquired territory.

Of all the *daimyo* who pursued this course, none was more vigorous than Toyotomi Hideyoshi, founder between 1581 and 1594 of no fewer than five castles: those at Himeji, Osaka, Yodo, Nagoya, and Fushimi. Each had a large, many-storied keep of wooden frame construction rising from the center of a walled and moated compound. To enhance its defensive capabilities, the keep was set on a high rectangular masonry base with concave sloping sides and tilted quoin stones—a design that was intended to resist the effects of earthquake

View from the keep showing the town below the castle (left). Roofs of the fortified castle at Osaka (right).

Today the Castle of the White Heron is set in exquisitely manicured grounds, its original military purpose all but forgotten (above). A decorative paneled interior in the castle keep (right).

shock, which is a factor that Japanese architects must allow for to this day.

Hideyoshi died in 1598, having seized control over the whole of Japan. His successor, Tokugawa Ieyasu, appointed his brother-in-law, Ikeda Terumasa, as the governor of the western provinces. Terumasa chose Himeji as his principal seat of government but found it inadequate. Determined to outshine his predecessors as a patron of military architecture, he set about remodeling the castle completely—and it remains virtually unchanged since the castle was finished in 1609.

STRENGTHENING THE DEFENSES

The original keep of 1581 was three stories high. Terumasa replaced this with a more impressive keep of five stories and seven floors, resting on a masonry base of far greater mass and height than that of the original building. To further strengthen the defenses, he added three more keeps, lower in profile than the main keep, but linked to it and to each other by two-story corridors. If the castle were attacked, defenders could move rapidly from one part of the complex to another, depending on where they were needed to fend off the enemy.

Considerable thought was given to making the compound around the core of the castle impregnable. The outer defensive line was a moat in a spiral configuration. Within this outer line was a series of strongly fortified gateways, and further in there was a labyrinthine system of inner courtyards and passageways calculated to confuse the enemy. Square and round openings in the walls were designed for firing muskets, triangular holes for firing arrows. Other fortified Japanese castles were planned along the same lines, but nowhere is the design more ingeniously contrived than at the castle of Himeji.

the soaring gabled roofs of the Japanese fortified castle in Osaka

73

Potala Palace

Lhasa, Tibet

Atop the Red Hill (Marpo Ri) overlooking the city of Lhasa stands Tibet's best known and most imposing building. The Potala Palace was founded by Ngawang Lobzang Gyatso, proclaimed the fifth Dalai Lama of the Gelugpa Sect of Buddhism in 1641 and, with the military and political backing of the Oelot Mongols, the ruler of a unified Tibet several years later. One of his reasons for select-ing the Red Hill as the site for his new palace was its association with the name of the much venerated king, Songtsan Gambo, who had built his own palace there in the early 7th century. The new Potala (known as the White Palace for the color of its outer walls) went up between 1645 and 1648, absorbing some of the ruins of the earlier palace.

The Red Palace was added in 1690–93. Positioned near the center of the White Palace, its greater height (13 stories) and the red-colored walls distinguish it from the rest of the complex.

FAST FACTS

■ DATE 1645–93

■ STYLE Tibetan Buddhist

■ MATERIALS Wood, earth, and stone

■ COMMISSIONED BY Fifth Dalai Lama

■ The palace walls were fortified against earthquakes by pouring molten copper into their cavities

Yet more additions were made by later Dalai Lamas, especially during the 18th century, when the Potala Palace assumed its present appearance.

Like those in most of the older palaces and monasteries of Tibet, the outer walls are of stone and diminish in thickness as they taper toward the top. The doors, windows, ceiling beams, balconies, and columns are of wood. The flat roofs can be used as outdoor living spaces. On its rear side and at each end the palace is fortified by circular towers. Stairways with dog-leg turns and flanking stone walls ascend from the plain below to various entrance gates in the southern façade. The palace contains a seemingly endless array of halls, terraces, chapels, corridors, and residential chambers. The audience hall that lies within the highest eastern block of the

This statue representing the Lord Buddha in one of his guises is one of some 200,000 statues in the complex.

The roofs are gilded (right), as are the sculptural features on the ridge lines and sloping edges (below).

White Palace was vital to the palace's former role as an administrative center. Important political and religious functions were held here, as well as ceremonies for the installation and the official recognition of each new Dalai Lama. Rising through several stories, the hall is subdivided, in customary Tibetan fashion, into three aisles by two lines of wooden columns carrying brightly painted and elaborately carved brackets, beams, and ceiling panels. The private apartments of the Dalai Lama were located on the top floor of the same block. Two large "sunshine" halls, facing east and west respectively, are complemented here by chapels, libraries, living rooms, and a bedchamber, all richly decorated and furnished. In the western side of the White Palace, accommodation was provided for more than 100 monks.

A PRECIOUS HERITAGE

The Red Palace was used almost exclusively for religious observances, meditation, and prayer. The largest of the many halls within is the so-called "West Hall" housing the monumental tomb of the fifth Dalai Lama. In the form of a chorten or stupa, this tomb is covered with gold plate inlaid with pearls and semi-precious gems. Over 650 fresco paintings adorn the walls. Other halls in the Red Palace contain chortens for the seventh to the thirteenth Dalai Lamas.

For symbolic reasons the temples of the Potala are located on the uppermost terraces of the building. They are free-standing, rectangular structures surmounted by pitched roofs with gables and deeply projecting eaves turning up at the corners like those in the traditional architecture of Nepal and China. The temples of the Potala are referred to in Tibet as the "Golden Roofs" due to their lavish gilding.

The importance of the Potala Palace both as a work of architecture and as a repository of Tibetan art and culture cannot be overestimated, for it is a rare survivor of the widespread destruction that befell Tibetan religious buildings during the Cultural Revolution of the late 1960s. A more enlightened attitude to heritage issues seems to prevail today. Sums of money are being spent on maintaining the Potala and its treasures, and pilgrims are allowed once again to worship at its shrines.

Residenz

Würzburg, Germany

I n the sum of its artistic and architectural qualities the Würzburg Residenz is the supreme example of Germany's 18th century Baroque palaces. That so fortunate a result was achieved at all says a great deal for the perspicacity and drive of the Prince–Bishops Johann and Friedrich von Schönborn who, as well as financing the construction of this glorious building, also managed to attract to it some of the most accomplished architects, painters, and craftsmen in western Europe.

FAST FACTS

■ DATE 1720–44

■ STYLE German Baroque

■ ARCHITECTS Johann Balthasar Neumann, Robert de Cotte, Germain Boffrand, and Lucas von Hildebrandt

■ An architectural tour-de-force involving artists from across Europe

A GRAND PLAN

Johann Balthasar Neumann, an architect from Würzburg, was employed to spearhead the planning of the Residenz and to coordinate its construction. French architects Robert de Cotte and Germain Boffrand and Viennese architect Lucas von Hildebrandt contributed most to the design of the façades of the building. Although Neumann had to make major concessions to the other architects with regard to the layout of the final scheme, it was he who conceived two of the Residenz's most outstanding architectural features: the court chapel in the south-west wing and the grand staircase leading from the main entrance vestibule on the ground floor to the main reception rooms on the first floor.

Considered as a whole, the Residenz is a four-story complex "of open and enclosed blocks and wings," laid out in a U-shape. The main entrance, which is approached from the west through a *cour d'honneur* ("court

Tiepolo's "Europa" fresco contains portraits of Tiepolo himself, Neumann, and Antonio Bossi, whose sculptures and stucco carvings helped forge the so-called "Wurzburg Rococo" style.

of honor"), features three doors of sufficient width and height to permit (in accordance with Prince–Bishop Johann von Schönborn's wishes) a coach to be driven through them into the vestibule beyond. Leading off the vestibule on its northern side is the grand staircase, a highly personal invention on Neumann's part, which was designed on almost theatrical principles. When viewing the stairs from the bottom visitors see only the first of its several flights. On climbing to the middle landing they see to their right and left another two flights, each doubling back on the first to reach the floor above. The other discovery they make at this point is that the staircase itself, and the gallery that surrounds it, are enclosed within an enormous, vaulted hall with big windows on three sides.

The effect of emerging from the relatively dark and low-ceilinged vestibule into the well-lit, soaring space of the stair hall is deliberately contrived and skillfully executed, and epitomizes the spirit of the Baroque. The same can be said of the Venetian painter Giovanni Battista Tiepolo's magnificent illusionist fresco on the ceiling of the stair hall. Its purpose is not only to add luster and prestige to what is

Neumann's monumental staircase zigzags from floor to floor (above). A Tiepolo fresco (left) adorns the ceiling of the Imperial Chamber.

already a magnificent interior, but also to create the impression that the stair hall is much more lofty than it actually is. This, "the largest fresco ever to be painted," has as its subject Apollo the sun god. He is depicted as the patron of the arts, presiding over allegorical representations of the four terrestrial regions into which the known world was then divided—America, Asia, Africa, and Europe.

On March 16, 1945, the Residenz suffered devastating damage by fire as a result of an air raid. Miraculously, the stair hall and apartments in its vicinity survived the conflagration. Since then, the building has been painstakingly restored, and in 1981 was included by UNESCO on the World Cultural Heritage List.

Castle of Neuschwanstein

Bavarian Alps, Germany

Dramatically perched atop a craggy hill, the castle of Neuschwanstein is the legacy of the "Dream King," Ludwig II of Bavaria (1845–86), and the embodiment of his passionate desire to give form to his fantasies. Ludwig grew up in a romantic Neo-Gothic castle, Hohenschwangau. The castle was restored in the 1830s from 12th century ruins associated with the legend of the Swan-Knight, Lohengrin. According to Ludwig's mother, Queen Marie, her son was interested in the arts from age six, built churches and monasteries with his toy bricks, and "loved dressing up as a nun, and enjoyed acting." In 1861, at the age of 15, Ludwig urged his father, Maximilian II, to commission a performance of Richard Wagner's opera *Lohengrin*. Utterly enchanted by Wagner's musical setting of the mythical exploits of Teutonic folk heroes, the boy became a passionate devotee.

FAST FACTS

- DATE 1869–92
- STYLE German Neo-Romanesque
- MATERIAL Stone
- ARCHITECTS Eduard Riedel, Georg Dollmann, and Julius Hofmann
- For all his influence over Ludwig, Wagner never set foot in the castle

MUSIC AND MAJESTY

In 1864 the whimsical prince became king. Very soon afterward, Ludwig wrote to Wagner asking to meet him. He offered to liberate the impoverished composer from "the tedious cares of everyday life." It was the beginning of a friendship and collaboration between the young king and the middle-aged composer that was to last until Wagner's death in 1883.

In 1867 Ludwig commissioned a new production of Wagner's *Tannhäuser*, an opera based on the medieval legend of a lustful German troubadour. Wanting the sets to be as authentic as possible, he visited the castle of Wartburg in Thuringia, believed to be the setting for the legend's famous song competition. In 1868 Ludwig wrote to Wagner about his

King Ludwig II's fairytale castle at Neuschwanstein and the road snaking up to it, viewed from above.

The Royal Bedroom is fitted out in Gothic style (above). Golden stars adorn the blue dome of the Throne Room (right).

plan to build a Wartburg of his own. It was to be "in the genuine style of the old German knights' castles ... [with] reminiscences of Tannhäuser ... and Lohengrin."

A CASTLE OF DREAMS

Construction began in 1869 under architect Eduard Riedel, in close consultation with Ludwig and scene-painter Christian Jank. After Riedel, two other architects were involved in the project: Georg Dollmann, from 1874, and Julius Hofmann, from 1884. The result is a powerful example of picturesque showmanship, the exterior detailing inspired by the German Romanesque, the interior combining the Romanesque with other medieval styles.

The richly carved royal bedroom, with its ornate four-poster bed, is Gothic. Hofmann's Throne Room is Byzantine, basilica-like in plan, with a two-story arcade on three sides and a semi-circular apse on the fourth. The walls are richly decorated with abstract and figurative designs. (Ludwig intended to place an ivory and gold throne on the dais of the apse, but the throne was never constructed.) The great ceiling candelabrum was modeled on that of the Palatine Chapel at Aachen, installed in 1168 by the Hohenstaufen king, Frederick Barbarossa. Wagnerian themes reach a climax in Ludwig's study, where paintings depict the Tannhäuser legend, and in the Minstrels' Hall, which is carefully modeled on that of Wartburg.

Toward the end of his life Ludwig spent more and more of his time in his fairytale castle. Here, on June 10, 1886, he learned he had been deposed on the grounds of insanity. Two days later, in the throes of a deep depression, he was taken to Berg Castle, a mental hospital situated on Lake Starnberg. The following evening, doctor and patient set out on a lakeside walk; both were later found drowned, and bruise marks on the doctor's neck suggested there had been a struggle. Out of sympathy for Ludwig most historians have stopped short of describing this event as a murder-suicide.

Julius Hofmann continued working on Ludwig's dream castle until 1892, but the interior was never to be completed.

The Disneyland Sleeping Beauty's Castle is modeled on Neuschwanstein.

Biltmore House

North Carolina, United States of America

Biltmore House, south of Asheville amid the mountainous scenery of North Carolina, represents American domestic architecture at its most grandiose. It was built for a member of one of the nation's wealthiest and most philanthropic families, the Vanderbilts. The entrepreneurial Cornelius Vanderbilt (1794–1877) left $100 million and 13 offspring—the makings of a dynasty.

Biltmore House became the most sumptuous architectural statement of a dynasty famed for their luxurious residences. It was constructed between 1888 and 1895, ostensibly to provide 28-year-old George Washington Vanderbilt (grandson of Cornelius) with a "healthy winter and spring residence." Still privately owned by George Vanderbilt's descendants, the house was opened to tourists in 1930 in a benevolent attempt to boost the local economy during the Great Depression; 90 of its 250 rooms can be visited.

FAST FACTS

- DATE 1888–95
- STYLE French Neo-Gothic
- MATERIALS Stone, glass, and wood
- ARCHITECT Richard Morris Hunt
- The house has 43 bathrooms and 65 fireplaces, as well as refrigeration and an Otis elevator

FRENCH SPLENDOR IN THE NEW WORLD

Biltmore's architect was Richard Morris Hunt (1828–95). He had trained at the École des Beaux-Arts in Paris and was especially enamored of the "French Château" style. Hunt accompanied Vanderbilt on a visit to the Loire Valley in 1889, hoping to persuade the young man to choose this style for his future house. The Château of Blois, with its widely varied wings in medieval, Gothic, and Renaissance styles, was the favored model. The late Gothic Louis XII wing (1498–1501) made the strongest impression and is reflected in Hunt's final design for Biltmore. Most of the details on the façades, and the configuration of the roofs, towers, and loggias, derive from this wing. The stairway to the left of the front door is based on the double-spiraled stairway of the François I

Richard Morris Hunt, architect of the French-château-inspired Biltmore House.

Great trees frame the house (above). The magnificent banquet hall features tapestries and a triple fireplace (right).

wing (1515–24), but in adapting the design, Hunt reversed the spiral, glazed the exterior openings, and replaced Renaissance details with Gothic ones.

GRACIOUS LIVING

The largest country house in the United States of America, some 775 feet (238 m) in length and equipped with the most up-to-date conveniences from refrigeration to a speedy Otis elevator, the four-storied Biltmore House cost an estimated $3 million to build. Thirty-two guest rooms alone were needed to sleep party visitors, while 43 bathrooms and 65 fireplaces were built to wash and warm the inhabitants. At ground level was the domestic sphere, containing the laundry, kitchens, and staff quarters, as well as recreational facilities—a bowling alley and a swimming pool. The second floor held reception areas, where guests were welcomed, fed, and entertained. On the third and fourth floors was the private realm—bedrooms, guest suites, and more intimate sitting areas.

Extended vistas through the house meet the eye at every turn, notably along the axis that runs the whole length of the first floor from the library to the banquet hall. The reception rooms—the entrance hall, music room, breakfast room, salon, and banquet hall—revolve around a central court, the glass-roofed "Winter Garden." All the public spaces are conceived on a princely scale, especially the vast banquet hall. Reminiscent of a medieval great hall, it measures 72 feet by 42 feet (22 x 13 m) and rises 70 feet (21.5 m) to a wooden, rib-vaulted ceiling hung with two large chandeliers.

Through the gallery that runs off the entrance hall on its southern side is the peaceful library, with its collection of around 20,000 volumes, many of them rare. On the northern side of the plan, the recreational wing resembles an English gentlemen's club, with its billiard room, gun room, and smoking room.

The Biltmore Estate itself provides a magical setting for the mansion: 8,000 acres (3,240 ha) of terraced gardens and forest plantations, all masterfully landscaped in 1888 by Frederick Law Olmsted. Originally covering 125,000 acres (50,600 ha), much of the estate has been sold or donated to the Pisgah National Forest. Visitors can experience the natural beauty of the forest depths along the 3 miles (5 km) of winding road that leads from the entrance gates to the esplanade in front of the house.

San Simeon

California, United States of America

The creation of San Simeon atop a hill overlooking the sea about 155 miles (250 km) south of San Francisco fulfilled the ambitions of two remarkable people: the newspaper magnate and sometime film producer William Randolph Hearst, and Julia Morgan, his architect. Hearst wanted a country house in which to entertain his friends and display his vast collection of antiques and art objects; Julia Morgan wanted a commission that would give her the opportunity to exercise her design powers with as much freedom as possible.

FAST FACTS

■ DATE 1919–30
■ STYLE Spanish Mission
■ ARCHITECT Julia Morgan
■ A building designed to be a glittering complement to the glamorous lives of William Randolph Hearst and his friends

Their collaboration was to last 28 years and produced one of the most extravagant and luxurious houses in the world. It was the perfect backdrop for parties with such famous guests as Winston Churchill, Charlie Chaplin, George Bernard Shaw, and many a Hollywood star.

MEDITERRANEAN SPLENDOR
The first buildings erected on the 250,000-acre (100,000-ha) site were three guest cottages constructed in 1919. Beautifully conceived in the Mediterranean style, they are the minions of the main house above, the Casa Grande, built on a monumental scale between 1922 and 1930. The western façade is framed by two massive towers containing the bedrooms that formed part of the Celestial Suite—Hearst's private suite. The towers are modeled on that of the Cathedral of Santa Maria la Mayor at Ronda in southern Spain. Beyond the entrance façade, the Spanish theme, redolent of the Gothic and Renaissance periods, continues in the ceilings, mantelpieces, architraves, and window details, many of which were removed from churches and castles in Spain and blended into the scheme by a skilled team of artisans.

plan of the estate

One of two pools, the Neptune Pool (above) has curving Ionic colonnades and a Corinthian temple façade, most of which was imported from Italy, as were the many antiques that surround it.

The entrance vestibule opens onto an assembly room, beyond which is an immense refectory, two stories high, containing a rich array of Gothic details and artifacts, also taken from churches and castles throughout Europe. The 28-foot (8.5-m) mantelpiece, stretching up to the ceiling at its western end, is balanced at the opposite end by a minstrels' gallery. From here, a door leads to the next wing of the house, which forms a T-junction. It has a morning room as its centerpiece, a billiard room, and a 50-seat theater on its northern side, and on its southern side a pantry and service area. There is no visually prominent staircase from the ground floor to those above; instead, the stairwells are discreetly tucked away or, in two instances, replaced by lifts.

Outside, on the lowest terrace of the garden, are the Roman Bath and the Neptune Pool, two structures that still astound visitors. Intended for use in winter, the swimming pool of the Roman Bath is enclosed in a building encrusted with blue and gold mosaics.

Hearst left San Simeon for the last time in 1947, and died in 1951. Morgan outlived him by six years. In the meantime, Hearst's sons had offered San Simeon to the state of California, a gift that was formally accepted in 1954. Four years later the property, which in the popular imagination became "Hearst Castle," opened its doors to the public.

THE FIRST MEDIA MAGNATE

William Randolph Hearst (1863–1951) was born in San Francisco. Educated at Harvard, he followed his father into the newspaper trade and rapidly acquired a nationwide chain of newspapers and periodicals. He introduced sensational innovations into journalism, such as banner headlines and eye-catching illustrations. Hearst's personality and career are believed to have inspired Orson Welles's 1941 film *Citizen Kane*, which concerns a power-mad media magnate who immures himself and his tragic wife in a splendid mansion called "Xanadu"—the stately pleasure dome of Coleridge's poem "Kubla Khan"—crammed with treasures looted from all over Europe.

Chapter Three
Centers of Power

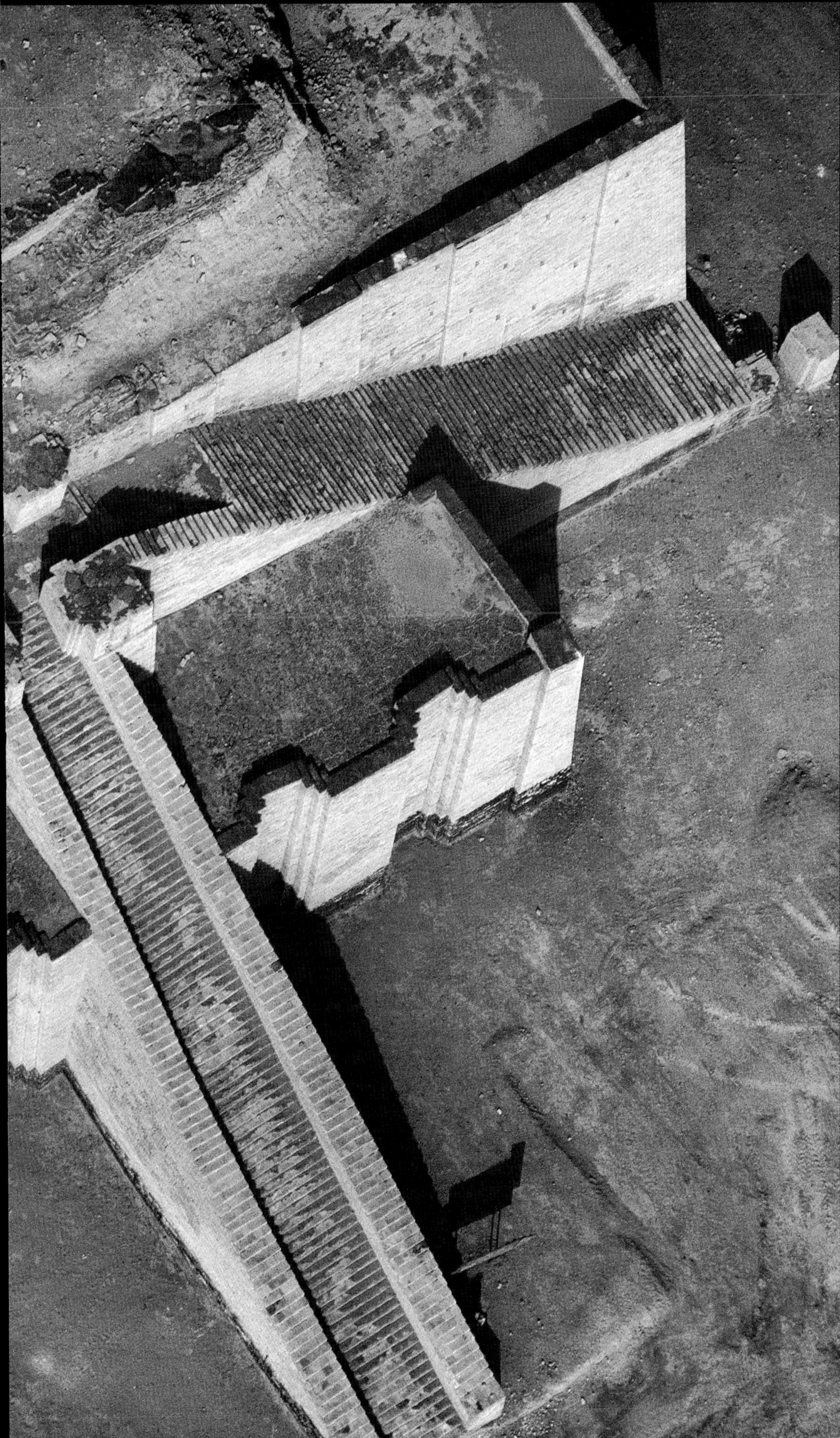

CENTERS OF POWER

Philosophers have traditionally divided power into two forms, public and private, and the buildings in this chapter have been chosen to exemplify the characteristics of each.

Public power, the rule of whole societies, has its origins in religious worship. Many ancient kings were also priests whose source of power resided in secret knowledge; such rulers could read the skies and predict the seasons, and could intercede with the gods on behalf of mortals. Thus the earliest examples of centers of power are always sacred sites, such as Stonehenge or the ziggurats of Mesopotamia.

Over thousands of years the temporal and spiritual powers of the rulers began to divide,

ROYAL OPULENCE *Versailles came to symbolize the decadence of the pre-Revolutionary French aristocracy.*

AN EXCLUSIVE DOMAIN *The Forbidden City, off limits to the populace, embodies the notion of autocratic rule.*

and priests became separate from kings. The royal court, home of the ruler and seat of government, developed its own unique architecture. The more powerful the rulers, the more mysterious and remote their dwellings became, as the Forbidden City in Beijing attests. Europe's most famous

example is the Château de Versailles. With its dramatic scale and inspiring use of landscape, Versailles became the model for many other royal courts, and (outwardly at least) for the capital of the new democracy of the United States of America. Washington retains the Neoclassical architecture and axial planning of its French sources, but the reason that Versailles is now a museum and Washington is not is the realization that power, to survive, must be shared. Rulers are now held accountable by the ruled in a completely new way.

The evolving idea of democracy in the Western world also underlies the stormy debates over the rebuilding of the Houses of Parliament in London in the 1840s. Parliament

FISCAL POWER *In the 20th century new centers of power developed, in the form of commercial buildings such as the Flatiron Building (inset) and the Hong Kong and Shanghai Bank (right).*

had always been a gentlemen's club, but its doors were forced open by the social up-heavals in Europe following the Industrial Revolution, and room had to be provided for members with very different political leanings. Since then, every new seat of government has been a politically charged symbol for the aspirations of the new nations that create it. Nowhere is this more true than in New Delhi, the capital that the British established in the 1920s for their Indian colony. Only a few years after New Delhi's completion the British Empire was no more, and the buildings designed to house India's British rulers now accommodate their Indian successors instead.

Private power has created empires of its own, based on trade and commerce. Ever since the trading

DEMOCRACY RULES
Though inspired by Versailles, the Capitol in Washington DC was the seat of an entirely different form of government.

cities and merchant princes of the Italian Renaissance in the 13th and 14th centuries, the rising middle class of traders, and later bankers, has sought to extend its control over large sections of the globe. All the European powers that estab-lished overseas colonies in the 15th and 16th centuries did so in the hope of commercial gain, and today the power of privately owned companies can rival or exceed that of many governments.

TEMPLES OF COMMERCE
For the past century the sky-scraper has been the symbol of this mercantile power, and buildings such as the Tribune Building in Chicago and the Flatiron Building in New York were designed to under-line it. But corporate power is itself changing. Once the skyscrapers bore the names of the men who built them, such as the Woolworth Building,

named after the retail king Frank Woolworth (who is depicted counting money in a sculpture on the building's façade), or the Chrysler Build-ing, commissioned by and named after the automobile tycoon Walter Chrysler. Now the private corporation often outlives its founder and reports to a board and shareholders, many of whom will never have direct contact with it. Such a corporation typically has its headquarters in the offices of anonymous institutions such as insurance companies and banks, some of which are known only by their street addresses. Increasingly these "cathedrals of commerce" are appearing around the world, and their American roots are being transplanted to foreign soil. As the power of the new economies of Asia continues to grow, so will the buildings that reflect the political realities of the 21st century.

Great Ziggurat at Ur

Iraq

More than 5,000 years ago, the fertile plain between the Tigris and the Euphrates Rivers was the site of some extraordinary and important developments in human history—the invention of writing and the wheel, the beginnings of law, medicine, astronomy, and architecture, and the first urban centers. All this was the work of the Sumerians of ancient Mesopotamia, and the impressive remnants of their city states can still be found in modern-day Iraq.

Perhaps one of the best preserved structures still left from this first urban civilization is the partially restored great ziggurat of the ancient city of Ur. A temple to the moon god, Nanna, it was built between 2125 and 2025 BC by King Ur-Nammu, a reformer, law-maker, and architect. Each

FAST FACTS

- DATE 2125–2025 BC
- PERIOD Sumerian
- MATERIAL Mud brick
- COMMISSIONED BY King Ur-Nammu
- Ziggurats, recalling the biblical story of the Tower of Babel, are found throughout Iraq

city had many temples, but that dedicated to the protective god of the city was the most important, being the link between heaven and earth. Along with the surrounding temples and palaces, it was the spiritual, economic, administrative, and political center of the city.

A HOLY MOUNTAIN

In earlier times, the principal temple had been set on a platform approached by a monumental ramp. Over time, the number of platforms increased, and the resulting stepped towers became known as ziggurats, or "holy mountains." The great ziggurat at Ur had three platforms. Though only the first platform remains today, it is still an impressive structure. It was about 70 feet (21 m) high, on a rectangular base about 200 by 150 feet (60 x 45 m). Three huge staircases led worshipers up to a great landing, from which further steps took the privileged few—including the king, who was also a priest and the intermediary between the Sumerians and their innumerable gods—to the shrine above. This was the focal point of the entire structure, where banquets would be set out for Nanna and offerings and human

This panel of the "Standard of Ur," made of shell and lapis lazuli, depicts a banquet as well as men herding livestock.

Access was via three ramps of stairs that met at the base of a central stairway leading to the upper levels (right).

sacrifices made. The shrine's design, however, is speculative because it no longer exists; the proposed reconstruction of the three supporting platforms, made by Sir Leonard Woolley, the English archaeologist who excavated the ziggurat in the 1920s, is more reliably based on existing evidence.

Unlike the great monuments of Egypt, this and all the other ziggurats were not built by slaves but by Sumerian farmers, working during the months between the planting and harvest seasons. The core of the enormous pile was constructed by heaping up millions of mud bricks, the most common building material in a land without substantial supplies of timber or stone. The sun-baked bricks were strong but porous, so further layers, up to 8 feet (2.5 m) thick, of harder kiln-fired bricks were needed as a waterproof casing. It was then covered in millions of glazed terracotta tiles, which would have made the ziggurat seem to glow in rich, deep colors.

The ziggurat and surrounding major public buildings formed the sacred precinct of Ur and were enclosed by a double wall. Just outside was a great mausoleum, known as the Royal Cemetery of Ur; in its 1,840 burial chambers were found fantastically rich grave goods (weapons and vessels in gold and silver, and objects inlaid with lapis lazuli and shell) and the remains of sacrificed retainers. Beyond the double wall lay the main residential areas and the two harbors of Ur, which provided access for shipping on the Euphrates. Like all Sumerian cities on the vast alluvial plain of Mesopotamia, which was prone to frequent flooding, the entire city was raised on a high earthen mound and enclosed by a heavily fortified wall to protect it from invasion. The wall and much of the city have disappeared, the landscape and even the course of the river have changed, but enough remains of the huge ziggurat of Ur to make it the characteristic building of Mesopotamian civilization.

three converging ramps led to the first level

89

Stonehenge

Wiltshire, England

The concentric circles of stones on Salisbury Plain, two miles (3.2 km) from the town of Amesbury in Wiltshire, have fascinated visitors for hundreds of years. Their precise function remains unknown, but continues to intrigue historians and archaeologists.

It seems reasonably certain that the circles originated in the Neolithic (New Stone Age) period, when the first farmers of Britain had begun to form permanent settlements. One theory is that the stones formed a primitive astronomical observatory. Stone Age

FAST FACTS
- DATE c. 2700–2000 BC
- BUILDERS Successive Neolithic and Bronze Age cultures
- The level of engineering needed to transport, shape, raise, and position the stones was extraordinarily sophisticated for the time

cultures throughout the world erected similar observatories to predict the best times for planting and harvesting. The temple of Karnak in Egypt, the temples of the Maya in Central America, and many smaller examples all around the Mediterranean were constructed to mark the time between specific astronomical events. The solstices—both summer (when the noon sun was at its highest) and winter (when it was at its lowest)—were of particular significance to early farmers. It is thought that the summer solstice may have signaled the new year for Neolithic communities.

In about 2700 BC the first builders of Stonehenge laid out the original circle of earthworks, with a large stone, the Friar's Heel or Heelstone, at the entrance to the north-east. The alignment between this stone and the so-called Slaughter Stone inside the circle gives the time of the summer solstice. Numerous small postholes near the entrance suggest that this point moved over the centuries and that the whole observatory was readjusted to

other standing stones include those at Callanish Outer Hebrides

From Neolithic peoples to present-day cults, Stonehenge has been a site of spiritual importance for about 4,000 years.

compensate. The center of the circle was probably empty, except for an altar of some kind.

The second phase of building at Stonehenge in about 2100 BC, by a culture named the Beaker People, produced the first monumental stones—huge bluestone blocks brought from the Prescelly Mountains in Wales, probably by water on a raft up the Bristol Channel and then overland by sledge from the River Avon. It is possible that the blocks were to have been arranged inside the earthworks in a double circle of standing stones, placed in pairs, but not all of this plan seems to have been carried out. There is no trace of such a configuration today.

A LINK TO THE PAST

What we now call Stonehenge is an Early Bronze Age structure that was built around 2000 BC. It consists of a ring of 30 sarsens (silicified sandstone blocks), with a diameter of 100 feet (30 m). Massive stone lintels surmount the sarsens. Within this ring is a series of trilithons (taller pairs of stones, each topped by a lintel), arranged in the shape of a horseshoe. Incredibly, these gigantic stones, each weighing up to 45 tons (46 t) were brought from a site on the Marlborough Downs, 25 miles (40 km) away. A few centuries later some of the original bluestone blocks from Stonehenge II were used to make additional circles inside the space defined by the trilithons. It seems that the function of the site, while still religious in character, was by now more symbolic than based on astronomical observation.

There are over 70 extant "henges" (a Saxon word that means a temple of stone or wood) in Britain alone, 12 of which have an internal stone circle. There is even a Woodhenge, where the Neolithic temple was constructed of wood. This might explain why stone lintels in Stonehenge III have mortise-and-tenon joints—more typically seen in wooden structures—but faithfully copied in a new, more permanent way.

The landscape around Stonehenge, with its many Neolithic tombs, is a link with the very first farming settlements in Britain thousands of years ago. The town of Avebury is built in the center of an even larger circle, nearly a mile (1.6 km) in circumference, and many stones are still standing or have been re-erected. Stonehenge was largely intact at the start of the 19th century, but it has suffered major damage in the intervening years. It is now strictly protected, with visitors viewing from a distance.

Forbidden City

Beijing, China

After driving the Mongols out of China in 1368, the Ming Dynasty restored China to the glories of an earlier era. The imperial city of Peking (now called Beijing), with the Forbidden City at its heart, remains an enduring symbol of Ming power and splendor.

Beijing, which lies close to the border between China and the Mongol Empire, was invaded by the Mongols under their leader Genghis Khan during the 12th century; later on, Kublai Khan, grandson of Genghis Khan, made his headquarters there. The third Ming emperor, Yung Lo, moved the seat of power from Nanking to Beijing in 1421 to be closer to the border in case of renewed threats from the north. Work began at once on the building of a magnificent new city.

Yung Lo's new capital was built over part of Kublai Khan's city. It centered on an artificial mound, Prospect Hill, which consisted of earth that Kublai Khan had excavated to form a series of ornamental lakes. The city plan—one of the first known—was based on a grid system and loosely followed ancient ideas of a propitious layout for a town. A high wall punctuated by watchtowers and monumental gateways surrounded the city. At a time when European cities were sunk in squalor, Beijing was a model of organization, with wide, hygienic streets patrolled by watchmen and fire fighters who maintained its regulations and safety standards.

> **FAST FACTS**
> ■ DATE 15th century
> ■ STYLE Ming Dynasty
> ■ MATERIALS Brick, marble, timber, and plaster
> ■ COMMISSIONED BY Yung Lo, third Ming emperor
> ■ The city has been rebuilt many times

A City within a City

Around a strict north–south axis passing through Prospect Hill was an inner enclosure, the Imperial City, filled with government offices and minor palaces. And at its very center, enclosed by a moat and a high wall, lay the Forbidden City itself: a huge complex that housed the emperor, his family, and his court. It was sometimes called Tzu Chin Ch'eng—the Purple Forbidden City—an allusion to the city's dazzling color scheme: The waters of its canals reflected red-plastered brick walls, white marble stairs and balustrades, yellow-glazed roof tiles, and brilliantly lacquered pillars.

No men except the emperor and his immediate family members were permitted to live inside the Forbidden City, so the ruler relied on a vast army of eunuchs to conduct the affairs of government. The eunuchs were practical and efficient administrators, but they were addicted to gossip and palace intrigue. Those who became

The Palace of Heavenly Purity (left), in the northern sector, was built in the early 15th century during the Ming dynasty. It was the core of the inner, residential area of the Forbidden City.

The Gate of Supreme Harmony (right) leads to the ceremonial halls. The Forbidden City is now a major tourist destination (inset).

troublesome were exiled to the provinces, sent overseas on embassies to other countries, or—if they had been particularly difficult—executed.

Inside the Forbidden City, the emperor held audiences for his subjects and received tribute from foreign states. Visitors traversed the axis that ran from the Temples of Heaven and Earth, outside the city, to the front gate; once admitted, they approached the Tianamen Gate and then passed through the Meridian Gate. This was the main entrance to the Forbidden City itself. The visitors then crossed one of the five marble bridges over the canal known as the Golden River, passed through a majestic gatehouse, and waited in the large paved courtyard beyond until they were summoned to an audience in the Hall of Supreme Harmony.

Once inside the hall, supplicants were expected to prostrate themselves nine times as they approached the imperial throne. This was the ceremony of *kow-tow*—a word that has found its way into English as a synonym for "grovel." The Forbidden City was rebuilt numerous times during the Ming and Ching dynasties. Few of the original buildings remain, but the layout carefully preserves Yung Lo's plan, and the grand structures are faithful copies of their 17th and 18th century originals. In this unique world apart, the last rulers of imperial China controlled the lives of millions of their countrymen, but their splendid isolation eventually cost them their thrones in 1912, with the creation of the Chinese Republic.

The imperial palace lay at the heart of the Forbidden City. On ceremonial occasions the courtyard in front of the palace was a scene of color and pageantry. The complex was a model of sophisticated urban planning.

Treasury at Petra

Petra, Jordan

Petra comes from the Greek word for "rock" and is a fitting name for this abandoned city surrounded by and carved out of rocky sandstone cliffs, whose glowing pinks, reds, purples, and pale yellows make it one of the most haunting and beautiful of lost places.

The city is located in southern Jordan, in the Wadi Musa—the ancient Valley of Moses. The first European to "find" it (in 1812) was Swiss explorer Jean-Louis Burckhardt. He thought that he had found a lost Greek city—many of the ruins of temples, tombs, and numerous public buildings, including a theater and palace, are indeed built in a Hellenistic style. Others show an Assyrian influence, while some combine elements of both, and of the Classical Roman style.

Petra was, in fact, the capital of an Arabic people named the Nabataeans who settled the valley and controlled the caravan routes between Arabia and the Mediterranean from about 300 BC. Contact with the outside world and its ways meant the inevitable adoption of new and valuable ideas, especially during Petra's greatest period, the rule of Aretas IV in the decades before AD 40, when the city center was constructed and a sophisticated water system,

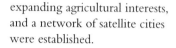

FAST FACTS

■ DATE 1st century AD

■ STYLES A mixture of Greek, Assyrian, and Classical Roman

■ MATERIAL Sandstone

■ BUILDERS The Nabataeans

■ This ancient city was carved out of a solid sandstone rock face

expanding agricultural interests, and a network of satellite cities were established.

A HIDDEN CITY

Entrance to Petra is through the Sik, a narrow sandstone gorge with sheer walls 300 feet (90 m) high that suddenly opens out into the brilliant sunshine of the valley and the imposing two-story façade of the Treasury. Possibly the most beautiful and famous of the Petra ruins, this is also the best preserved, as the soft sandstone rock face from which it is carved is sheltered from the wind and rain. It is named for the urn that sits atop the façade of columns and cornices and which, according to local belief, holds a great treasure. The urn is marked by many bullet holes made by people who have tried to shatter it and release its booty.

Despite its name, the building was probably a temple or tomb, but never a treasury. It appears to belong to the period of Aretas IV and its style recalls contemporary buildings at Pompeii and especially Alexandria, the largest city of the region. The second story of three carved pavilions, including a central, round kiosk with a tent roof, prevents the building from being dwarfed by the huge wall of rock behind it without the lower story having to bear too great a weight. The spacious portico of the lower story forms an outer chamber, while two doorways under the colonnade lead to small, sumptuous rooms. Inside, the great central chamber leads to two small side rooms and, at the rear of the chamber, the sanctuary.

Detail of carving (right). Rooms are cut from solid rock (below). The façade of the Treasury, 92 feet (28 m) wide by 130 feet (39 m) high, dwarfs visiting tourists (facing page).

It may have been covered in hard plaster, then painted, a practice common to the Nabataeans, although no such decoration remains today.

After the Romans conquered Petra in AD 106, the city continued to flourish until changes to the caravan routes brought about its decline. An earthquake in 551 destroyed half the city. Thereafter, apart from a visit by the Crusaders in the 13th century, Petra was known only to local tribes for more than 1,000 years until Burckhardt rediscovered it. The descendants of these tribes were still living in the ruins up to the 1980s.

Piazza del Campidoglio

Rome, Italy

When the rebuilding of Rome began in the 16th century, Michelangelo, the unquestioned architectural master of the city, was commissioned to reorganize the Capitoline Hill. His brilliant design for a difficult space became the Piazza del Campidoglio.

The Capitoline Hill had been a focus of spiritual and temporal power since the Latins founded the city in the 6th century BC. A steep and narrow bluff, it was ideal as a temporary refuge but too small for permanent habitation, so it became the site of a series of

FAST FACTS
- DATE 1539–64
- STYLE High Renaissance
- MATERIALS Stone and marble
- ARCHITECT Michelangelo
- Michelangelo's design gave a clear view across the city to the new center of power, the Vatican

temples to Rome's presiding deity, "Jupiter the best and the greatest, of the Capitoline Hill."

PAPAL POWER
With the decline of the Roman Empire, the Capitoline Hill fell into ruin for over 1,000 years, until Michelangelo accepted his challenging commission in 1537. The reigning pope, Paul III, insisted that he retain and restore the medieval Palazzo dei Senatori and the 15th century Palazzo dei Conservatori, which stood on the site at an angle of 80 degrees to each other. Michelangelo also had to reorient the piazza to face the Vatican—now the city's power base. His solution was to build a new palace, the Palazzo Nuovo, at an angle of 80 degrees on the other side of the Palazzo dei Senatori, to balance the design. This generated a striking trapezoidal plan for the new piazza, which was connected to the streets below by a magnificent flight of steps, the Cordonata. The Palazzo dei Senatori, on the eastern side, faces the Cordonata. On the south side is the Palazzo dei Conservatori,

The Cordonata and piazza (above). Fresco (c. 1525) of the founding of the Temple of Jupiter on the Capitoline Hill (left).

fitted out with Michelangelo's façade and loggia, and to the north is Michelangelo's Palazzo Nuovo. These two buildings—now the Capitoline Museums—are two-storied, with identical façades: Immense pilasters decorate both levels, and at ground level the pilasters enclose loggias framed by pairs of structural columns supporting flat arches. The three-storied Palazzo dei Senatori dominates the piazza. Michelangelo's restoration uses design elements similar to those of the other two buildings but in a more imposing mode.

Defying the conventions of the time, Michelangelo did not plan a building for the fourth side of the piazza; instead, he defined the "fourth wall" with statuary and a balustrade, leaving an open vista from the piazza to the Vatican.

The demanding Pope Paul also insisted that the piazza contain Rome's only surviving bronze equestrian statue, the AD 165 likeness of the benevolent Roman Emperor Marcus Aurelius, suggesting a symbolic connection between the power of the Caesars and that of the Popes. Michelangelo was reluctant to comply—perhaps because he wanted to crown his design with a sculpture of his

own—but was obliged to give in. He placed the statue at the very center of the square, on an oval plinth that was the focus of an oval pavement design. Marcus Aurelius and his horse remained there until 1981, when they were removed because pollution was threatening to erode them. They are now housed in the Capitoline Museums that flank the square.

A CITY'S HISTORY IN STONE

Michelangelo died before his design was realized, but his successors followed his ideas and created one of the finest of all Renaissance urban spaces—and one that epitomizes the whole history of this great city. The Capitoline Museums contain a bronze statue (c. 500 BC) of the she-wolf that suckled Romulus and Remus, legendary founders of Rome; nearby are the blackened remains of Rome's first temple; and the piazza itself is a triumphant monument to an era in which architectural and structural skills flourished.

Michelangelo's oval pavement design for the piazza (above). The Etruscan statue of the she-wolf that suckled the legendary founders of Rome (left).

97

Château de Versailles

Paris, France

The Château de Versailles, just outside Paris, is one of the most impressive demonstrations of royal power and prestige in the world. Here the French Sun King, Louis XIV, dazzled everyone with the opulence and extravagance of his court.

The palace had its beginnings in 1668 in a humble hunting lodge. Louis recruited architect Louis Le Vau, landscaper André Le Nôtre, and painter Charles Le Brun to create his "City of the Sun." The great task was to involve thousands of workers, plus the army when needed, as well as huge sums

Louis XIV (left) ruled France from 1651 to 1715. The building of the Château de Versailles (above) took most of his reign.

FAST FACTS

■ DATE 1668–1710

■ STYLE French Classical Baroque

■ MATERIALS Stone, timber, and stucco

■ COMMISSIONED BY Louis XIV

■ Versailles served as a model for royal palaces throughout Europe

taxed from the poorest levels of society. The original buildings were continuously enlarged until the palace was more than a quarter of a mile (400 m) long, set in an immense park.

SAFETY AND SPLENDOR

In Paris, the traditional seat of French kings had been the Palace of the Louvre, but in 1682 the entire French court moved to Versailles, partly because of fear of civil unrest. Angry mobs had forced Louis XIV to flee Paris in his youth, and he hoped to find safety outside the city. Here, under Louis' watchful eye, the most powerful families in France congregated in surroundings of unsurpassed splendor.

The buildings and gardens were laid out on an east–west axis passing through the king's bedroom. To the east, a straight line leads to Paris; to the west, the Grand Canal seems to disappear into infinity. The palace has hundreds of rooms; the most famous is the Galerie des Glaces (the Hall of Mirrors), which extends along most of the western façade. Designed as a reception space for state occasions, it was here that World War I officially ended with the signing of the Treaty of Versailles in 1919.

The Galerie des Glaces (above)—the Hall of Mirrors—233 feet (72 m) long, is a triumph of Baroque design. Visitors must remove high-heeled shoes to protect the delicate parquet flooring.

DEGREES OF DISCOMFORT

Grand though it was, the palace, crowded with courtiers, administrators, soldiers, and servants, was never comfortable. Its sanitation was primitive, and its huge rooms were stifling in summer and bitterly cold in winter: On one occasion, the water froze in the glasses at the royal table. Nor was it politically relaxed. "The King's establishment is like a vast market," wrote a French nobleman of the time, "where there is no choice but to go and bargain, both to maintain one's own existence and to protect the interests of those to whom we are attached by duty or friendship."

Intrigue flourished at Versailles. A favorable word from the king could repay years of waiting, or a dark look spell instant ruin. There were affairs, plots, suicides, even poisonings. The king himself came to prefer his estate at Marly, a few miles away, where he could lead a slightly more normal life.

Maintaining this luxurious life-style eventually consumed a tenth of France's annual tax revenues. But all Versailles' glory could not protect the monarchy; when a popular uprising took place in

1789, a century after the move to Versailles, the Sun King's great-grandson, Louis XVI, was told that the Prison of the Bastille had fallen and a mob was marching on Versailles. "This is a revolt!" said the king. "No, sire," said the messenger. "It is a revolution."

MARIE ANTOINETTE AT VERSAILLES

Marie Antoinette of Austria was just 14 when she married Louis XVI of France. Clothes and jewels were her passion, but it was her ardor for landscaping and building that earned her the nickname "Madame Deficit" after the royal couple set up court at Versailles in 1774.

In a remote corner of the palace grounds, the queen created a land of make-believe (left) with the help of her favorite architect, Richard Mique.

It included a labyrinth, a grotto, a Temple of Love, and a tiny farming village, "Le Hameau," stocked with real peasants and farmyard animals. Dressed in simple clothes, Marie Antoinette and her friends played at farming, milking cows into Sèvres porcelain bowls. Whatever peace the queen found here ended with the Revolution. With rare and surprising courage she stood by her husband, following him into prison and then to the guillotine.

Capitol Building

Washington DC, United States of America

Considering that eight architects had a hand in its creation over a period of 70 years, the Capitol Building of the United States in Washington DC is remarkably coherent in style. What is more, this great American landmark became an influential model for later civic and public buildings. Its grand Neoclassical design is intimately tied to the ideals ascendant during the founding of the new republic, and bears the influence of similar ideals fermenting in pre-Revolutionary France during Thomas Jefferson's term as ambassador there.

In 1791, President Washington chose a 10-square mile (26 sq km) plot along the Potomac River as the site of a capital city. A French engineer, Pierre Charles L'Enfant, was selected to create an overall city design. His monumental plan accommodated present and future buildings balanced with lawns, gardens, and pathways in a geometric grandeur reminiscent of Versailles. This, he felt, would express the symbolic importance befitting the seat of this young democracy.

FAST FACTS

■ DATE 1793–1874
■ STYLE Neoclassical
■ MATERIALS Sandstone and marble
■ ARCHITECTS William Thornton, Benjamin Latrobe, and others
■ The building has some 540 rooms, 658 windows, and 850 doorways

A TEMPLE TO DEMOCRACY

However, Thomas Jefferson, a noteworthy "gentleman architect" and by now Secretary of State, put his own imprimatur on the project. Jefferson was an ardent proponent of the Neoclassical esthetic that had captured the romantic imagination of the age. He believed that the elegant proportions of ancient structures would evoke the chief values of the Enlightenment: reason, order, and democracy. "Embellished with Athenian taste," he declared, the Capitol Building would become "the first temple dedicated to the sovereignty of the people."

Meanwhile, L'Enfant, who found himself butting heads with authority, was dismissed before he had drawn up a plan for the Capitol Building itself. In 1792 Jefferson proposed a competition for the building's design. A late entry from William Thornton, an amateur

The Rotunda, 180 feet (55 m) high and 96 feet (29 m) in diameter, is the symbolic heart of the Capitol.

architect and physician, won the approval of all. Thornton's design featured two rectangular wings connected by a central dome. Its echoes of the Roman Pantheon, with its columns and pediments, must have been especially pleasing to Jefferson, who had modeled his design for Virginia's state capitol after a Roman temple.

President Washington laid the cornerstone for the Capitol Building in 1793 in a grand Masonic ceremony. The proceedings reflected the Founding Fathers' membership of this secret society, whose beliefs harked back to the master builders of ancient Greece and Egypt. Construction proceeded in fits and starts with a succession of early architects. But in 1803, Jefferson, who was now president, brought in Benjamin Henry Latrobe, a professional architect trained in Britain. Latrobe oversaw design and construction for 14 years, including the reconstruction required after the building's near ruin by British arsonists during the war of 1812.

Later architects continued the lengthy process. Charles Bulfinch completed the Rotunda and first

Floor plan (left). The "whispering wall" in National Statuary Hall (below) reflects faint sounds around the room.

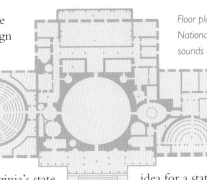

dome, and Thomas U. Walter expanded the north and south wings, fashioned a new, larger dome, and put forward the idea for a statue to top it. The installation of the Statue of Freedom in 1863, accompanied by gun salutes, marked a culmination of sorts. In 1873 Frederick Law Olmsted, the landscape architect who masterminded New York's Central Park, was put in charge of designing the terraces and grounds. The Italian artist Constantino Brumidi worked for more than 25 years on much of the building's extraordinary art and decoration, including the fresco on the dome's canopy and the frieze in the Rotunda.

Today this stately five-level building with its approximately 540 rooms sprawls across some four acres (1.6 ha). The Capitol houses vast historic art and statuary collections, not to mention the U.S. Congress, and attracts millions of visitors each year.

Palace of Westminster

London, England

When London's old Houses of Parliament burned down in 1834, it was an opportunity to replace a hotchpotch of buildings dating back to the 12th century with an up-to-date complex suitable for governing an empire and dealing with the dramatic social changes that followed the Industrial Revolution. The government also wanted the building to be a showplace of the finest achievements in British art, demonstrating the greatness of Britain's past and the limitlessness of its future.

In 1835, a design competition was announced. The rules specified a Gothic or Tudor design—to the indignation of leading architects, who had made their reputations designing classical buildings. The winner, Charles Barry, was one of these, but he supplied a Gothic design as requested. His main collaborator in the project was

Big Ben is the name of the large bell in the Clock Tower, not of the clock itself.

FAST FACTS

■ DATE 1835–67

■ STYLE English Gothic Revival

■ MATERIALS Stone and timber

■ ARCHITECTS Charles Barry, Augustus Pugin, and E. M. Barry

■ Built around the remains of the seat of the medieval kings of England

Augustus Welby Pugin, a virtual unknown but a master of the Gothic idiom: For him the Gothic Revival represented a return to the unified Christian world that existed before the Industrial Revolution.

Around the surviving parts of the old buildings—particularly the magnificent Westminster Hall and the ruins of the medieval St. Stephen's Chapel—Barry planned new chambers for the Commons and Lords, with ancillary spaces such as committee rooms, libraries, kitchens, and smoking rooms. His greatest success was in making the design work as a whole, giving the complex an impressive river frontage, 914 feet (289 m) long, dominated by two towers: The Victoria Tower to the south—the ceremonial entrance to Parliament for the monarch—and the Clock Tower to the north. Pugin was in charge of the interiors, generating inspired designs and training craftsmen to produce them.

By 1840 the old Painted Chamber had been re-roofed to be a temporary House of Lords, while the Lords' original chamber became an interim House of Commons. Barry then faced various difficulties, from how much seating the House of Commons required, to a protracted

The building is an imposing sight when viewed from the Thames (above). The building's architect, Sir Charles Barry (left). The House of Lords (below).

dispute over heating and ventilation, and whether women visitors should be sheltered from view by a metal grille. (The grille was eventually omitted.) Barry pressed on, plagued by endless investigations into costs, criticisms in the press, and social unrest—in 1848, the year of revolutions in Europe, the new buildings were garrisoned to withstand a siege. But by 1846 the Lords were installed in their chamber and by 1852 the Commons in theirs. There were instant complaints about ventilation, acoustics, and costs. (The Leader of the Opposition, William Gladstone, suggested hanging Barry to prevent further debacles—but the government knighted him instead.) In 1852 Pugin died. Barry carried on until his death in 1860, when his son, Edward Barry, took over.

Even installing Big Ben, the great bell in the Clock Tower, caused problems. The first casting broke, and the bell was not raised until late in 1858. But its sound drowned out the parliamentary speakers, and there were plans to get rid of it until a simple adjustment in the angle of the hammer solved the problem.

A POLITICAL STATEMENT

The Palace of Westminster is England's greatest example of Victorian Gothic architecture and a powerful political symbol. Built between the Parliamentary Reform Bills of 1832 and 1867, it represents an attempt to recreate Britain's past stability in a time of political turmoil. Democracy and revolution were in the air, and the problem was how to permit one without having to undergo the other. Historians now agree that the extension of voting rights in Britain helped avert the revolutions that rocked the rest of Europe. The building both looks back to an idealized medieval past and reflects the contemporary agitation for parliamentary reform. Designed as a club for the aristocratic elite, the Palace of Westminster now houses their democratic successors in imperial splendor.

Flatiron Building

New York, United States of America

The Flatiron Building was an instant sensation when it was completed in 1902, quickly joining the Brooklyn Bridge and the Statue of Liberty as an icon of modern New York. It was not the first skyscraper built in the city and, at 285 feet (87 m), only briefly was it the tallest, but its commanding presence on the junction of Broadway and 23rd Street has made it an enduring symbol of the America of Theodore Roosevelt, of burgeoning wealth and power, and industrial pre-eminence.

Built by a prominent construction company, George A. Fuller, on an island site in downtown Manhattan, the Fuller office tower was immediately dubbed the "Flatiron" because of its triangular design. Daniel Burnham, the architect, exploited the fact that its unique, irregular site meant that the building could never be hemmed in, and designed it to be

The building was one of the first in New York to be supported by a steel cage (right). The corner site (below) before building began.

FAST FACTS

- DATE 1902
- STYLE Beaux-Arts
- MATERIALS Steel, terracotta, and limestone cladding
- ARCHITECT Daniel H. Burnham
- The oldest remaining skyscraper in Manhattan

viewed unencumbered as a dramatically sheer freestanding tower, 22 stories high.

From the beginning the new building attracted both critics and admirers. Passers-by complained that the high winds that it deflected down to street level knocked them off their feet, while the men who gathered to watch the effect of the winds on women's skirts caused traffic jams and had to be moved on by police officers. Architects themselves were divided over "Uncle Dan's" latest achievement.

SOMETHING OLD, SOMETHING NEW

The Flatiron Building was a fascinating mixture of the thoroughly up-to-date and the backward-looking. Like the first skyscrapers in Chicago, it used the new structural possibilities of steel-framed buildings to build high. Its invisible structural framework of a vast steel cage, combined with its great height, made New Yorkers fear that it would tumble, but Fuller boasted that it was the strongest building ever constructed. It reflected the new technologies in many other ways as well, from structural engineering to fireproofing, from its innovative service and communications systems to its actual financing and construction, which were expertly organized. This was, indeed, one of the new "cathedrals of commerce," a symbol of the modern age. As the photographer Alfred Stieglitz observed, it "appeared to be moving toward me like the bow of a monster ocean steamer—a picture of new America still in the making."

However, Daniel Burnham had been trained in the ideals of the Beaux-Arts school, of monumental buildings designed in the styles

of the past, and he therefore gave his very modern building a very old-fashioned exterior. Lofty façades topped by a prominent cornice, undulating walls of limestone and terracotta decorated in flowers and Grecian urns, executed in a style reminiscent of 16th-century Renaissance France adapted to 20th-century New York—it was over these aspects of the building that the bitterest controversy raged. That the vast walls should look like load-bearing masonry instead of the stone cladding they really were seemed especially unforgivable to many at the time.

More than 100 years later, when viewed from a contemporary perspective, the Flatiron Building seems like a happy synthesis of old and new—its technical innovations made it a practical and durable building, but the concern for context and scale that Burnham took from the Beaux-Arts tradition has also served it well. The three bottom floors feature wide windows and rough-hewn limestone facings, and serve to visually anchor the building. The middle stories are pierced with rows of narrower windows that emphasize the building's slender, vertical lines and draw the eye upward to the ornate columns, arches, and cornice that embellish the top two stories.

Burnham died in 1912, and the Fuller Company moved out (to an even grander building) in 1929, but the Flatiron Building has continued to attract admirers to this day. Endlessly photographed, it represents both a confident and exuberant era and a vanished ideal of civic good manners. In 1979 it was formally added to the U.S. National Register of Historic Places.

Floor plan (above). The building's rounded summit gives the tower (right) the appearance of an enormous free-standing column.

Viceroy's House

New Delhi, India

I n 1911 the British staged a vast ceremonial gathering, or *durbar*, in Delhi to honor the new king, George V, and to present him to his Indian subjects. The British Empire, which was at the height of its power, extended over one quarter of the globe, and the British directly or indirectly controlled the lives of hundreds of millions of people.

At this *durbar* the king announced plans to transfer the seat of British power in India from Calcutta to Delhi. A few months later the king appointed Sir Edwin Lutyens (1869–1944), best known for his grand Edwardian country houses, to the Delhi Planning Commission. He and the rest of the commission im-mediately set sail for India on the first of several trips to survey

FAST FACTS

■ *DATE 1913–30*

■ *STYLE British Colonial*

■ *MATERIALS Sandstone and marble*

■ *ARCHITECT Sir Edwin Lutyens*

■ *Roman buildings or Bramante's plans for St. Peter's in Rome may have been the sources for the palace*

the site for New Delhi. They also inspected the historic cities of the north-west to look for inspiration. By 1913 the site had been chosen and Lutyens and two others were appointed to do the detailed design work. The third member of the team, an art historian, did not last long, and Lutyens and the second man, Sir Herbert Baker, formed an uneasy partnership. They had long been rivals, and their relationship was difficult from the start.

HEADQUARTERS OF AN EMPIRE

The Viceroy's House (really a palace) was to be the heart of the new city, combining the Viceroy's official residence and the headquarters of the vast bureaucracy required to run the Indian colony. The complex was to lie at the end of a processional way, 2 miles (3 km) long, that led to a vast square in front of the Viceroy's House. The house was Lutyen's job, with Baker designing the two Secretariat buildings on either side and the Council building nearby.

Lutyens made initial designs for the Viceroy's House in 1914, before World War I stopped work on New Delhi. When work resumed in the early 1920s, Lutyens refined his

Lutyens was also known for his professional partnership with garden designer Gertrude Jekyll.

Sir Herbert Baker was responsible for the Secretariat Buildings (above). Iron gates (right) guard the presidential area.

design, producing an eclectic mixture of classical European forms and traditional Indian architecture. The result was an oddly satisfying building, well adapted to the extremes of the Indian climate, beautifully built of red and white Vindhyan sandstone, with 100,000 cubic feet (2,830 m³) of marble used in the interiors. The centerpiece of the complex was the huge Durbar Hall, where the viceregal couple held their official receptions in a setting of great splendor. The whole complex was surrounded by magnificent gardens with many fountains.

Lutyens was a traditionalist; he did not subscribe to the avant-garde architectural movements of the time, but drew his inspiration from the great buildings of the past. Historians are still debating whether he used Roman buildings or Bramante's plan for St. Peter's in Rome as sources for this huge palace, but whatever the inspiration, the results were appropriately grand.

The relationship between Lutyens and Baker deteriorated steadily, and there was a final quarrel over the scale of their respective buildings. Their argument seems irrelevant now, for the group of buildings they produced did form a harmonious whole and made a suitably impressive capital for the British Raj. Work was completed in 1930 and New Delhi was inaugurated with consider-able pomp in January 1931.

However, the capital that the British hoped would emphasize their rule over India lasted a mere 16 years. India won its independence in 1947 and the Viceroy's House became the home of the President of the Republic instead. Ironically, the new Indian government took better care of Lutyens' work than the British had. To Lutyens' dismay the various Vicereines had redecorated his grand interiors to their own taste, but the Indians restored the rooms to their original form and otherwise left the house largely as it was.

To some architects New Delhi is a great missed opportunity. They believe Lutyens turned his back on the most exciting ideas in modern architecture and town planning of the 1920s, but in his defense these ideas were only put into practice after World War II, in the new cities of Brasilia, Chandigarh, and Dacca. Lutyens' work has worn well, and its traditional sources, feeling for place, and careful craftsmanship have commended it to future generations.

Chicago Tribune Tower

Chicago, United States of America

In the history of architecture, a building can mark a turning point for reasons not obvious to the eye. In the case of Chicago's Tribune Tower, its enormous influence on the future of the skyscraper lies less in its own design than in the activity from which it emerged.

In 1922, the very notion of what a skyscraper should do and be was much debated. Should it aim to be a utilitarian "machine for living" or an elegant "cathedral of commerce?" Into this debate came Colonel Robert R. McCormick, the outspoken owner of the *Chicago Tribune*. On the 75th anniversary of his newspaper, he announced an international competition to design "the most beautiful and distinctive office building in the world." It was to be located by the new Michigan Avenue Bridge, which joins the city's north and south sides. Situated at this critical junction, the Tribune Tower would anchor the gateway to Chicago's "Miracle Mile."

With $100,000 in prize money, the competition would be the first major design contest since World War I and one of the great architectural events of the century. A host of impressive entries poured in from around the world, but in deference to McCormick's preferences the awards committee selected a relatively traditional design.

Two American unknowns, Raymond M. Hood and John Mead Howells, were awarded first prize for a design that clearly echoed the motifs of New York's Woolworth Building, a 1913 Gothic Revival structure that was then the

FAST FACTS
- DATE 1922–25
- STYLE Skyscraper Gothic
- MATERIALS Steel and limestone
- ARCHITECTS Raymond M. Hood and John Mead Howells
- Officially designated a Chicago landmark in February 1989

tallest building in America. They clad their steel-framed structure in customary limestone masonry, and decorated it with flying buttresses and gargoyles in the style of France's medieval Rouen Cathedral. Its crowning octagonal tower ornamented with open tracery was reminiscent of a campanile soaring heavenward.

Yet the design was not merely derivative. The tower was innovative in setting windows rather than columns in its rounded corners, creating prime corner offices with sweeping views. It also introduced a new skyscraper form, one that shoots straight up from its base, forgoing the use of setbacks.

A LASTING INFLUENCE

Despite its merits, many disagreed with the committee's choice. Architects of the influential Chicago School, who favored steel-frame technology and minimal ornamentation, saw it as a virtual denial of their existence. The popular favorite was the second-prize winner, designed by the Finnish architect Eliel Saarinen, a more modern structure emphasizing solid verticality and graduated setbacks. In any event, all the entrants had their day in the sun when viewers across America had the opportunity to see this encyclopedic compendium of designs during the competition's extraordinary traveling exhibition. In fact, the influence of this seminal competition was so far-reaching that in 1980, contemporary architects paid homage to the great 1922 contest by offering their own designs for the Tribune Tower.

Raymond Hood went on to codesign several major New York skyscrapers, including the McGraw-Hill Building and portions of the Rockefeller Center, while Eliel Saarinen, the second-prize winner, set up shop in the United States, where many of his designs were realized. All told, the Tribune Tower competition produced far more than a single winner.

Raymond Hood, co-architect of the tower (above). The competition to design the tower attracted 263 submissions from 23 countries, from both great architects and unknowns.

Chrysler Building

New York City, United States of America

Crowning the skyline of Manhattan with its radiant arcs and sunbursts, this 1930 Art Deco icon is a celebration of the machine age and a fitting beacon for "the city that never sleeps." By day, its elegant steel top gleams in the sun; by night, its glowing lantern promises stylish after-dark excitement in the ever-restless metropolis of New York.

The building was conceived and constructed during the skyscraper frenzy that reached its apogee in the period between the two world wars. Fueled by the booming stock market, real estate developers, architects, and wealthy sponsors joined hands in the race to pierce the sky. Among them was Walter Chrysler, founder and head of the newly established Chrysler Motors Corporation. Chrysler was eager to erect a structure whose size and splendor would be a worthy symbol of his empire. He bought the site at 42nd Street and Lexington Avenue, conveniently situated near Grand Central Terminal, and told architect William Van Alen what he wanted: "Make this building higher than the Eiffel Tower."

A MONUMENT TO THE MACHINE AGE

Van Alen proposed a bold Art Deco design. His plan was approved, but he encountered an unexpected challenge in the quest to erect the world's tallest building: H. Craig Severance, Van Alen's former partner—and current rival—was a step ahead of the game; he had already broken ground for a soaring bank tower at 40 Wall Street that aimed to become the tallest structure in the world. The rival architects altered their plans to outdo each other in mid-construction. But when the completed Wall Street tower reached a record 927 feet (282.5 m), Van Alen delivered his *coup de grâce*: He secretly built a 185-foot (56-m) spire inside the building, then shocked the media and the public by hoisting it up through the roof and bolting it into place. Now reaching a staggering 1,046 feet (319 m), the 77-story Chrysler Building was finally the world's highest.

Van Alen's creation would become one of the quintessential embodiments of Art Deco style.

Steel, the material of machinery and industry, cloaks the summit (above). Streamlined steel eagles (right) are a 20th century update on the medieval gargoyle.

The building's summit is adorned with arcs and sunbursts, both common Art Deco motifs reflecting the optimism of the era.

FAST FACTS

■ DATE 1929–30

■ STYLE Art Deco

■ MATERIALS Steel frame; brick and stainless steel cladding

■ ARCHITECT William Van Alen

■ Tallest building in the world for just 12 months—overtaken in 1931

Art Deco utilizes streamlined forms, geometric patterns, and stylized ornaments to convey the sleek, modern elegance of machinery and industry. The Chrysler's signature steel crown displays a striking geometry of triangle and arc, narrowing in a series of setbacks to its gleaming spire. The building was one of the first to use stainless steel over a large exterior surface. Its shaft, clad in white glazed brick with dark trim, emphasizes both traditional verticals and modern horizontal lines. The façade is adorned with designs that reflect Art Deco's obsession with ornament as well as the building's "theme": a frieze of hubcaps, a band of abstract automobiles, and huge gargoyles styled after Chrysler's eagle's-head hood ornaments and winged radiator caps. These extraordinary new-fangled steel gargoyles leaping out from the corners of the building are one of its most notable eccentricities.

The drama and flamboyance continue inside. Passing through the three-story black granite entrance has been likened to being swallowed up by a coffin. The muted, vault-like interior stands in stark contrast to the brightness of the façade. Here, the visitor is overwhelmed by extravagant finishes and designs. Richly patterned, deeply hued red Moroccan marble lines the walls, and a subdued ambience is cast by onyx panel lighting. Exotic wood inlays decorate the doors of the building's 32 elevators, while a massive ceiling mural depicts airplanes, an automobile assembly line, and the building itself.

THE COMPETITIVE SPIRIT

A Chrysler brochure from the period boasted that the building provided "every contribution to efficiency, sanitation, comfort, and even inspiration, that human ingenuity can conceive or money can buy." Yet just a year after the Chrysler Building was completed, the Empire State Building claimed the title as number one. The two towers continue to vie for position as leader in the pantheon of Manhattan iconography, but in a competition for sheer visual splendor, many feel that Chrysler remains the victor.

Elaborate Art Deco designs embellish the elevator doors in the lobby.

Empire State Building

New York, United States of America

John Jacob Raskob had a score to settle. The creator of General Motors simply could not live with the idea that his rival, Walter Chrysler, had recently built the tallest building in the world. But Raskob had a plan. He went to William Lamb, a partner in the architectural firm of Shreve, Lamb, and Harmon, and shared his dream of a skyscraper that would eclipse the Chrysler. The question he asked was ingenious in its simplicity and breathtaking in its ambition: "How high can you make it so that it won't fall down?"

Before long, the old Waldorf–Astoria Hotel at Fifth Avenue and 34th Street was being demolished to make room for the Empire State Building. The name was inspired by George Washington, who had observed while sailing up the Hudson River that the region was "the key to the new empire."

AN AUDACIOUS PLAN

Only two criteria were specified: that the building look like a pencil and soar higher than any other structure on Earth. Even more astounding than the scale of the project was the magnitude of its risks. The location was deemed commercially "undesirable."

FAST FACTS

- DATE 1930–31
- STYLE Art Deco
- MATERIALS Brick, steel, concrete, and limestone
- ARCHITECT William Lamb
- The onset of the Depression halved the estimated cost of the building

Not a single tenant was enlisted. And the stock market had just begun a downward spiral that would plunge the nation into the Great Depression.

Given such a shaky foundation, a stronger one was needed. It was provided by the granite bedrock of Manhattan Island, into which 210 concrete and steel columns were sunk. Though only two stories deep, this platform would support a tower 102 stories (1,250 feet/380 m) tall and weighing some 365,000 tons (370,000 t).

An architect once said: "Building skyscrapers is the nearest peacetime equivalent of war." For this battle, an army of laborers and craftsmen was assembled, 3,000 of them at work on the site at any given time. The heroes among them were the ironworkers, many from the Mohawk and Iroquois tribes—Native Americans are famous for their fearlessness. Working 13 hours a day for $1.92 an hour, these brave souls dangled from dizzying heights, riveting into place more than

A construction worker (c. 1930) balances precariously (above). (Below) The tallest building in Manhattan, the Empire State Building is a landmark on the city skyline.

NANTUCKET

The lobby (above) is three floors high. (Right) The building's steel framework rose at the impressive rate of four stories per week.

50,000 massive, 1-ton (1-t) steel beams—enough to lay railroad tracks between New York and Baltimore. Finished to tolerances of less than ⅛ inch (3 mm), these beams were hoisted into place and fitted together just eight hours after they had left their Pittsburgh mill.

Despite 16 changes in its design and construction while the project was underway, the building was completed 45 days ahead of schedule and $5 million under budget. The $41 million marvel went up in record time (under 14 months), at a speed that has never been surpassed. Never swaying more than ¼ inch (6 mm) off center, the building comprises 10 million bricks and 5 acres (2 ha) of windows. Enhancing its sleek Art Deco design are graceful, gradually recessed walls, or "setbacks," which were legally required by New York City's cautious building codes.

SYMBOL OF A CITY

Soon after its completion, the building had so few tenants for its 2 million square feet (186,000 sq m) of office space that it was dubbed "the Empty State Building." But today it hosts 15,000 office workers and countless visitors. After taking a one-minute elevator ride up to the observation deck, they can see for up to 80 miles (128 km).

The building remained the world's tallest until 1972, when the former World Trade Center was built. It still defines the Manhattan skyline, and has never failed to lose its luster. "The Empire State Building," noted one critic, "seems almost to float, like an enchanted fairy tower, over New York. An edifice so lofty, so serene, so marvelously simple, so luminously beautiful, had never before been imagined. One could look back on a dream well planned."

Hong Kong and Shanghai Bank

Hong Kong, China

Foster and Partners is arguably a paradigm of modern architectural firms. With a head office in London and branch offices in Europe and Asia, the firm has undertaken more than 1,000 projects around the world. Led by the brilliant and exacting Sir Norman Foster, the firm has worked at every kind of design problem on every scale, from furniture systems to large urban redevelopments. His designs have been called "high-tech," but he dislikes the term, saying: "Since Stonehenge, architects have always been at the cutting edge of technology. And you can't separate technology from the humanistic and spiritual content of a building."

The philosophy of his company is that because architecture is a public art, each project must be "sensitive to the culture and climate of its place." Early regarded as one of the most talented British architects to emerge in the 1960s, Foster made his name with industrial buildings of unusual quality but small scale. When he won the international competition in 1979 to design the new headquarters for the Hong Kong and Shanghai Bank, his firm had created nothing higher than three stories. Now they had a commission to construct a 41-story building that would provide office space for the biggest bank in Asia. The result has been acclaimed as one of the most significant buildings of the 20th century.

THE ESTHETICS OF COMMERCE

The building is a bravura demonstration of Foster's fascination with a commercial esthetic. His first idea was to incorporate the grand banking chamber of the old bank in the new building. This plan was abandoned quite early, but it suggested to Foster the key idea of a building hovering over a dramatic public space. Unlike conventional office buildings, with their central core of service spaces and elevators, the Hong Kong and Shanghai Bank is designed with large,

FAST FACTS
- DATE 1979–86
- STYLE High-Tech Modern
- MATERIALS Steel and glass
- ARCHITECT Norman Foster
- Principles of feng shui were taken into account in the course of designing the building

clear spans, with the services pushed to the edge of the building. This provides interiors of great flexibility and adaptability, free of any obstacles to future changes in arrangements.

To carry this idea throughout the building, it was necessary to create an exceptionally bold structural scheme. Tall steel masts at each corner of the building support huge, double-height trusses that bear the weight of the floors below without any further division of the interior space. These giant, beautifully finished structural elements dramatically define the building inside and out. The result is that even from a workspace deep within the building, everyone has a view that is never more than half a building width away.

The exception to the uniform office floors of the higher levels is the 10-story atrium, entered from the public plaza below. This, the largest space in the building, is lit by daylight, which is captured by a computer-controlled "sunscoop"

The building is designed around a huge, light-filled atrium above a public plaza (above). Norman Foster (left) was knighted in 1990 for his services to architecture.

on the outside of the building and reflected inside and down by a sophisticated system of mirrors. From inside this huge, light-filled space, the thousands of people who visit the bank every day glide up a series of escalators to their destinations.

SYMBOLIC LINKS

The bank wanted a building that would signal a British connection with Hong Kong even after its return to Chinese control in 1997. The design also takes symbolic and cultural considerations into account. Like the original building, the new Hong Kong and Shanghai Bank sits on a north–south axis, with the harbor and the Chinese mainland to the north and the old colonial city center to the south. Other symbolic factors were important too: Chinese geomancers deemed the first design to have unfavorable feng shui, and the structural configuration on the façade was changed as a result.

Though dazzling, the Hong Kong and Shanghai Bank is a building of many contradictions. It is very much a Western building in the heart of Asia, designed by a British architect, intended to symbolize the faith of the British in the future of Hong Kong and their place in it. It looks forward to boundless prosperity through the 21st century, but its internal organization reflects some very old-fashioned ideas about control and hierarchy. The open spaces of the office floors give everyone a view—but they also mean that everyone can be constantly observed, and there is a deliberate progression from the large public areas below to the increasingly private executive suites above. (The chairman's suite on the top floor even has its own helipad.) Foster and Partners have gone on to do major work in ecologically sustainable buildings elsewhere, but the Hong Kong and Shanghai Bank remains a monument to high technology: highly insulated, heavily serviced, and one of the most expensive office buildings ever constructed.

The building's enormous metal trusses support the structure and define the internal spaces, as well as giving the building its distinctive appearance.

Petronas Towers

Kuala Lumpur, Malaysia

Tall buildings are technological marvels of the modern world, but they are also commanding symbols of money and power. They first appeared in the thrusting American cities of the late 19th century such as New York and Chicago, where the new wealth from industry and commerce found its boldest expression. The most famous building of them all, the Empire State Building in New York City (1931), held the record for the tallest building for over 40 years until it was eclipsed by another American building, Chicago's Sears Tower (1974), which held the record for another 20 years.

The tapering twin towers, each 88 stories tall, have an Islamic-influenced polygonal plan and are linked by a skybridge.

FAST FACTS

- DATE 1998
- STYLE Post-Modern
- MATERIALS Reinforced concrete and stainless steel cladding
- ARCHITECT Cesar Pelli, Thornton-Tomasetti (engineers)
- The world's tallest twin building

TWIN TALL TOWERS

The project that finally broke the Sears record was not another skyscraper in Atlanta or Dallas but a pair of dramatic towers in Malaysia. With the rise of the "tiger economies" of Asia a new center of money and power has appeared, and the seemingly inevitable result is a rash of ever more spectacular buildings in China, Korea, Taiwan, and Singapore. Once only a Western (and specifically American) phenomenon, tall buildings have appeared around the Pacific rim as symbols of national pride and economic prosperity.

The Petronas Towers in Kuala Lumpur are the visible evidence of the determination of the former Prime Minister, Datuk Seri Mahathir bin Mohamad, to make Malaysia a fully industrialized economy and a leading regional power by the year 2020. The towers are the focus of a huge redevelopment of the Kuala Lumpur city center, simultaneously announcing the destruction of the colonial past and the beginnings of a radically different future for Malaysia.

Designed by the American architect Cesar Pelli and structural engineers Thornton-Tomasetti, the towers are the headquarters of Petroleum Nasional Berhad, a government-owned oil company. They contain 8 million square feet (750,000 sq m) of office space, 1.5 million square feet (140,000 sq m) of retail and entertainment facilities, parking for 4,500 cars, a conference center, a petroleum museum, and

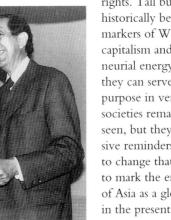

another and acts as an emergency exit for these supertall towers. Such buildings tend to twist and sway in the wind, so the skybridge is linked to the towers by flexible joints that allow up to 12 inches (30 cm) of movement at each end. With the skybridge, the towers constitute a monumental gateway to the rapidly redeveloping city behind them.

Petronas Towers is no longer the world's tallest building. In 2004 that reord passed to Taiwan's Taipei 101, and other towering giants are under construction in South Korea and Shanghai. Whether these buildings are worth the enormous amounts of money, materials, and energy invested in them is a political question not easily answered. Dr. Mahathir expressed the view that Asians can have development without democracy and prosperity without political rights. Tall buildings have historically been the markers of Western capitalism and entrepreneurial energy. Whether they can serve the same purpose in very different societies remains to be seen, but they are impressive reminders of the will to change that is likely to mark the emergence of Asia as a global power in the present century.

a concert hall. A requirement of the project was to provide space in which the Muslim office workers could hold their obligatory twice-daily prayers.

The buildings, uncharacteristically for towers this tall, are largely built of reinforced concrete, which was specially developed for this project. They rest on a raft of piles sunk more than 300 feet (92 m) below the buildings into the soft rock beneath; these unusually deep foundations support the 1,482-foot (452-m) high towers above.

BLOWING IN THE WIND

Apart from structural stability, vertical transport for buildings of this scale is the biggest problem. The large number of elevators that are needed to service the upper floors consume a very large amount of floor space, so the two "bustles" on the towers—44-story buildings attached to each base—add the area necessary to make the buildings workable as office space.

The towers are linked by a 192-foot (58-m), 738-ton (750-t) double-decked "skybridge" halfway up the structure that allows access from one high-level elevator lobby to

Tall buildings of the world: From left to right, St. Peter's Basilica, 1612; Pyramid of Khufu, 2700 BC; Eiffel Tower, 1889; Empire State Building, 1931; Sears Tower, 1974; Petronas Towers, 1998; Taipei 101, 2004. The Sears looks taller than Petronas Towers, but its antenna is not considered an architectural feature and so is not counted when calculating its height.

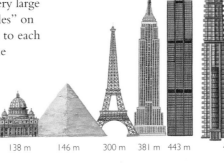

138 m   146 m   300 m   381 m   443 m   452 m   508 m

DESIGNS FOR LIVING

Domestic buildings reveal the lifestyles and preoccupations of entire cultures, as well as the personalities and aspirations of the individuals who built and inhabited them.

Throughout the world the way people live is always in response to their physical and cultural environment. The structures in which we dwell tell not just of the great men and women of history, or of powerful kingdoms and wealthy individuals, but also open a window into the everyday life of the whole variety of humankind.

Shelter is the one theme that unifies all our designs for living—in other words, our housing—but a number of other ideas appear regularly in housing design over the centuries. These ideas include the community, the individual, the classical ideal, and the liking or disliking of decoration. Firstly, there are the two kinds of architecture behind the designing of our homes. Vernacular architecture, or "architecture without architects," is design which has evolved in a particular community through adaptation to environment and need—examples in this chapter are Çatalhöyük and Machu Picchu. On the other hand, architect-designed dwellings may also respond to the perceived needs of a community, as is evident in the design of Habitat Montreal. However, in this case the architect formally identified community needs and set about to respond to these needs in a relatively short space of time, compared

DISPLAYS OF WEALTH *The House of the Vettii, in Pompeii, is richly decorated with frescoes such as that depicting scenes of a Dionysian mystery cult (above). The house of a king, the Royal Pavilion in Brighton (right) took its inspiration from Asian architecture.*

to the centuries taken to arrive at the housing form of, for example, Çatalhöyük. These examples of mass housing form entire towns or units of habitation within a city, but community housing may also be created for specific groups such as the religious community of Mont Saint-Michel.

INDIVIDUAL RESPONSES

Other housing responds to the individual, often in consultation with an architect. The Royal Pavilion at Brighton became the orientalist house of a king; the Villa Capra the retirement home of a Papal

advisor; Hardwick Hall the expression of social ambition. Because people have different priorities in deciding how they wish to live, so housing takes on diverse forms. Architectural ideals span the ages and the search for purity of form can be seen in such designs as the Villa Capra and Farnsworth House, both providing fresh interpretations of classical ideals. Different approaches to organic design for living spaces

the hedonistic lifestyle of the period. This can best be seen in dwellings such as the House of the Vettii, Pompeii. Pleasure of another kind can be seen in the Royal Crescent at Bath, a collection of conjoined permanent and seasonal homes for the wealthy and the well-connected, which gains its character from its combination of external visual harmony and luxurious internal decoration, designed around a huge, grassy park suggesting a country estate.

So the designs in which we have lived over the millennia take diverse forms, responding to our esthetic and practical needs. The very variety found in just this small selection of our greatest dwellings gives an indication of the great variety of the human experience, just as the unifying factors of these buildings tell of the community of human endeavor.

are demonstrated by Baron Victor Horta's designs for van Eetvelde House and Frank Lloyd Wright's Fallingwater. Both architects responded to the client's brief, but Horta had been asked to consider the internal requirements of the house, whereas Wright found the key to Fallingwater in the natural environment of Bear Run, Pennsylvania.

SEASONAL LIVING

If the inhabitation of housing is seasonal, again the design must respond to this way of living. The Farnsworth House was constructed as a holiday dwelling, so did not need the considerable storage and formal sleeping areas of a permanent dwelling, leaving the architect free to work with clean, uncluttered lines and visually transparent spaces in the house's natural setting. In

contrast, a permanent dwelling that responds to its urban environment and its inhabitants' lifestyle may be rich in detail, cocooning its residents in a microclimate created by the use of internal gardens, water features, and murals suggesting

COMMUNITY LIVING *Some mass housing grows randomly, but other examples, such as the Habitat apartments in Montreal, were designed to cater to the needs of a particular community.*

Çatalhöyük

Konya, Turkey

Thirty miles (50 km) south-east of the city of Konya lies Çatalhöyük, the remains of a complex and highly sophisticated prehistoric civilization dating from at least 7000 BC, whose level of culture and productive economy far surpassed that of other countries in the Near Eastern "cradle of civilization." Çatalhöyük has been progressively excavated since it was first identified by British archaeologist James Mellaart in 1958.

The site, a mound rising 57 feet (17 m) above the surrounding plain, covers about 32 acres (130 sq km). Over a dozen levels have been exposed, indicating that the settlement was inhabited for as long as a thousand years. It is not clear whether the entire site was occupied at any one time, but the possible population has been estimated as several thousand—the largest prehistoric settlement in the Near East.

NEW HOUSES FOR OLD

The architecture of Çatalhöyük is entirely of mud brick and wood. The settlement was a dense, unified structure, the buildings completely joined, one to the other, so the only access was by ladders through roof-openings. The linking of the buildings made them more stable and created an easily defended fortlike structure. Heavy timber beams supported the roofs; over these rested an arrangement of smaller beams, reeds, and mud. Across the top of the standard rectangular units that made up the town were the pedestrian "streets."

New houses were continually built over the ruins of the old, so buildings were often on different levels, resulting in open courtyards and high windows in some of the walls. The courtyards

> **FAST FACTS**
> ■ DATE c. 7000 BC
> ■ PERIOD Bronze Age
> ■ MATERIALS Mud brick and wood
> ■ Possibly occupied for as long as a thousand years, Çatalhöyük has been called the Neolithic city, and even the first known city

around which the single-storied buildings were often arranged were used as dumps, where garbage was burned. Within each building, the rooms were roughly square, the interior walls finished in white plaster. Red-painted pillars set in the walls supported the roofs.

Furniture comprised mud brick "built-ins;" there were platforms for sleeping, for sitting, and for food preparation. Ovens and hearths were found in the living areas, and the houses contained burnished, cream-colored pottery vessels, used to hold grains, pulses, and seeds.

A baby's skeleton found in a Çatalhöyük burial chamber wears a bracelet and anklet (above). The streets were at rooftop level, and ladders led from the roofs to the living areas (right).

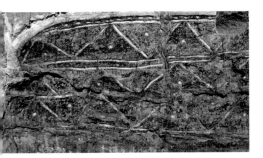

The people of Çatalhöyük produced many artifacts, including carved and painted wall frescoes (left), carved figurines, wooden and basketwork vessels, and high-quality woolen textiles.

BURIAL SITES

Beneath the plaster floors of their houses, the people of Çatalhöyük buried their dead. Rooms became shrines and were decorated with vivid wall frescoes, both painted and carved. These were part of the ritual of burial— they were not meant for permanent display and they were regularly painted over. The decorative themes indicate the importance of cattle to the economy of the region: Cattle horns were attached to modeled bulls' heads, and cattle appear in the murals, along with hunting scenes and wild animals such as leopards and stags. Mellaart believed that a picture of the erupting volcano

Hasan Dag was the first landscape painting in history. The inhabitants also produced clay and carved stone mother-goddess figurines in every feminine aspect—youth, marriage, pregnancy, giving birth, old age; women were even depicted commanding wild beasts. Eventually the entire building containing the burial chambers was demolished and a new house built on its site, the occupants continuing to live above the graves of their ancestors.

RISE AND FALL OF A CITY

Domesticated sheep and cattle provided meat and skins, but the people of Çatalhöyük were also hunters and gatherers. They traded with their neighbors for objects and materials from the coastal areas and further afield. Industries included chipped stone tools, bone artifacts such as needles and beads, and the first mirrors, made of the black volcanic glass called obsidian.

Çatalhöyük was a community in transition between a hunter–gatherer society and a settled city. By about 5700 BC an agrarian economy was wholly in place, but less than a century later the site was abandoned, possibly because it lacked the civic institutions such as a centralized administration that allow a city to function. But Çatalhöyük has been called "a premature flash of brilliance a thousand years before its time."

House of the Vettii

Pompeii, Italy

Pompeii, the ancient Roman commercial and resort town so famously destroyed by the eruption of Mount Vesuvius in AD 79, provides a remarkable record of life in the early Imperial period. The volcanic ash that buried the city also preserved it, as if frozen in time—excavations almost 1,700 years later revealed a prosperous city of 20,000 people caught in the midst of going about its business. There is the usual Roman forum, an amphitheater and gladiators' barracks, and streets laid out on a grid system with

> **FAST FACTS**
> ■ DATE 1st century AD
> ■ STYLE Early Imperial Roman
> ■ MATERIALS Brick, stone, and stucco
> ■ BUILDERS The people and artisans of Pompeii
> ■ Excavated from the volcanic ash left by an eruption of Mt. Vesuvius

public baths, shops, temples, theaters, and brothels. Private homes lie behind the shops—some with plaster casts of victims' bodies, made from the shapes left in the ash as people tried to shield themselves from volcanic dust, or lay where they had fallen, asphyxiated by fumes.

A LIFE OF LUXURY

The House of the Vettii is one of the best preserved houses in Pompeii. Its graceful design and decor are evidence of the luxurious taste and comfortable lifestyle enjoyed by the upper classes of ancient Rome. It belonged to wealthy freedmen, Aulus Vettius Testitutus and Aulus Vettius Conviva, as indicated by the bronze seals that were found in the atrium and the election slogans painted outside the high, enclosing walls protecting the house from the noise and dust of the street.

The entrance portal of the two-story house leads from the

section and floor plan

The peristyle was adopted by the Romans from the Greeks (above left). Murals in many rooms incorporate illusionist effects (above and below). Plaster cast of a victim of the eruption (inset).

vestibule to the atrium, an inner courtyard open to the sky, lined with elegant frescoes and at its center, an impluvium. On either side were the family strongboxes—safes encased in iron and bronze.

On the southern side is a corridor containing steps to the upper story and also leading to the stables and latrine. The northern side opens onto the servants' quarters, a number of smaller rooms that wrap around a secondary atrium. The kitchen is reached from here; a bronze grill, tripods, and other utensils can still be found in the hearth.

A GREEK INFLUENCE

The atrium had, in earlier styles of Roman houses, been the center of family life. But the 1st century BC–1st century AD saw a fusion of the atrium house with the Greek style of housing, which centered around the peristyle, a courtyard garden that was surrounded by a columned portico and various rooms. This design so appealed to the Roman appreciation of nature that the peristyle soon became the focus of the household.

In the House of the Vettii, the main atrium opens through a pair of columns onto the much larger peristyle, 66 feet (20 m) long, around which the main living rooms of the house are arranged. The complex, formal garden was planted with large trees (probably fruiting varieties such as olives, nuts, lemons, and soft fruits), as well as vines, and dotted with statues, pillars, and fountains.

Rooms off the peristyle garden include a reception room strikingly decorated in black-banded frescoes on red walls. This would have been used for dining in good weather, when the atmosphere of the garden could be enjoyed. There are two other dining rooms (*triclinia*) opening onto the peristyle, plus a much smaller, separate peristyle, part of a "suite" that includes a bedroom and a living–dining room. All these rooms are decorated with murals. The lavish use throughout of decoration to extend the sensory experience in the House of the Vettii is typical of Pompeii's rich atrium houses, so often the centers of appreciation and patronage of the arts—and of a hedonistic lifestyle.

Mont Saint-Michel

Brittany, France

In medieval France, Michael the Archangel was a figure to be taken seriously. Leader of heaven's armies and conqueror of Satan, he was the mightiest of all created spirits, the one nearest to God. So in 708, when Aubert, the bishop of Avranches, had three dreams in which Michael the Archangel appeared to him, he listened carefully. According to legend, the archangel commanded the bishop to build a chapel on top of a steep cliff—a suitable place of high honor—to celebrate his memory. At first Aubert doubted his senses,

FAST FACTS

■ DATE 8th–19th centuries

■ STYLE Romanesque (original buildings); Gothic (later additions)

■ MATERIAL Granite

■ COMMISSIONED BY Bishop Aubert

■ Inspired by visions of the Archangel Michael.

but when a series of miracles convinced him of the authenticity of these visions, he set about his task.

A PLACE OF PILGRIMAGE

The site Aubert chose was a granite mound 256 feet (80 m) high in the bay between Brittany and Normandy. By 966 a Benedictine abbey was erected there. For medieval Europeans who were in search of the archangel's blessing, it would become a mecca. To reach it, however, some would have to pay the ultimate sacrifice. Mont Saint-Michel becomes an island only when the tides are very high. Most of the time it is surrounded by vast sandbanks. Before the 3,000-foot (915-m) long causeway that connects the island to the mainland was built, quicksand and tides racing faster than a galloping horse claimed the lives of many pilgrims.

Over the centuries, the faithful erected ever grander monuments to the Almighty, but limited space required them to build vertically, turning earlier structures into a labyrinth of

The cloisters and colonnade of the 10th century abbey, which is once again in use by the Benedictine order that built it.

foundations and crypts. In the 13th century, more monastic buildings were added. Known collectively as La Merveille ("the marvel"), they form a three-story Gothic masterpiece. The monks lived on the top floor, and the abbot, noble guests, and knights on the second. On the lower level came the humble pilgrims to pay homage. Later, around the slopes below the abbey, a compact little township evolved.

One visitor, the American historian Henry Adams, observed that "No one is likely to forget what Norman architecture was, who takes the trouble to pass once through this fragment of its earliest bloom."

A TURBULENT HISTORY

Because of its strategic military location, Mont Saint-Michel grew in its importance to the French monarchy. At the heart of many conflicts, it was attacked by both English and French troops, yet its mighty fortifications held strong. In 1203 the abbey was partly burned when King Philip II of France tried to capture it. The fortress also survived sieges during the Hundred Years War (1337–1453) and the French Wars of Religion (1562–98). It was turned into a prison during the

French Revolution (1789–99), and remained so until 1863. Only after a crusade by novelist Victor Hugo was it restored and declared a historic monument.

In the late 19th century, more than a millennium after its birth, the abbey was finally graced with a tower and spire, fittingly crowned with a statue of St. Michael. Monks returned to the island in 1966. Once again a Benedictine community, it houses some 75 cloistered residents who go about their prayers and chores amid throngs of tourists.

Today, the greatest danger to Mont Saint-Michel is not war but water; the causeway has allowed silt to accumulate in the bay, threatening to fill in the short distance between the island and the mainland. The French government hopes to preserve the island's ethereal setting by replacing the causeway with a footbridge.

A walkway around the island passes through an arch in the lowest level of this house, built right out onto the water (left). An aerial view of Mont Saint-Michel at low tide (above). A carving in the abbey (inset).

127

Machu Picchu

Peru

High and remote in the Peruvian Andes, often swathed in the mists of the surrounding cloud forest, stands Machu Picchu. Built by the Inca, it is an engineering masterpiece rendered in stone and a place of the most arresting beauty. Machu Picchu is perfectly synthesized with its site, a narrow saddle of land perched 1,500 feet (455 m) above the fertile Urubamba River valley, between two peaks, Huayna Picchu (New Peak) and Machu Picchu (Old Peak).

FAST FACTS

■ DATE *Late 15th century*
■ MATERIAL *Granite*
■ BUILDERS *The Inca*
■ *Demonstrates the extraordinary ability of the Inca to shape their settlements as an organic part of the environment in which they were built*

It is from the latter peak that the site takes its name, for no one knows what the Inca called it. Probably built and inhabited some time after the mid 15th century, its main purpose is still unclear—it may have been a city, a palace, a fortress, or an important ceremonial site, used for the sun-worship that was so fundamental to the Inca civilization. The entire complex covers roughly 5 acres (2 ha) and is divided into three sections: urban, agricultural, and religious. These are linked by more than 3,000 steps and reflect the divisions of the city and of Inca society, which was hierarchical and ruled over by an emperor (regarded as a living god, son of the sun).

A STRATIFIED CITY

On hundreds of stepped terraces and irrigation channels on the steep slopes below the city, peasant farmers grew maize, potatoes, and other produce; the terraces greatly increased the area available for crops and helped prevent erosion and mudslides. A wall separates this section

Some of the most striking Inca works of art were carved into living bedrock, such as this small grotto in a royal tomb.

Machu Picchu seen from Huayna Picchu (above). This rock (inset) bears tool marks that show how the Inca split stones. The Intihuantana (below) was used as a sundial.

from the residential section of narrow alleys lined with single-roomed private dwellings that would have once been covered with thatched roofs. This section also contains artisans' workrooms, schools, a garrison or jail, and the royal cemetery. Finally, a series of flattened grassy plazas leads to the domain of the nobility and priests, a complex of temples, palaces, and the Temple of the Sun, centered around a grotto and a spur of rock that rises from the mountainside to be enclosed by the curved stone Military Tower. A long staircase leads to the Sacred Plaza. Here, the Temple of the Three Windows stands alongside the Central Temple, which has huge boulders fitted under niches that may have held mummies. Behind this temple is the most intriguing of Machu Picchu's shrines, the Intihuantana, or Hitching Post of the Sun, a thick stone pinnacle atop a hewn pedestal 6 feet (2 m) high, which functioned as a ceremonial sundial.

Perhaps the most amazing thing about this site is its actual construction. Huge granite blocks were cut so precisely that their contours fitted together perfectly, with almost imperceptible joints, to create walls and buildings that needed no mortar but have withstood numerous earthquakes. And yet the Inca had no iron tools. They shaped and dressed the stone using hammerstones, with pumice sometimes used for a final polish. And they managed to move these massive slabs into place, though they had no beasts of burden beyond llamas and no knowledge of the wheel either.

The Inca empire lasted for about 100 years, from the 1430s until its destruction by the Spanish in 1532. But the conquistadores who looted so many other Inca cities never found Machu Picchu; its inhabitants probably abandoned the site some time after the invasion. And so it stood, empty and unknown to the outside world, until the American Hiram Bingham "discovered" it with the help of a local Quechua Indian almost 400 years later, in 1912. Today, the legendary Machu Picchu is much visited and yet it remains an enigma, like the civilization that built it but left no written records as a key to deciphering such awe-inspiring achievements.

129

Villa Capra

Vicenza, Italy

O f the many villas that Andrea Palladio designed during the Italian High Renaissance, perhaps the most celebrated and influential was the Villa Capra. It was begun in 1566 for Monsignor Paolo Almerico when he returned to Vicenza upon his retirement from the papal court of Pius IV and commissioned Palladio to design him a rural retreat.

Palladio's style was a refined Classicism that reached its most formal expression in the Villa Capra, where the geometric forms of square, circle, and rectangle were arranged according to precise mathematical formulae—as explained by the architect in his 1570 publication *I quattro libri dell'architettura* (*Four Books on Architecture*). The villa is a cube surmounted by a dome above a circular hall—this is the source of its other name, the Villa Rotonda—surrounded by rectangular rooms with loggias in the form of porticos on all four sides.

A Room with a View

The Villa Capra was designed as a belvedere, or a place with a beautiful view. It was built at the edge of the city, crowning a hill

A cutaway view shows the precisely symmetrical layout of the villa, based on the architecture of classical Greece and Rome; the ornate frescoes in the circular hall; and the circular gallery above it.

FAST FACTS
- DATE 1566–71
- STYLE Italian High Renaissance
- MATERIALS Brick and stucco
- ARCHITECT Andrea Palladio
- The model for many 18th century country houses throughout England and America

and surrounded by vineyards, orchards, and a river. This almost Arcadian landscape was visible both from the porticos and from the central circular hall. The porticos are supported by Ionic columns, with pedestals lining the broad staircases decorated with statuary by Lorenzo Vicentino, and overlook the surrounding countryside in all directions. The villa, although symmetrical, is asymmetrically positioned atop its hill, so that each loggia relates differently to the landscape it overlooks.

Palladio described the interior in his *Quattro libri*: "Under the floors of [the loggias], and off the hall, are the rooms for the conveniency and use of the family. The hall is in the middle,

The villa is rotated 45 degrees to the south on its hilltop, enabling all rooms to receive some sunshine.

is round, and receives its light from above … Over the [vaulted] great rooms there is a place to walk around the hall, fifteen foot and a half wide." And so it remains today. However, the plan of the villa in the *Quattro libri* shows the dome above the central hall to be high, with a steeply pitched roof, whereas the finished building has a low-pitched roof with a stepped dome, thought to be the work of Palladio's assistant, Vincenzo Scamozzi, who completed the villa after Palladio's death. The existing lantern on the dome

THE CLASSICAL IDEAL

Andrea Palladio (1508–80), who trained as a stonemason and sculptor, became the Western world's first professional architect—and the only one after whom an architectural idiom has ever been named. Palladianism drew on three beliefs: That a universal language of architectural form is desirable and possible; that this language has its roots in the forms of ancient Roman architecture; and that the skillful employment of these forms will result in beauty. Beauty, usefulness, and durability were Palladio's prime objectives, and they were realized in buildings of absolute symmetry and proportion, evoking calm and serenity.

was also a late addition; when the English architect Inigo Jones, a great devotee of Palladio's work, visited the villa in 1614, he noted that the dome's oculus, or "open eye"—a circular hole in the dome's center, modeled on that of the Pantheon—was open to the sky, screened only by net, as Palladio had planned it. Likewise, the hall, decorated in 1581 in lush stucco and fresco work by Agostino Rubini, Ruggiero Bascape, and Domenico Fontana, was not part of Palladio's original cool, precise vision.

SMALL IS BEAUTIFUL

Grand as it is, the Villa Capra is not large. It was built quite simply, using brick and stucco almost exclusively. Stone was employed only for the purpose of carving major decorations—for example, it was used very cleverly on the corners of the entablature to give a crisp and detailed profile, while the rest of the entablature was built in brick and stucco. But despite its modest scale and materials, the refined elegance of Villa Capra, its way of integrating classical harmonies with the natural landscape around it, has made this one of Palladio's most copied buildings—a model that was replicated again and again in the grand country houses of 18th century England and America.

Hardwick Hall

Derbyshire, England

Hardwick, the great manor house on a hill in north-central England, was built for Elizabeth Talbot, Countess of Shrewsbury (1520–1608). The Countess, who came to be called Bess of Hardwick, was a formidable figure, a four-times widowed dowager who was one of the wealthiest and most influential women in England—after Elizabeth I. Following a long legal dispute with her fourth husband, the sixth Earl of Shrewsbury (whom she accused of conducting a lengthy affair with Mary, Queen of Scots), Bess received a substantial settlement, giving her the means to embark upon a grand project: to reinvent Hardwick Hall, the rather modest country house that was her birthplace and family home.

Bess returned to Hardwick Hall, Derbyshire, in 1584 and soon began making improve-ments to the original house. Alas, these early design "experiments" created something of a shambles. Around the time of her husband's death in 1590, she decided she would build a new mansion on the same site, one that would fully reflect her tastes and her status. This time, she hired Robert Smythson (c. 1536–1614) to help execute her ideas. Smythson, a freemason noted for his work on such distinguished manors as Longleat, Wiltshire, and Wollaton Hall, Nottinghamshire, is widely regarded as the greatest house designer of the Elizabethan era.

A PERSONAL STYLE

Smythson's plan for Hardwick is basically a wide H, with a two-storied hall that crosses through the center and divides the structure into two wings. Three massive square towers rise up from each arm of the H, giving the house its

FAST FACTS
- DATE 1590–97
- STYLE Elizabethan
- MATERIALS Sandstone and timber
- ARCHITECT Robert Smythson
- Bess of Hardwick acquired the hall after her brother, the former owner, died in a debtors' prison

distinctive profile. Bess's initials, "ES," appear in pierced stonework on the tower balustrades. The sandstone building has a rigorous symmetry; its squareness, generous glazing, and overall austerity combine to create a curiously modern effect.

At the same time, Hardwick is decidedly eclectic, owing to its builder, its owner, and most of all, its era. Elizabethan architecture is a transitional style that borrows elements from Italian early Renaissance, French Loire style, and Flemish ornamentation, as well as local design. So while the towers of Hardwick's exterior are reminiscent of English castles, the interior plan is that of an Italian villa, the ceiling strapwork reflects a Flemish influence, and certain furnishings are based on French designs. Inside, the house is spatially dramatic. The rooms become vaster and brighter as one ascends from the service area on the ground floor through the family and formal entertaining quarters on the first and second floors, respectively, to the third level, where the roof and upper towers begin. The Long Gallery runs the entire 162-foot (54-m) width of the second floor and is lined with portraits and tapestries. Hardwick still contains most of its original furniture and fittings, which thoroughly reflect its owner's taste and temperament. One of the most striking pieces is the "sea-dog table" in Bess's withdrawing room, named for the fantastical creatures that support the table, bearing wings, fishtails, and enormous breasts.

The hall's H-shaped floor plan (left). Hardwick Hall (above) is set amid the Derbyshire countryside. "Hardwick Hall, more glass than wall" is the lyric inspired by the house's dramatic windows that stretch almost from floor to ceiling (facing page).

Hardwick was completed in 1597 and has scarcely been altered since. It is a triumph of Elizabethan architecture and one of the finest manor houses of the period. The house was lived in until the onset of World War I and in 1959 was turned over to the National Trust.

A major restoration effort was embarked upon in honor of Hardwick's 400th anniversary in 1997, with masons and conservators busily plying their trades to restore the hall to its original state. Today, the grand old house is a popular destination for tourists.

Royal Crescent

Bath, England

Designed and constructed in the middle of the 18th century, the Royal Crescent in Bath is one part of a much larger plan of the two John Woods (father and son), whose scheme for the town revolutionized the concept of town planning in Britain. Their work became a reference point for many later architects and planners, including George Dance and John Nash.

The importance of the Royal Crescent lies in its fluid articulation with the town. It was here that the concept of buildings extending around a crescent and a circus—an open space, usually circular, where several streets converge—was first seen in Georgian England.

The Crescent (foreground) and the Circus are integral elements in the design of Bath.

FAST FACTS

- **DATE** 1767
- **PERIOD** Georgian
- **MATERIAL** Golden Bath stone
- **ARCHITECT** John Wood the younger
- **The design of Bath and the Royal Crescent marked a revolution in British town planning concepts**

A NEW ROMAN CITY

Bath was named for the health-giving hot springs that drew first the Celts and then the Roman occupiers of Britain to the site. By AD 43 the Romans had built a temple to Minerva at the springs, and a spa developed. The spa buildings, still largely complete today, fired the imagination of the eccentric and idealistic John Wood the elder (1704–54), who dreamed of recreating Bath as the Roman city it had once been. He designed Queen Square, with its façades evoking a rustic palazzo; the Circus, with its integrated radiating streets, employing the classical orders of architecture carried through each level in the manner of the Colosseum; a forum; and a gymnasium.

Only Queen Square was completed before Wood died, though he did at least lay the foundation stone of the Circus, which was completed by his son. John Wood the younger (1728–82) went on to plan and build the Royal Crescent, where the elite of Bath sojourned, their "Season" punctuated by the evening balls held at his new Assembly Rooms (1769).

A walk along Brock Street leads from the Circus to the Royal Crescent—a series of

30 houses constructed of golden Bath stone around a semi-ellipse, overlooking the Royal Victoria Park, a green sward beyond the cobbled street and traditional iron railings.

THE ITALIAN INFLUENCE

In designing the Royal Crescent, Wood was strongly influenced by Palladianism—a style of architecture derived from the work of the 16th century Italian architect Andrea Palladio, who revived and developed Roman ideas of symmetrical planning and harmonic proportion.

The unity of the massive unadorned pediment that forms the ground floor of the houses, running like a broad ribbon around the curve, draws the eye around the crescent. Above this, gigantic Ionic columns create an optical rhythm along the façade. At the same time, this single order of columns gives each section of the façade great height as the colonnade continues, unbroken, through the upper floors. Together, the plain lower pediment

Neoclassical façades

and the grand repetitions of the upper levels present a sophisticated variety of surfaces and decorative elements.

The Royal Crescent houses were built for the wealthy, the influential, and royalty— George III's son, the Duke of York, was a sometime resident—who came to Bath for relaxation, to view the Roman ruins, and for society. Consequently no expense was spared in the construction and decoration of the houses, with master craftsmen employed to work on the opulent interior decoration.

No. 1 Royal Crescent is now a museum, its rooms set up as if the occupants have briefly stepped out. Visitors can glimpse how life was lived when the houses were first built. A leisurely dessert is laid out in the dining room; across the hall the drawing room, with its enviable view of the crescent's curve, is set for a ladies' tea party; while upstairs a four-poster bed awaits tired ball-goers. It vividly evokes the society so penetratingly portrayed in the novels of Jane Austen.

Palais Royal

Paris, France

W hen Cardinal Richelieu was made Chief Minister of France by Louis XIII in 1624, he decided that a new residence at a new address was required, one that was worthy of his new position. He chose a site just across the road from the Louvre, the then home of the French kings, and commissioned his favorite architect, Jacques Lemercier (c. 1585–1654), to build the sumptuous Palais Cardinal, as it was originally known, as a classical-style *hôtel*.

A *hôtel* (private house) was a town residence for a single wealthy individual or family. This style of dwelling had evolved throughout France during the 16th century, an adaptation of the castle to an urban setting. The Palais Cardinal was one of the finest and most expensive examples of its time.

Work was begun in 1624. A quite plain entrance front, a two-story screen, faced the street; an archway led through to a narrow entrance forecourt surrounded on three sides by two-story buildings with *lucarnes* (a type of dormer window) set into their steep-pitched slate roofs. To the right was the Salle de Spectacle, a private theater built to satisfy Cardinal Richelieu's ambitions as an actor and author. Beyond the entrance forecourt was the wider "court of honor," with wings containing the living and reception rooms. On the northern end a massive arcaded screen separated this courtyard from an enormous garden of formal avenues of mulberry trees on either side of a broad central path. Off to the right of this was the "base court," the second courtyard, where the servants' quarters, outhouses, and stables were located.

> **FAST FACTS**
> - **DATE** Begun 1624
> - **STYLES** French Renaissance and Neoclassical
> - **MATERIAL** Stone
> - **COMMISSIONED BY** Cardinal Richelieu
> - Once used as a gambling den

A contemporary engraving depicts revolutionaries attempting to destroy the Palais Royal during the 1848 uprising.

The colonnaded courtyards (above and left) and arcades (right) are now popular public spaces.

Richelieu willed his home to the royal family upon his death in 1642, when it became known as the Palais Royal. Jacques Lemercier was placed in charge of subsequent extensions, of which only one interior wing remains. Indeed, this was to be the fate of much of Lemercier's original building. Interior renovations between 1717 and 1720 were followed by extensive interior and exterior remodeling in the 1750s. Additional work by Pierre-Louis Moreau-Desproux in the 1760s gave the building's main façade its Tuscan and Ionic columns.

TIMES OF CHANGE

Perhaps the most controversial changes were instigated by Louis-Philippe d'Orléans, also known as Philippe Égalité for his revolutionary ideas. Between 1781 and 1783, he employed the architect Victor Louis to turn the Palais Royal's large gardens into their present form, a vast annexed garden with arcaded pavilions around three sides. The grand façades lined with Corinthian pilasters, the arcades full of shops, cafés, and restaurants, and the upper floors of private apartments quickly became the place to rendezvous in Paris. Louis-Philippe also built a new theater at the southern end of the building (this later became the Comédie Française, headquarters of France's national theater) before he was guillotined in 1793.

The Palais Royal went on to become a gambling house before being reclaimed in 1815, and only just escaped being burnt down in the 1871 uprising. After more restoration work, it was finally made the property of the state. The Jardin du Palais Royal retained its status as a Parisian hotspot, full of gambling dens, brothels, good restaurants, and carnival attractions, for many years. Nowadays, its arcades, with their expensive boutiques and hotels, are altogether more dignified.

The Palais Royal is now home to various government bodies, such as the Constitutional Council and the Ministry of Culture. Another controversial (although ultimately successful) development occurred in the 1980s, when the artist Daniel Buren laid out the main courtyard with black and white stone pillars of varying sizes, standing above flowing water. Previously a car park, the courtyard has been transformed into a popular pedestrian space, with the columns doubling as an adventure playground for children and a good perch for adults.

Royal Pavilion

Brighton, England

The extravagant Gothic Oriental palace that is the Royal Pavilion began life as a simple farmhouse leased to the young Prince of Wales, the future George IV, who escaped there with his mistress, later his secret wife, Marie Fitzherbert.

The pavilion's rejuvenation began in 1787 under architect Henry Holland and continued into the 1820s under the eccentric John Nash. Holland added a colonnaded, circular, domed saloon. A further extension mirrored the old house, creating three sections.

The Prince's fascination with the Orient influenced the style of ensuing renovations,

FAST FACTS

- DATE 1787–c. 1821
- STYLES Regency Hindoo, Chinese
- MATERIALS Iron, resin, and stone
- ARCHITECTS Henry Holland, William Porden, Humphry Repton, and John Nash
- Originally a country retreat for the Prince of Wales and his mistress

with architects and designers such as William Porden and Humphry Repton contributing fantasies of China and India.

The pavilion's final form, of picturesque turban domes and minarets, was the perfect setting for the prince's lavish parties. Sea-bathing had become a holiday fad, and the elite were deserting spa towns such as Bath in favor of England's first seaside resort.

AN ORIENTAL VISION

The largest project was Porden's domed stable building, designed in the Indian manner with exotic pinnacles and pointed arches. In 1807 Repton suggested continuing the Indian theme to the pavilion by surmounting it with domes, pinnacles, and minarets. But the building program lapsed, Repton's plans unrealized.

In 1815, the Prince Regent, concerned that the pavilion was overshadowed by the Indian stables, invited John Nash to review the work. Nash's solution was to raise the pavilion's profile by crowning it with a series of domes,

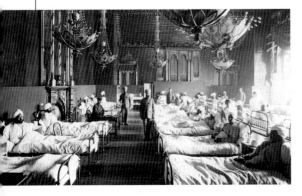

Originally the retreat of the hedonistic Prince of Wales, the Royal Pavilion has also seen service as a military hospital.

as first suggested by Repton. Nash designed a music room and banqueting room, whose concave cones of molded plaster on the roofs give the feeling of an exotic tent. Oriental themes prevailed, even in the huge new kitchens, where the iron supporting columns were decorated with copper palm leaves.

The exterior conversion that created the pavilion of today began in 1818, when the iron frame of the "Hindoo" dome was erected and covered in sheet iron and ornamentation molded from mastic resin. Lesser domes followed over flanking rooms, and minarets of Bath stone pierced the sky, while the old colonnade was replaced with one based on an illustration of a hall at Allahabad in India.

More Indian elements were added across the entrance façade, and in 1820 Frederick Crace and Robert Jones began the interior decoration in the Chinese style, from the red and gold mural in the music room to the dragon-themed banqueting room, in which a magnificent crystal chandelier hangs from the grip of a huge ceiling dragon.

In 1850 the pavilion was stripped of most of its fittings and sold to the town of Brighton. It has been restored, and many of the original pieces have been recovered or replaced with reproductions,

such as the bed in Queen Victoria's little-used apartments. Visitors stroll through the lavish interiors or, in quintessentially English fashion, view Nash's exotic confection from the striped deckchairs in the gardens opposite. Here, the domed Indian stables are now a concert hall.

A PLAYFUL ARCHITECT

John Nash (1752–1835), the most entrepreneurial architect and planner of his day, introduced a quirky and theatrical vision into Regency England. He flirted with the picturesque, Gothic, and rustic and classical Italianate styles to design everything from thatched cottages to whole streets. Nash flourished under the patronage of the Prince Regent and in 1813 became Deputy Surveyor General of Works. In London, he is best known for his 1812 design of Regent Street. This was the "royal route" that George IV took from his Carlton House palace to the newly landscaped Regent's Park, and is an exceptional example of town planning. The curve of the "Quadrant" is particularly famous, as are the cream-colored stuccoed terraces lining Regent's Park's Outer Circle.

Nash's Orient-inspired 1814 rotunda in Woolwich, London, is now the Museum of Artillery.

Van Eetvelde House

Brussels, Belgium

FAST FACTS

■ DATE 1895–98

■ STYLE Art Nouveau

■ MATERIALS Iron, stone, and glass

■ ARCHITECT Baron Victor Horta

■ Horta created buildings that rejected historical styles and marked the beginning of modern architecture

From 1892 Brussels was an important center for European avant-garde art and home to one of the major proponents of Art Nouveau: Baron Victor Horta. The van Eetvelde House, designed by Horta as a family home for Edmond van Eetvelde, Secretary of State and advisor to King Leopold II, represents a high point of Art Nouveau domestic architecture.

Born in Ghent, Victor Horta (1861–1947) was Belgium's most renowned architect and the designer of many Art Nouveau buildings in Brussels. Horta's major contributions to Art Nouveau were his interior designs, which are a synthesis of the Modernist exposure of structure using materials such as iron with intricate surface decorations (arabesques) and a dramatic use of interior lighting. The malleability of iron suited his curvilinear style, enabling him to create his distinctive fluid spaces flooded with natural light filtered through glass roofs; the cool tones of marble in the interiors enhanced this airy feel.

USING THE SPACE

Horta's style of domestic architecture was partly dictated by the constraints of small sites. The Industrial Revolution had caused rapid population growth in Brussels since the 1870s. As surrounding rural land and villages were subsumed by the city, land prices increased in the city center and only small blocks of land, narrow but long, were available. Houses were inevitably conjoined, greatly reducing lighting potential, so Horta's ability to create a feeling of spaciousness and light was very important.

Horta's client, van Eetvelde, required large public rooms for his official entertainment duties, and more modest private rooms on the upper floors. The house was built in three sections: First the main block (1895), then extensions on either side. (The 1898 western extension is now a separate residence.) Externally, the upper three levels of the central main section are slightly cantilevered over the stone first-floor entrance level. Garden fences, upper floor panels, and window treatments are visually united by fine, graceful linear design. Further unity is supplied by the curtain wall façade that extends across the two main floors, and the vertical strength of the building finds expression in the use of a visible iron frame.

The main reception rooms are half a level above the street, and are approached by a stairway to the octagonal Winter Garden, which carries the eye up through the main floors to the natural light that is diffused through a patterned glass dome. The rooms spin off the octagonal shape of the Winter Garden, creating a swirling architectural space that echoes the refined arabesques that Horta employed in the detail of every part of the building. The fluidity of the design and the associated play of light through glass afford an

A NEW ESTHETIC

The ethos of the Art Nouveau movement was that the applied arts should abandon the revival of earlier styles and seek inspiration in the organic forms of nature. Undulating lines suggesting waves, flames, vines, flower stems, and tresses of hair were favorite motifs. Drawing on the design concepts of William Morris and the English Arts and Crafts movement, Art Nouveau began in the 1880s and influenced architecture, furniture, iron work, glass, jewelry, wallpaper, clothing, typography, and book illustration.

Ironically, some advocates of Art Nouveau, such as Glasgow architect Charles Rennie Mackintosh and Belgian Henri Clemens van de Velde, came to prefer geometric rather than naturalistic designs. These developments toward a 20th century Modernist esthetic eventually led to the decline of Art Nouveau.

Windows on the south façade of the Scotland Street School, Glasgow, designed by Charles Rennie Mackintosh.

endless variety of views across and between
rooms from the perimeter stair. As well as the
fine glass, Horta used a wide variety of materials
to express his esthetic vision—marble, rare
African timbers, and iron are all finely worked
into the structure in sinuous organic patterns.

*Generous natural lighting,
a feature of Horta's
architecture, was achieved in
the van Eetvelde house by
the beautiful glass ceiling
over the central hall (right).*

Raffles Hotel

Singapore

Somerset Maugham, English novelist and dramatist, once claimed that the legendary Raffles Hotel "stands for all the fables of the exotic East." Raffles certainly is famous not so much for its architecture—best defined as eclectic—as for its political and social history and ambience. The hotel was named for the founder of modern Singapore, entrepreneur and orientalist Sir Stamford Raffles, who transformed the small island

FAST FACTS

■ DATE 1899

■ STYLE Victorian eclectic with Classical details

■ ARCHITECT R. A. J. Bidwell

■ A byword for the luxury and glamor of high society in the early 20th century

on the Straits of Malacca into a thriving port. In 1819, Raffles signed a treaty with the Sultan of Johor to establish a trading outpost there for the British East India Company.

HIGH SOCIETY

As a center for free trade and a burgeoning rubber export industry, Singapore grew rapidly, its position at the crossroads of the region bringing people of many communities to the port and establishing the Singapore of today. In what is still called the Colonial District, the British built churches, theaters, a cricket ground, a City Hall, a House of Parliament, and a Supreme Court. In this very British setting, Raffles Hotel became the center of Singapore high society for more than 40 years.

The original hotel opened on December 1, 1887 in an old, two-level bungalow set on prestigious "Twenty-House Street" (Beach Road) facing the harbor—now reclaimed land.

Guests can still enjoy a Singapore Sling, a drink including gin and cherry brandy, that was invented in this bar in 1915.

It was later renovated by the Sarkies brothers, Martin, Aviet, Tigran, and Arshak, members of the prosperous Armenian community. In 1899, the elegant new Raffles Hotel was built around the old bungalow. Two accommodation wings were added, along with the Palm Court and Billiard Room annexes. The three-story main building was designed by R. A. J. Bidwell, of Swan and Maclaren, a popular firm for colonial work. The latest word in luxury, Raffles was the only hotel in the Straits Settlements that could boast electric light and fans. The grandeur of the hotel's façade—a free interpretation of Classical references—is somewhat eccentrically modified by its colonial context.

From its earliest days, the hotel attracted the rich and famous. Eight of its suites are named for "personalities" who stayed there, including writers Somerset Maugham, Rudyard Kipling, Noel Coward, and Joseph Conrad, and film stars Ava Gardner and Charlie Chaplin. One of the grandest is named for Sir Stamford Raffles.

Peaceful tropical gardens and courtyards add to the ambience of the site, the landscaping helping to visually isolate guests from big city life. Maugham wrote several short stories while seated beneath one of the garden's frangipani trees. This separation from the city evokes the

The Tiffin Room (above) evokes the glamor of Raffles (left) in its heyday. Raffles is one of the few remaining 19th century hotels in south-east Asia.

period when the hotel faced directly onto the water, as it did when Noel Coward was a guest in 1930. "I sat on the veranda of the hotel ... there was a thunderstorm brewing. The sky split in two; the sea lost its smooth, oily temper and rushed at the hotel as though it wanted to swallow it up, and then the rain came ... its impact on the roof of the veranda was terrific."

DECLINE AND RISE

Raffles' heyday, however, was over by 1931. The Sarkies' empire fell victim to the Depression and the hotel became a public company. When the Japanese invaded Singapore in 1942, hotel guests found themselves prisoners of war, while Japanese officers made Raffles their headquarters. In 1945, the hotel became a camp for freed Allied prisoners. Much deteriorated, but still imposing, it earned its nickname "Grand Old Lady of the East."

In 1987 the Singapore government declared Raffles a national monument. A government-funded renovation project began in 1989. When the hotel reopened in 1991, the section built in 1899 was largely returned to its former glory.

143

Fallingwater

Bear Run, United States of America

Fallingwater was designed by Frank Lloyd Wright (1869–1959) as a weekend retreat for Edgar J. Kaufmann and his wife, Liliane. Wright, one of the most original and influential architects of the 20th century, began his career in Chicago, working for the innovative architect Louis Sullivan. Sullivan's axiom, "form follows function," influenced Wright's work, as did the simple, expressive lines of the Japanese prints that he had begun to collect.

Fallingwater was commissioned at a period when Wright's practice was severely affected by the Great Depression and the international influence of his famous "Prairie Houses" had long passed. However, despite this inauspicious start, the house was to become the most celebrated of the 300 that he created.

"PRAIRIE HOUSES"

Wright's "Prairie Houses," built between 1900 and 1910 in suburban Chicago, revolutionized domestic architecture. His approach was both Naturalist in the way that the building and its site appeared to blend—the long, low lines of the exterior echoing the surrounding flat mid west (hence the name of the complex)—and Cubist in the asymmetry of the exterior and in the interiors, where the concept of space dominated over mass. Wright's aim was to create a total environment, not merely a house; in many of his commissions, the landscaping of the

FAST FACTS
- DATE 1935–36
- STYLE Organic
- MATERIALS Stone, concrete, timber, and glass
- ARCHITECT Frank Lloyd Wright
- Designed over a waterfall, and to integrate with its environment

site, the interior fittings and decor were all part of his creative vision and under his control.

A HOUSE OVER WATER

In July 1933, Kaufmann acquired the title to land at Bear Run in Pennsylvania. He was committed to the area's conservation and had visions of a log-cabin retreat, but Wright persuaded his client to allow him to experiment with the latest technologies for using reinforced concrete and glass.

Wright procrastinated over the plans for Fallingwater. Finally, in September 1935, they were completed in a 24-hour burst of activity, illustrating Wright's capacity for developing an architectural concept in his mind, through all the processes of organization, analysis, elimination, and refinement, before committing the idea to paper. As Wright said, "by way of concentrated thought, the idea is likely to spring into life all at once and be completed eventually with the unity of a living organism."

The house is partially cantilevered over Bear Run, a fast-flowing stream tumbling down a series of falls. Kaufmann wanted the house as close to the falls as possible, among the boulders, rock ledges, and trees. The waterfall became the prevailing motif of the design, Wright later stating: "In a beautiful forest was a solid, high rock ledge rising beside a waterfall, and the natural thing seemed to be to cantilever the house from that rock bank over the falling water."

The strong, horizontal lines of the house rise over three levels in a series of terraces and cantilevers, echoing the form of the rock bank. Dominating the first-level main floor is the living room, which centers on a huge hearth. Balancing the horizontal bands of concrete are vertical walls and pillars of massive rusticated local stone. Inside, glass windows in horizontal panels maintain the connection with nature. Stairs provide internal access to the waterfall, and exterior and interior have a seamless continuity of materials—stone, glass, concrete, and wood—that refer directly to the natural environment of the house.

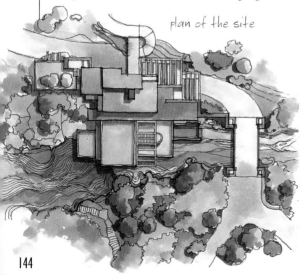

plan of the site

In Fallingwater, balanced over a waterfall as if it were part of the landscape itself, Frank Lloyd Wright brought architecture and nature together as an organic whole (facing page).

Farnsworth House

Illinois, United States of America

Farnsworth House, created by Ludwig Mies van der Rohe (1886–1969), is famed for its functional living spaces enclosed in a light, pure, fragile-seeming glass envelope with an extended terrace hovering above the building's setting in the placid meadow country of Plano, Illinois.

Commissioned by Edith Farnsworth in 1945 as a weekend getaway, the single-story, open-plan building was pared down to the simplest elements needed for services and accommodation. The house was intended for the use of one person, so interior privacy was not a consideration. But external privacy was another matter. The huge 10-acre (4-ha) site initially guaranteed seclusion. But the design's fame spread rapidly, and practical considerations overrode the architect's vision of translucency; drapes had to be fitted to shut out sightseers fascinated by the architect's literally visionary concept.

FAST FACTS

■ DATE 1946–57
■ STYLE Modern International
■ MATERIALS Glass and steel
■ ARCHITECT Ludwig Mies van der Rohe
■ Visionary in concept, the house proved almost impossible to live in

FORM AND FUNCTION

Structure was of fundamental importance to the International Style, in which concrete and steel frames allowed formerly weight-bearing walls to become mere "curtains." Functionalism (that the building's function determines its form) was all-important, generating original design concepts to serve individuated needs.

Farnsworth House is constructed mainly of glass with a steel frame, modern materials with which Mies van der Rohe demonstrated his feeling for construction, materials, and new building technologies. He had the conviction that "there could be no architecture of our time without the prior acceptance of these new scientific and technical developments." In this project, his perfectionism is evident in the finish of the materials and the precision of the workmanship.

Mies van der Rohe has been compared to the abstract painter Mondrian in his "absolute pitch" in

detail of glass curtain wall

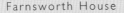

Designed to be completely visible from the outside, the interiors are brightly lit by the glass walls (right).

determining proportions and spatial relationships. The interior of the main rectangular envelope of Farnsworth House, which measures 28 feet by 77 feet (8.5 x 23.5 m), is divided into sleeping, eating, sitting, and service areas, with partitions of natural timber. One end of this rectangle is open to form a large covered terrace. The white-painted steel frame, suspended by eight I-shaped columns exterior to the main envelope, shows as a grid against the surrounding tall trees. A second floating rectangular podium, faced with the same travertine stone as the interior, is slightly offset from and lower than the main house, forming a second, open, terrace.

NATURE TRIUMPHANT

From inside the house, the view is of the meadow, the trees, and the Fox River beyond, the relationship to nature interrupted only by the narrow steel window frames. As Mies van der Rohe said: "Nature should also live its own life, we should not destroy it with the colors of our houses and interiors. But we should try to bring nature, houses and human beings together in a higher unity." But nature, for all the respect the architect paid it, struck back. The glass envelope created a climatic nightmare for the owner—cold with condensation in winter, stifling and insect-infested in the summer. (The architect would allow no screening of doors or terraces.) The architectural tourists and nature itself turned paradise into a nightmare.

THE INTERNATIONAL STYLE

Ludwig Mies van der Rohe was one of several brilliant German architects who fled Nazi Germany in the early 1930s for the United States, their innovative work denounced by Hitler as *nichtdeutsch*—"un-German." The International Style—which was highly influential in Europe, and epitomized in Le Corbusier's architectural philosophy of creating "machines for living"—finally reached America due to the influence of such architects as Mies van der Rohe (left, c. 1958) and Walter Gropius, both of whom had taught at the famous Bauhaus art school in Dessau.

Habitat

Montreal, Canada

Habitat, built at Mackay Pier on the St. Lawrence River, was the first modern apartment building to consider its potential inhabitants in creating a built environment. Designed by Canadian–Israeli architect Moshe Safdie (born 1938), the building was completed in 1967 as part of Expo 67, the International Exhibition at Montreal.

The development consists of 158 apartments with from one to four bedrooms; altogether, there are 15 different plans. The apartments are constructed from 354 individual prefabricated concrete units, each 70–90 tons (71-92 t) in weight, stacked in "confused order" and connected by internal steel cables.

FAST FACTS

- DATE 1967
- STYLE Modern
- MATERIAL Prefabricated concrete modules
- ARCHITECT Moshe Safdie
- Designed to integrate living spaces with the external environment

QUALITY OF LIFE

Nearly 1,000 apartments were originally planned: It was only on such a scale, in Safdie's view, that the scheme could fulfill his vision of affordable, mass-produced family housing that would be comfortable and pleasant to live in. Ironically, in the 21st century a two-bedroom "condo" in the city's "most prestigious apartment building" has recently been advertised at a price of $795,000.

Habitat looks rather like an informal pile of boxes, seemingly thrown together higgledy-piggledy. It has been likened to a Pueblo Indian town and to an untidy ziggurat, but its design origins may well lie in the vernacular architecture of the Palestine of Safdie's childhood. Each apartment has an outdoor living space of similar dimensions to the interior space,

usually on the roof of the apartment directly below. Apparently random but rhythmic recesses and projections created by the systematic arrangement of the modules create privacy, access to views, and protection from weather. Pedestrian "streets" allow horizontal movement around the site, and the whole effect evokes echoes of L'Unité d'Habitation, built by Le Corbusier in Marseilles from 1947 to 1952, which the French architect described as aiming to "give freedom to the individual within a collective organization."

Habitat's intricate spaces are perfectly articulated with the outdoor environment. Environmentally sensitive management of the water-cooled air conditioning system allows the construction of a series of terraced pools and water sprays suitable for children's play. The patterns of light entering the spaces between, under, and over modules bring the immediate environment alive, encouraging changing uses and providing visual variety.

Habitat represented a new way of thinking about housing in urban centers— an approach driven by consideration of how

people would live there and the environment in which they would live. In Safdie's own words, he intended to create "the rhythms and variety of urban experience essential to community experience." Habitat needed to provide both privacy and outdoor living, just as a house would, and yet be cost-effective to build and maintain, like high-rise apartments.

Safdie wrote a series of conditions required for apartment buildings, which developed into a code for environmental amenity—in effect, he was creating an environment, not just a building. To design and construct such a complex, he experimented with prefabricated concrete, designing boxlike "space cells" that could be endlessly arranged in a complex system to suit a variety of sites and conditions. Habitat was to be the prototype for a system that would fast-track the building process and thus pare down the cost of providing family housing in urban environments.

FAILURE—OR SUCCESS?
To some extent Habitat was an expensive failure, largely because of the innovative nature of the project. The cost of prefabrication was huge and construction was difficult. But people continue to enjoy living there—so Safdie's environmental project can be judged a success.

Safdie has continually revised his modular concept: After Habitat Montreal, he used the same principles in Habitat New York I and II; in the 300-unit Habitat Puerto Rico, set on a hill in San Juan; and in a massive project in Israel that contains 4,500 units. The student union of San Francisco State College takes the repetitive use of modular units a step further— hexagonal-shaped units can be rearranged to create a flexible building capable of adapting to a variety of human needs.

Habitat's architect, Moshe Safdie (above). Habitat was the first of several of Safdie's explorations into the possibilities of prefabricated and mass-produced modular units (left).

149

LEARNING AND LEISURE

The idea of culture is inseparable from the idea

of civilization, and the history of civilization

is a record of the cultures of the past.

A key aspect of culture is memory, and those things that preserve our memory of the past, such as art and writing, are the basis for the transmission of culture to future generations.

The earliest art is based on magical and spiritual explanations of the world; the earliest architecture on shrines for the gods that ruled that world. For people to live together in large numbers, laws and government were necessary, both of which required writing. The survival of written records is the definition of history. Thus some of the centers of culture discussed in this chapter are libraries and museums, which house the records of the past and are used to teach the young about the societies in which they live.

The library at Ephesus in Turkey is one of the best preserved of the libraries of the ancient world. The museum of the Louvre in Paris, once the home of kings, is now the repository of priceless works of art collected to display royal grandeur. The close connection between the functions of these two buildings and that of education is apparent in Thomas Jefferson's famous design for the University of Virginia, where the library, housed in the great Rotunda, is the focus of the whole complex, and the buildings themselves are a kind of museum of architecture.

PASTIMES OF THE PAST *The plays of ancient Greece brought to life the gods and myths of Greek culture in theaters such as the splendid open-air theater at Epidauros (above), which is still in use today. The ancient Romans placed great emphasis on learning and established public libraries such as that at Ephesus, in Turkey (right).*

This instinct for a culture to define itself by its art is by no means dead, as shown by three very contemporary buildings. The Pompidou Center in Paris, which combines a museum, archives, galleries, and teaching facilities in one space, is the most visited building in Europe, while Frank Gehry's startling Guggenheim Museum in Bilbao has given new vigor to the city and helped to redefine the Basque identity. Like its famous namesake in New York, built by Frank Lloyd Wright, the new Guggenheim Museum has attracted attention as much for its own sake as for the art it contains.

DRAMA AND SPECTACLE

Another way in which the past has been evoked is through ceremony and ritual, and the performance of these ceremonies over centuries speaks of enduring human concerns.

The Greeks of Periclean Athens in the 5th century BC regarded drama as the noblest way of explaining the world and the mysterious workings of the gods to men. Our Western idea of theater was born here, and at the theater of Epidauros in Greece spectators can still see the great plays of the classical past, with their eternal lessons for humanity, performed in one

MODERN INTERPRETATIONS
One of the most ancient forms of shelter, the tent, was the inspiration for Olympic Park in Munich (left). The Pompidou Center (below) caused great controversy because of its inside-out design.

of their original settings. Similarly in London a 20-year labor of love on the part of one man to re-create Shakespeare's Globe Theater reminds us of the power that the setting has on the performance.

THE BUSINESS OF SPORT
Several buildings illustrated here demonstrate this power for performances of a different kind. Sport, though as thrilling as any drama, rarely has a script, but it shares with drama the idea of spectacle. The stadiums of the past, such as the Roman Colosseum, were the setting

for the cruelest spectacles, and according to some historians these had a moral of their own—the folly of defying the power of the Roman state.

Present-day international sporting competitions also mix athletic contests with politics, most notably in the Olympic Games. For most of their history the modern Olympics have involved political bargaining on a global scale, and the 1936 Games in Berlin, capital of Hitler's Nazi Germany, haunt the memory. The 1940 Olympics were to be held in Tokyo, another aggressor

nation, and only the outbreak of World War II prevented them from going ahead. Thus the stadiums built for the 1964 and 1970 Olympics, held in Tokyo and Munich respectively, are important not only for their outstanding design but also for their symbolic marking of the readmission of Germany and Japan to the world community.

ART HOUSE *The value of many museums, such as the Guggenheim in New York, lies as much in their own esthetic qualities as in the works of art that they house.*

Theater and Temple of Apollo

Delphi, Greece

Delphi, at the end of a long and arduous climb 2,000 feet (600 m) up the slopes of Mount Parnassus, was one of the most famous holy sites in the classical Greek world. Built on the site of a spring that was sacred to Ge, the Mycenaean earth-goddess, Delphi was a place of pilgrimage even before the Greeks built the first of six temples to Apollo there. In its spectacular mountain setting, the cult of Apollo attracted visitors from all over the Mediterranean, brought to Delphi by the fame of its oracle.

FAST FACTS
- DATE 4th century BC
- STYLE Greek Classical
- MATERIAL Stone masonry
- Zeus, king of the gods, wishing to find the center of the Earth, let loose two eagles from the two ends of the world. The sacred birds met at Delphi

THE WORD OF THE ORACLE
In an age of sibyls, oracles, and prophesies, the Delphic oracle was considered the foremost among its peers. It was believed to be the most prescient, able to foretell the future with remarkable accuracy, if one could decipher the enigmatic utterances of its priestess. Through this priestess, Pythia ("Pythoness"), visitors—kings and commoners both—could learn what the fates held in store for them. After first visiting a sacred cave, and bearing the appropriate tributes for the god, petitioners would be received within the temple, in a small enclosure (really a small building of its own) that was known as the *adyton*. The *adyton* was built above the sacred spring and contained a statue of Apollo, a three-legged seat (known as a *tripod*) for the priestess, and a bench for advisors. Steps led down into the crypt which contained the spring.

Pythia answered all questions in the same way—ambiguously—and the temple priests would then interpret these responses for the questioner. Any questions of a political nature tended to receive vaguer answers than more everyday ones, and these answers had to be treated with some caution. Everyone remembered what had happened to King Croesus: When he asked whether he should invade

The ruins of the theater (above), and those of the temple in front of it (above right). A statue of Nike, the goddess of victory, from the temple (right).

a neighboring state, the oracle had replied that a great empire would fall if he did so. It was only after the invasion had gone disastrously wrong that Croesus realized the empire referred to by the oracle was, in fact, his own.

DIONYSIAN REVELS

Delphi was also the legendary home of Dionysus, the god of fertility and hospitality, known to the Romans as Bacchus, the god of wine. Every winter, while Apollo the sun god was away, Dionysus ruled in Delphi. The theater situated above the temple of Apollo was filled with followers of Dionysus, the women and girls known as the Maenads, who abandoned themselves to frenzies of worship by torchlight. Their revels continued until Apollo's return in the spring, when visitors in search of answers to life's questions again made the long journey up the side of Mount Parnassus.

With the spread of Christianity, and the realization that its priests could be bribed, Delphi began to lose its spiritual authority. Julius the Apostate was the last ruler to send an ambassador to consult the oracle, but by the time of the emperor Theodorus Delphi was in decline. Centuries of plunder and earthquakes reduced the city once known as the center of the Earth to rubble, and it was rediscovered only at the end of the 19th century by French archaeologists.

Archaeologists have used contemporary accounts of Delphi at the height of its fame to identify many of the ruins, with one exception. Though the temple of Apollo and many other famous buildings were located and explored in this way, the sacred cave used by the oracle has never been found.

reconstructed view of Temple of Apollo

155

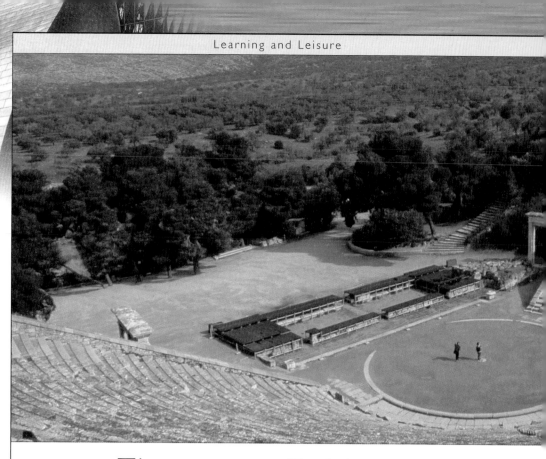

Theater at Epidauros

Epidauros, Greece

The theater at Epidauros is the best preserved and the most beautiful of the ancient Greek theaters—and it is still in use today. Epidauros was the Lourdes of the ancient world; in the hope of healing, thousands of sick pilgrims came here every year to the shrine of Aesculapius, the god of medicine and, for Greeks and Romans alike, the most respected of the gods. Aesculapius was generally portrayed carrying a staff festooned with serpents. His cult had been popular in Greece since the 5th century BC, notably at Epidauros. The town was a busy commercial center as well, with numerous important buildings, including its magnificent theater.

FAST FACTS

■ PERIOD 4th century BC

■ STYLE Greek Classical

■ MATERIAL Stone masonry

■ ARCHITECT Polyclitus the Younger

■ The secret of the remarkable acoustics of the theater at Epidauros remains a mystery

THE BEGINNINGS OF WESTERN DRAMA

Built around 350 BC by Polyclitus the Younger, the theater at Epidauros could seat 12,000 spectators in a setting of unsurpassed natural beauty. Like all Greek theaters, it evolved from a natural site at the foot of a hill, where performances could take place in the valley, with the audience looking down from the hillside above.

Over time this arrangement became more permanent, with tiers of stone seats (the *cavea*) arranged in a semicircle around the *orchestra,* the flat performance area. A long, low building—the *skene*—which served as both dressing room and backdrop, backed onto the orchestra. The front row of seats was reserved for the priests of Dionysus; other dignitaries had permanent seats behind them.

One of the most outstanding achievements of these ancient theaters was their sheer practicality as playing spaces. Using the hillside

Actors performed wearing masks made out of fabric stiffened with plaster. The large mouths helped carry the actors' voices to the back of the theater.

theatrical masks

setting meant that everyone had a clear view of the stage. But facial expressions were difficult to see at such distances, so Greek dramatic performances became highly stylized; the performers wore large masks and brilliantly colored costumes and acted by means of large formal gestures, rather like Japanese Noh and Kabuki plays. There was a set number of masks available to ancient Greek actors, each with an easily recognizable expression. These masks could double up for different roles. Women's roles were played by men, a dramatic convention that continues in the East to this day.

The theater's remarkable acoustics still amaze visitors to Epidauros. Even a whisper on stage could—and still can—be heard clearly by the spectators high above on the outermost tier of seats. How this was achieved continues to fascinate and mystify historians: The playing area, paved in stone or marble, seems to have acted as a reverberating surface, while the structure of the tiered seating was designed to minimize resonance and echo. Vitruvius, the first architectural theorist, writing about theater design, mentions that vessels partly filled with water were often placed under the seats in order to improve the acoustics.

The Greek dramatic tradition, which evolved from fertility rites in honor of the god Dionysus, became a powerful medium of expression under the great playwrights of classical Greece, Aeschylus, Sophocles, and Euripides. In *The Eumenides, The Bacchantes,*

and *Oedipus the King*, these writers brought to life the fickleness of the gods and the fates of those who dared to defy them. At the theater of Epidauros today, audiences can watch these unchanging stories in a theater where they were first staged over 2,400 years ago.

The rectangular foundations to the left of the circular area (above) are the ruins of the skene, the building that housed the dressing rooms. A performance of Euripides's Hippolytus, staged in the theater at Epidauros in 1954 (below).

Library at Ephesus

Ephesus, Turkey

One of the best preserved Roman libraries is that at Ephesus, on Turkey's Mediterranean coast. Ephesus was one of the original 13 Greek colonies in Asia Minor and for centuries was a great trading port. The city's Temple of Diana was one of the wonders of the ancient world and attracted pilgrims from all over the Mediterranean. When the library was built, about AD 151, Ephesus had become a Roman colony and had acquired some Roman features, including a geometric plan, an amphitheater, and a large town square.

FOR LEARNING AND FOR PLEASURE

The library was sited near the gate of the town square. Dedicated to the memory of a generous benefactor, Tiberius Celsus, it was a handsome two-storied building with a heavily modeled façade. Niches in the façade on either side of the doors displayed statues representing Wisdom, Virtue, Reason, and Knowledge. A broad flight of steps led into a single, large space lined with books and dominated by a statue of Athene (Minerva in Roman mythology), the Greek goddess of wisdom. We can only speculate as to the interior finishes used, but very likely they were as lavish as money would allow, with a fine molded stucco ceiling, a mosaic floor, and walls depicting mythological scenes.

Floor plan (right). The books were housed and the readers accommodated in the building's central open space (below). A colonnade around the edge of the space once supported a mezzanine above (facing page).

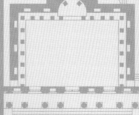

FAST FACTS

- DATE 2nd century AD
- STYLE Imperial Roman
- MATERIALS Stone masonry
- DEDICATED TO Tiberius Celsus, who is buried below the library
- A public library as well as a place where copies of books were made

This space was the reading room. The readers sat on high-backed chairs or folding stools and the scribes at tables, hand-copying books. In the room was a catalog based on the original one developed by Callimachus in the great library of Alexandria, with books divided into eight classes (drama, oratory, history, lyric poetry, legislation, medicine, philosophy, and miscellaneous) and arranged, for the first time, in alphabetical order. The librarian and his assistants spent their time updating the catalog and collecting more volumes, by soliciting donations of either books or of money so that copies could be made.

At this time books were still in the form of papyrus rolls, each about 30 feet (9 m) long, 10 inches (25 cm) wide, and two inches (5 cm) thick when rolled up. All would have had a central wooden rod (ivory or gold in the case of more important books) to help unfurl the scroll, and were identified by a parchment tag. Reference books were made wholly of parchment for longer wear. The rolls were stacked on cedar shelves along the inner wall; the most prized books were probably kept in wooden chests to which only the librarian held the key. There were books in both Greek and Latin— the classic tales, Euclid's geometry, and works on science, law, history, and philosophy. It is unlikely, given the persecution of Christians, that any Christian works were held by the library at this time, but some Hebrew religious texts may have been allowed in the collection.

Most city inhabitants, even women and slaves, were able to read. Literacy and numeracy were considered essential for the commercial transactions carried out daily in a busy port, but reading was also a pastime—for pleasure and reflection. Private libraries, many extensive, were the preserve of most patrician families, but Vitruvius, the Roman architectural writer, was not alone in recommending that libraries be established for the public to enjoy. Tiberius Celsus, who is buried in the crypt below the library, clearly agreed.

The Colosseum

Rome, Italy

The Colosseum is both a monument to the organizational genius of ancient Rome and a very stark reminder of the cruelty and power of the Roman Empire. Yet the Emperor Vespasian (AD 69–79), who commenced the Colosseum in AD 71, was a commonsense man of the people; not a city noble, like Nero, his hated predecessor, but a country aristocrat. His simple tastes coincided with the people's: In rebuilding a city ravaged by fire (allegedly caused by Nero), he finally provided a permanent home for the Romans' favorite entertainment, the blood-thirsty gladiatorial games.

The Romans had adopted the Etruscan custom of staging elaborate funeral games on the death of an important person, in which prisoners and slaves would be sacrificed to the memory of the deceased. It was believed that shedding the blood of the living honored the dead; the more people sacrificed, the greater the honor. As the practice developed of having the doomed men sacrifice each other, some prisoners were specially chosen and trained to be gladiators. Survivors might win their freedom; cowards were tortured instead.

> **FAST FACTS**
>
> ■ DATE AD 71–80
> ■ STYLE Imperial Roman
> ■ MATERIALS Stone and concrete
> ■ COMMISSIONED BY The emperors Vespasian and Titus
> ■ The Colosseum could be emptied of 50,000 spectators in minutes

At first confined to funerals, these combats quickly became a spectator sport. Magistrates, public officials, and election candidates staged them to win popular approval. Games were held originally in market places or town squares, but as crowds increased so did the need for better settings: Amphitheaters— theaters in the round—could accommodate thousands of spectators. Temporary wooden versions were built, but as audiences reached tens of thousands there were dramatic collapses.

A Symbolic Site

The building of the Colosseum on the site of Nero's Golden House was symbolic: a mass entertainment venue, seating 50,000, arising from the elitist palace of a despot. Nero's ornamental lake was drained to provide a stable foundation for the gigantic elliptical building in concrete and stone. The façade was decorated with travertine, a sedimentary limestone. Rising steeply to a height of 160 feet (50 m) were four tiers of seats. The bottom row was for the emperor, high officials, and the vestal priestesses; the next for wealthy citizens; with women and the poor at the top. The building could be emptied in minutes through an expertly planned system of corridors and exits. A huge canvas awning protected spectators from the elements.

The façade is a series of round arches flanked by half-columns (left). Four stories high and 620 feet long by 500 feet wide (190 x 154 m), the Colosseum (right) encloses an arena measuring 290 feet by 180 feet (89 x 55 m).

CARNAGE IN THE COLOSSEUM

Vespasian's son Titus completed the building in AD 80. The inauguration celebrations lasted 123 days, during which 5,000 wild beasts were slain. Eventually the spectacles became even more terrible. Animals—bears, lions, tigers, even elephants—were chained together to fight to the death. Men were pitted against animals, or giants against dwarves. Cruel deaths, by crucifixion or burning alive, always drew crowds. Greek myths were enacted, in which Orpheus or Oedipus would really die. Many Christians were martyred, but they were unpopular with the crowds because of their eagerness to die for their faith; criminals, deserters, and other kinds of religious heretics were more inclined to fight. By the time of Domitian, Titus's brother, knights and women, as well as gladiators, participated in the games.

Some have theorized that this carnage was deliberate, to accustom Romans to the realities of war and conquest: To see was to believe in the power of the Roman Empire. With the fall of the empire and the rise of Christianity the Colosseum fell into disuse. Left to decay, it was plundered for its marble and stone to rebuild a later Rome.

Below the arena, a labyrinth of chambers held the animals and the stage machinery, and provided quarters for the gladiators; multiple trapdoors opened directly into the showground.

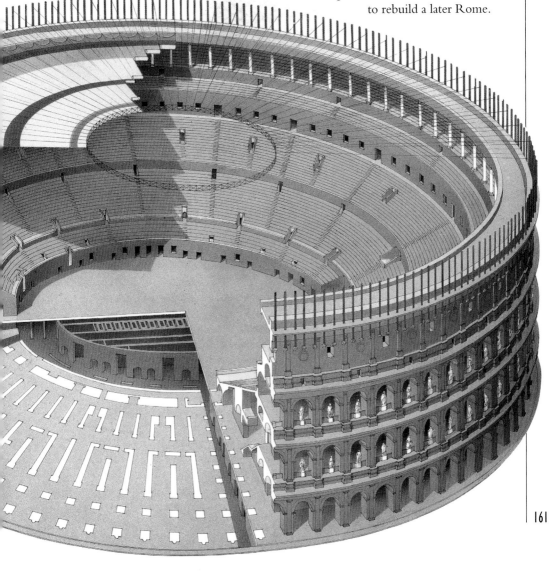

Louvre Museum

Paris, France

The Palais du Louvre, the Louvre's full name, is actually a complex of buildings built over a period of 700 years by the kings of France. It was the royal headquarters in Paris until Louis XIV (who disliked it) built Versailles to live in instead. The core of the complex is the Old Louvre, a medieval quadrangle on the eastern end; Henri IV built the Grand Galerie, 1,500 feet (457 m) long, running west from this block overlooking the Seine, and Catherine de Medici built another large palace, the Tuileries, at the western end.

FAST FACTS

■ DATE 1667–1989

■ STYLE French Classical Baroque

■ MATERIALS Stone and timber

■ ARCHITECTS Le Vau, Perrault, and Pei

■ The Louvre is now one of the world's great art museums

FIT FOR A KING

Louis XIV's chief minister, Jean Baptiste Colbert, understood the importance of grand public buildings to a king's dignity. He and Louis extended the Louvre initially by creating a vast parade ground, the Place du Carrousel, west of the Old Louvre and behind the Grand Galerie. Louis Le Vau, the future architect of Versailles, was commissioned to design some new buildings around the old quadrangle, the Cour Carrée, but the eastern façade was left unfinished. This was to be the main entrance to the royal palace from the city and Colbert wanted something suitably grand for its 600-foot (182-m) length.

Le Vau submitted a design but it was rejected. The great Italian Baroque architect Bernini was then invited to try but was also unsuccessful. The competition to design the eastern façade was becoming the biggest of its day; Jules Hardouin Mansart, the King's architect, was favored to win it, but in the end an unknown designer, Claude Perrault, was the surprise—and controversial—choice.

The Louvre houses hundreds of thousands of art works from all periods, including the Mona Lisa and Victory of Samothrace.

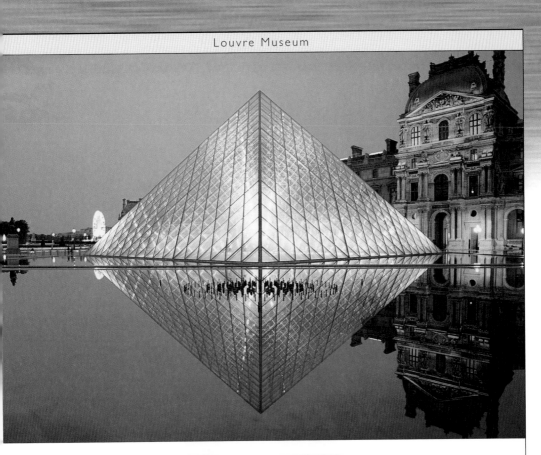

The Richelieu wing of the Louvre (above left). Two views of the controversial Pyramide du Louvre (above and right).

Perrault was a doctor and writer as well as an amateur architect. He obtained the commission over the greatest architects of the day, even of the century, by the advantage of being both a courtier and well connected—his brother was Colbert's secretary. The brothers actively intrigued against Bernini, arguing that his design was impractical, and Colbert eventually came round. Perrault was also, crucially, a member of the design jury.

Perrault's solution was a synthesis of various earlier schemes, and was influenced by his fellow committee members (and professional architects) Le Vau and Le Brun. But his work impressed Colbert, who gave instructions for work to begin in 1667. By 1670 the eastern façade was largely completed, but Louis XIV was now concentrating on Versailles and the Louvre was no longer his major interest.

After the French Revolution the Louvre became the national gallery of France. Napoleon enlarged it further until he, too, was overthrown; later his nephew, Napoleon III, completed the series of buildings along the northern edge of the site. In the Paris Commune of 1871 the revolutionaries tried to burn down the Louvre but only succeeded in destroying the palace of the Tuileries. When the ruins were cleared the Louvre became essentially the building we see today.

A MODERN ADDITION

Controversy erupted again in 1985 with the announcement of plans to extend the Louvre. American architect Ieoh Ming Pei's design—four pyramids in steel and glass in the Cour Napoleon, the main courtyard to the Louvre—is in starkly modern contrast to the ornate Classicism of the original building. The main pyramid rises 71 feet (21.5 m) above the ground and is partially sunken into the courtyard, creating a subterranean area that comprises the entrance to the expanded main galleries as well as much-needed support spaces. The main pyramid is clad in reflective glass tinted a pale ocher to complement the honey-colored stone of the Old Louvre. Three smaller pyramids provide further light and ventilation to the underground spaces. Although Pei's "intervention" has been criticized by some for disrupting the Louvre's classical harmony, others have praised it for reinvigorating the more traditional building behind it.

University of Virginia

Charlottesville, United States of America

Thomas Jefferson, founder of the University of Virginia, was a towering figure of the American Revolution. Trained as a lawyer, he had a matchless public career—he wrote the Declaration of Independence, served as Governor of Virginia and Secretary of State, was special envoy to France, was twice elected President of the United States, and once President of the American Philosophical Society. His ideas about the new American republic that he helped to found influence citizens and legislators to this day.

FAST FACTS

■ DATE 1817–25
■ STYLE Neoclassical
■ MATERIALS Brick, timber, and stucco
■ ARCHITECT Thomas Jefferson
■ Jefferson called the University "the last of my mortal cares and the last service I can render my country"

Jefferson was born in 1743 to a wealthy Virginia tobacco planter and was raised as an 18th century gentleman. He was a gifted amateur architect: He designed his house at Monticello, as well as an early version of the Richmond Penitentiary (later built by Benjamin Latrobe) and the Virginia State Capitol. He also took an active interest in planning the new federal capital of Washington and, most impressive of all, singlehandedly brought about the creation of the University of Virginia when he was over 70 years old. Jefferson found the site, raised the money, designed the buildings, supervised their construction, planned the curriculum, and hired the professors. Building began in 1817, the university was granted its charter in 1819, and it opened in 1825.

THE IDEAL OF A UNIVERSITY

Jefferson's university brilliantly demonstrates his convictions about the role of education in a new democracy. The focus of his passion was

Jefferson, an advocate of free public eduation, devoted his retirement to the University of Virginia—the realization of the ideal university that he had planned in 1805, while President.

Jefferson, the university's founder, is commemorated by this statue (above). Detail of a Neoclassical column in the Rotunda (left).

not a church or a chapel but a great library. The planning of the university harks back to the Classical ideals of symmetry and order, renewed in the Renaissance and embodied in the work of Jefferson's favorite architect, Andrea Palladio (1518–80). It was laid out in deliberate contrast to the medieval universities of Oxford and Cambridge. On both sides of a great central space, the Lawn, were houses for professors and dormitories for students, linked by long colonnaded walkways. On the third side, dominating the whole, was the Rotunda, a half-scale replica of the Pantheon in Rome. The fourth side was left open, linking the "academical village" to the open country beyond.

A NEW RENAISSANCE

Jefferson's planning may have been influenced by ideas about making knowledge visible, in the way that the museums of the Renaissance tried to locate all human knowledge in precisely defined spaces. Jefferson no doubt had something such as this in mind with the 10 pavilions that housed the university professors and their various branches of knowledge grouped round the great library—"the memory of the world"—which was housed in the Rotunda. Even the pavilions themselves were designed as visualized knowledge, each one representing a different example of the classic buildings of the past, suitable for lectures on architecture.

The Rotunda was more than merely the physical focus of the university. Its lower floors contained lecture rooms and a gymnasium while the upper floor was the symbolic heart of the university. It contained not only a library—for which Jefferson personally selected the books—but also a planetarium with movable stars and planets. Jefferson felt that in such a place, "based on the illimitable freedom of the human mind ... we are not afraid to follow the truth wherever it may lead or to tolerate any error so long as reason is left free to combat it."

The university was opened in the winter of 1825. Jefferson died the following summer, fittingly enough on the Fourth of July. He left a last design to be executed by his heirs—his own memorial. An obelisk 8 feet (2.5 m) high was to list his three proudest achievements: not his Presidency, nor the Louisiana Purchase, but the Declaration of Independence, the Statute of Religious Freedom—and the founding of the University of Virginia.

Opéra Garnier

Paris, France

According to historians, every self-consciously modern capital in the 19th century needed three things: a railway station, a telegraph office, and an opera house. Paris was to acquire all three under the Second Empire. Napoleon Bonaparte's nephew, Napoleon III (Louis Napoleon, 1808–73) was elected president of the Second Republic after the revolutions of 1848. In 1851 he proclaimed himself emperor, and for the next 20 years devoted himself to the nation's modernization. Paris was to be the most glittering capital in Europe: The Prefect of the Seine, Baron Haussmann (1809–91), was given unprecedented power to remodel the city. Haussmann laid out the grand boulevards that now divide Paris, ruthlessly uprooting whole communities

Charles Garnier spent 14 years working on the opera house.

FAST FACTS

- **DATE** 1861–75
- **STYLE** Beaux-Arts
- **MATERIALS** Stone, timber, and stucco
- **ARCHITECT** Jean-Louis Charles Garnier
- Home to the Phantom of the Opera

and demolishing ancient quarters of the city to do so. But it is the vast and ornate Paris Opéra that best epitomizes the showy wealth of the Second Empire. Its exterior, with its paired columns (copied from the Louvre), its decorative sculptures and friezes, and its roof topped by three cupolas, is an eclectic mix of Classical, Renaissance, and Baroque styles. The lavish façade is considered stylishly opulent by some—but it has also been compared in its vulgarity to a wedding cake.

AN ERA OF GRAND PLANS

A new opera house had been mooted for some time, and under the Second Empire the time seemed ripe to revive the idea. Napoleon III had already embarked on the enlargement of the Louvre and was open to grand plans; Haussmann led the way with his new thoroughfares. The Place de l'Opéra had been laid out in 1858; all that was needed was the right building. In 1861 Charles Garnier won the second competition for a design that satisfied the emperor and his empress, Eugénie, and commenced work on a project that was soon beset by difficulties.

The interiors are lavishly gilded (above). The vast building covers 3 acres (1.2 ha) (right).

Problems began with the charges that Garnier had plagiarized his design from other entries. Then excavations revealed that a tributary of the Seine ran beneath the site, requiring complicated structural work to isolate the building from the water below. There was also constant government pressure to contain costs. Garnier had promised that the building would be ready for the Paris Universal Exhibition in 1867, but when the time came only the shell was complete. The sumptuous interiors were also taking longer than had been anticipated; bureaucratic obstacles, a fire, and the Emperor's constant suggestions caused further delays.

Garnier's severest test came in 1870, when the Prussians laid siege to Paris. Napoleon III was forced to sign a humiliating peace treaty in January 1871 and promptly abdicated. The newly elected government was not popular and there was an uprising in Paris. The revolutionaries took over the unfinished opera house and flew the Red Flag from the roof; the building was used as a barracks, a storehouse, and a field hospital before the revolt was finally crushed in May 1871.

Garnier now had to persuade the new government to complete a building commissioned by its hated predecessor. Honing his diplomatic skills, he convinced them that the Opera House was not a memorial to a fallen emperor but a noble expression of the glory of France.

A MODEL THEATER

The inauguration in January 1875, a selection of operatic excerpts, was a triumph. Garnier's magnificent interiors were immediately recognized as masterpieces—the curving marble Grand Staircase, High Baroque in style; the mosaic ceiling of the Grand Foyer; and the velvet-and-gilt auditorium, seating 2,200 patrons in five tiers. The Paris Opéra was rapidly imitated in capitals all over Europe, from Vienna to Bucharest to Odessa, and was regarded as a theatrical model until at least World War I.

L'Opéra Garnier, as it has been known since the 1989 opening of the contrastingly stark, monumental glass Opéra Bastille, now focuses on ballet classics, performed under Marc Chagall's magical ceiling, painted in 1964. Tours are available, or visitors can admire the exterior from the pavement tables of the Café de la Paix opposite, also designed by Garnier.

Sydney Opera House

Sydney, Australia

The sails of a yacht, the wings of a bird, shells fanning outward—these images have all been evoked by Sydney's Opera House. It has become an icon of the city, its gleaming white sails arcing into the sky while the massive granite podium moors it to a narrow strip of land, lapped on three sides by the waters of Sydney Harbor.

Sydney acquired its extraordinary Opera House because of a decision, in the early 1950s, that the city needed a proper performing arts center. In 1957 the Danish architect Jørn Utzon (born 1918) won an international design competition with a vision for a building like no other—organic, sculptural, and wonderfully evocative, perfect for a site and a city so dominated and determined by a large expanse of water. Even then, the judges thought it "capable of becoming one of the great buildings of the world." But it was a controversial decision, too, because of the enormous technical difficulties involved—the project's English consulting engineers called it "a structure that could barely be built."

> **FAST FACTS**
> ■ DATE 1957–73
> ■ STYLE Expressionist Modern
> ■ MATERIALS Granite, concrete, and glass
> ■ ARCHITECT Jørn Utzon
> ■ The architect has never visited the finished building

CONTROVERSY AND CRISIS

Utzon's design was a unique one that broke many rules. Its construction therefore demanded that new techniques be developed when work began in 1959, and perhaps not surprisingly, it resulted in controversy and drama. When increasing costs and delays were used by a new government interested in making political capital out of the unpopular project, Utzon was forced out in early 1966 and left Australia. For a few months it was thought that perhaps the towering empty shells on their podium should be left as a giant unfinished sculpture. But work was finally completed in 1973, the interiors being reworked to a changed brief. The Opera House was opened amid great public support that same year, though Utzon was notably absent.

final stages of construction

His building is designed to be viewed from every angle, including from above and, like a sculpture, always to reveal something slightly new. It comprises three clusters of interlocking shell vaults atop a massive terraced podium of granite slabs that houses the working areas—the rehearsal and dressing rooms, recording studios, workshops, and administrative offices—plus the drama theater, and a small performance space. Two side-by-side shell clusters hold the two main auditoriums: the larger concert hall, which has a hanging ceiling with radial segments, and the opera theater, used for opera and ballet. The third shell cluster contains a restaurant. These shells, up to 197 feet (60 m) high, are supported by fanlike concrete rib beams, with 2-inch (5-cm) thick concrete walls. They are covered in over a million matte and glazed ceramic tiles that accent the shells' radiating shapes and glisten like fish scales in the sun. Glass walls fill the open ends and sides of the shells, creating the impression of glass waterfalls and providing spectacular views all round. A concourse links all the performance spaces and encircles the entire building; the two main auditoriums are also approached via grand external staircases.

Though it has acoustic problems and may be a flawed masterpiece because of its compromised interiors, the competition judges have been proved right about the Sydney Opera House. Today, it is variously described as one of the iconic buildings of the 20th century and as the eighth wonder of the world. And it is almost impossible to imagine Sydney without it.

The glass-walled bar area of the Concert Hall provides sweeping views (above).

JØRN UTZON

Born in Copenhagen, Denmark, in 1918, Jørn Utzon studied architecture in Copenhagen from 1937 to 1942 before continuing his studies in Sweden and the United States, and working with the Finnish architect and designer Alvar Aalto. Utzon developed a style of architecture known as Additive Architecture. Domestic work forms an important part of his oeuvre. However, it is for the Sydney Opera House (though the crisis surrounding its construction was to mar his career and his life) and projects such as the Kuwait National Assembly that he is internationally renowned—as an architect of imaginative monumental buildings that opened Modernism to concepts of organic form, for which he has received numerous awards.

Guggenheim Museum
New York, United States of America

A great white snail, a space-ship, a funnel, a salad spinner, a nautilus shell, a giant drum, a … washing machine? Frank Lloyd Wright's innovative spiral showcase has been tagged with odd monikers by scores of admirers and detractors, but on one point there is no argument: The Guggenheim is simply provocative.

It was commissioned to house the growing art collection of Solomon R. Guggenheim, one of seven sons of a mining magnate whose fortune fueled a wealth of distinguished endeavors. He began collecting paintings in the 1920s, and soon amassed one of the most extensive modern art collections in the world. He had Kandinskys, Modiglianis, Mondrians, Klees, and Picassos, but no permanent home in which to display

FAST FACTS
- DATE 1956–59
- STYLE Organic
- MATERIALS Reinforced concrete and glass
- ARCHITECT Frank Lloyd Wright
- The museum's radical, helix-shaped design offered a new way of viewing works of art

them. So his art advisor and collection director, Baroness Hilla Rebay von Ehrenweisen, contacted the famed 76-year-old architect. "I want a temple of spirit," she instructed him, "a monument!"—in short, a structure as ground-breaking as the art it would house.

A NEW WAY OF SEEING
A prime site was selected, extending the full width of a Manhattan city block on upper Fifth Avenue and facing Central Park. Wright, who was never comfortable with urban environs, had deemed New York City an undesirable choice of location, and at one point lobbied to have the museum moved into the park. Nevertheless, he seized the opportunity to further experiment with his notions of organic architecture and open-plan designs. He began with nature's primordial form, the spiral. The specific shape he had in mind was

A light sculpture by Dan Flavin pierces the central space directly under the apex of the building's glass dome.

A long ramp gradually ascends toward the dome (above). Wright displays a model of the museum (c.1950) (right).

that of a ziggurat (an ancient, stepped pyramidal temple), only turned on its head. He felt the shape's fluidity would complement abstract art.

Wright's design exploited the sculptural possibilities of reinforced concrete and also pushed the technology to its limits. Much engineering know-how was required to build the vast molds for the poured concrete and to achieve the "no visible means of support" effect. In fact, Wright's plans were so formidable that they frightened off several contractors. Some suggested the architect's aging imagination had simply run amok, losing touch with the practical realities of construction. Plans were submitted in 1943, then came the war. Construction did not begin until 1956 (by which time Guggenheim had died) and was completed in 1959, six months after Wright's death. Yet the result is one of the most extraordinary interiors of the 20th century.

Wright's design offers visitors a new way of moving through a museum and looking at art. The great spiral ramp that defines the main gallery widens as it ascends toward a huge domed skylight, creating, in Wright's words, "one great space on a single continuous floor." So instead of moving from one room to another (and inevitably retracing one's steps) in the usual way, here one can take a one-way trip and view multiple levels of art simultaneously. Many visitors head to the top by elevator, then work their way down. Others climb upward, gradually approaching the extraordinary light. However viewers choose to proceed, they soon discover a curious sport: gazing first at the artworks mounted on the spiral's outer walls, then turning to hang off the balustrades of the inner spiral, checking out the paintings—and the people—across the way.

Does architecture that invites this much attention and "play" enhance or detract from the museum-going experience? Critics argue that art cannot be properly viewed when floor and wall are not at right angles. But Wright's aim was for something more: "... to make the building and the painting an uninterrupted, beautiful symphony such as never existed in the World of Art before." To him, the museum's helical form echoed nothing so much as an unbroken wave, nature's perfect circle.

Yoyogi National Sports Center

Tokyo, Japan

Set in Tokyo's largest park, Yoyogi-koen, the Yoyogi National Sports Center was built for the 1964 Olympics by Kenzo Tange, one of the most distinguished Japanese architects to gain international prominence after 1945. The hosting of the 1964 Games was an important political breakthrough for Japan; it marked the country's readmission to the international family after World War II, in which Japan had been an aggressor nation. (The 1940 Olympics were to have been held in Tokyo, but were canceled after war broke out in Europe.) Japanese athletes were not invited to the first post-war Games, in 1948, but by 1952 they were gradually reappearing in international competitions.

Tange's work owed a huge debt to Le Corbusier's strongly sculptural architectural forms and his use of reinforced concrete as a

FAST FACTS

■ DATE 1960–64
■ STYLE Expressionist Modern
■ MATERIALS Concrete and steel cable
■ ARCHITECT Kenzo Tange
■ Considered to be among the most graceful sports arenas ever built

building material. Concrete in its roughest state, first seen in Le Corbusier's Unité d'Habitation apartment building in Marseilles (1946–52), became something of a Tange trademark. But he also developed his own idiom, brilliantly combining features common to traditional Japanese architecture (which was strongly geometric in form) with the most advanced ideas in structural engineering: In his first major design, the Hiroshima Peace Hall (1949–56), he took the typical Japanese post-and-beam construction and inflated it on a vast scale.

ART IN THE SERVICE OF SPORT

Tange designed two buildings for the Tokyo Olympics. The larger, seating 15,000, housed the swimming; the smaller, with 4,000 seats, accommodated the boxing and basketball. Both used the same structural idea of a suspended, cable-net roof, slung from supporting masts. This design provided elegant,

Massive anchoring cables and the curving form of the roof help resist winds that can reach up to hurricane force in the region.

tentlike interiors of great intimacy and charm. Linked underground, the whole complex was built on an elevated concrete platform, and combined areas for competitors, spectators, and officials in a satisfying whole. The swooping roof of the larger building is hung in two sections from steel masts on either side of a slit-shaped skylight. South-west of the pool building, the roof of the smaller circular pavilion hangs from a single mast; the wood-clad interior resembles a giant shell.

EAST MEETS WEST

Kenzo Tange, born in 1913, began his career as an architect in 1945 under Kunio Maekawa. Maekawa, along with several other Japanese architects, had worked in the office of the Swiss–French master architect, Le Corbusier. Tange's career was a long one, both at home and abroad. Notably, after winning a United Nations competition, in 1965 he replanned the city of Skopje in Yugoslavia. In 1991 he was responsible for Tokyo's tallest building, the massive Tokyo Metropolitan Government Offices in West Shinjuku, housing 13,000 workers; its matching 48-story towers were inspired by Notre Dame in Paris.

At the 1964 Olympics, the pool was the scene of some spectacular swimming feats, dominated by the United States, whose team won 16 out of 25 events. Don Schollander of the United States was the outstanding male swimmer of the Games, and Dawn Fraser of Australia the outstanding female. Fraser had achieved the rare Olympic feat of winning a gold medal in the same event, the 100 meters freestyle, at three successive Games.

ORGANIC ARCHITECTURE

The buildings attracted attention from architects around the world. The Australian critic Robin Boyd asked: "How much higher than this can modern architecture aspire? For what else had the 20th century been searching during 64 years? A functional stance, a consistent order, variety within unity, a compelling structure, a sculptural form, a transcendental space, universal principles but a regional flavor, all achieved simultaneously and with a Spartan simplicity." Several younger Japanese architects—Kazuo Shinohara, Fumihiko Maki, Kiyonori Kikutake, and Kisho Kurokawa—were greatly influenced by Tange and formed the Metabolism Group, which strove for flexibility over fixed building forms.

Olympic Stadium

Munich, Germany

Structure and architecture are inseparable, but modern architecture has sometimes been slow to realize the possibilities that modern engineering has created. The example of Sir Joseph Paxton's Crystal Palace of 1851 has been repeated many times; the greatest architects of the day simply ignored Paxton's innovative use of iron and glass to create a totally new building, and continued working in the tired old styles of the past.

A number of outstanding engineers, such as Buckminster Fuller, Robert Maillart, and Pier Luigi Nervi, have led the way in demonstrating the expressive and creative powers of the new materials and structural systems of recent times. Another such engineer, who is also an architect, is the German designer Frei

FAST FACTS

- DATE 1972
- STYLE Expressionist Modern
- MATERIALS Acrylic, steel, and glass
- DESIGNER Frei Otto
- A striking experiment in tensile structures and in designs that create one environmental entity

Otto, born in 1925. His work continues an important tradition in experimental structures that was begun in the 19th century by people such as Paxton and Gustave Eiffel. Like them, Otto is fascinated by buildings made not by following a given style but by the working out of a logical process.

ARCHITECTURE AS SCULPTURE

The son and grandson of sculptors, Frei Otto deeply admires the craftsmanship and inventiveness of sculptors such as Constantin Brancusi. Like Brancusi, Otto takes a minimalist approach that is both beautifully simple and wholly rational.

Otto studied architecture before taking his engineering degree with a thesis on suspended roofs. His interest in new ways of enclosing space started with the humblest structural system of them all: the tent. He developed an amazing and sophisticated way of making

Seen from the air, the stadium complex's roof resembles a giant, fantastical cobweb (above). The roofs are made of steel supports, nets of wire, and acrylic panels (right).

The architect, Frei Otto, was involved in the design of every element in the stadium's roof, from the supporting masts and cables to the clamps that held the glass panes to the net..

shelters of every type, from temporary covers for garden shows and ice rinks to visionary schemes to enclose entire cities in the Arctic.

He had been conducting his research quietly and largely unknown for 10 years before his luminous roofs for the German pavilion at Expo 67 in Montreal brought him international notice. He was involved in Berlin's bid to stage the 1972 Olympics, but when Munich was chosen as host city for the Games that year, Otto's enormous acrylic tents for the Munich stadiums became famous around the world.

The stadium had to be designed with television transmission in mind, and Otto's translucent roofs seemed the ideal answer, covering spectators without obscuring their view, or—crucially for the television cameras—plunging them into deep shadow. But Otto's radical structure, though the clear winner of the competition for the new stadium design, was almost too much for the judges, who delayed confirming it for nearly two years.

Otto worked with the architects to develop the final scheme for the Olympic site. The arenas are sunken into the ground,

and the earthen banks create the seating for the spectators. The undulating cable-net roofs link the various arenas and define the site in a graceful and effective way.

RESPECTING THE ENVIRONMENT

Frei Otto was a pioneer in the reawakening of Western ideas about structure in the 20th century, but his work also reflects a paradoxical desire to make buildings that do not dominate the earth. He perceives his task as providing shelter for transient needs while damaging the environment as little as possible. Otto has made a virtue out of the necessity for temporary structures; nevertheless, his great designs for the Munich stadium are still in place more than 30 years after the 1972 Olympiad.

example of tensile structure

Centre Georges Pompidou

Paris, France

In 1971 two young architects, Renzo Piano and Richard Rogers, won an international competition to design a new building in Paris. The Centre National d'Art et de Culture was to be a monument to Georges Pompidou, the late French President, containing art exhibitions, archives, research centers, offices, and large public areas.

Piano and Rogers decided that their concept should be as bold as possible. Like London's Crystal Palace 120 years earlier, their cultural center would be both popular and instructive, as unlike a traditional art museum as they could make it—more like a machine, even a fun palace. Their gamble was successful and they

FAST FACTS

■ DATE 1971–77
■ STYLE High-Tech Modern
■ MATERIALS Steel and glass
■ ARCHITECTS Renzo Piano and Richard Rogers
■ A fusion of technology, architecture, and art

won first place over more than 600 competitors. The win was a tribute both to their design and also to the far-sighted jury, which stood by its decision even when it was sued six times by disgruntled competitors.

A BUILDING FOR EVERYONE

The architects intended the Pompidou Center to be for all the people, not just the art-loving public. To this end they persuaded the city to allow them to create a large piazza on the western side of the site, giving this densely settled quarter of Paris some much-needed open space. The design of the building itself also strongly reflected their desire to make the center accessible; the building was to be transparent—a diagram, easily read—where there was no doubt about how to get in or where to go once you were in. The result is that the Pompidou Center is now the most visited building in Europe.

Piano and Rogers developed another important idea: They wanted the building to be an industrial object, like something made in a factory (as indeed most of it was), a utilitarian shell that was flexible and could

A detail of the fountain sculpture in front of the Pompidou Center.

be put to a wide variety of uses. They pushed all the service functions out to the perimeter of the building to create an interior of huge open spaces, the size of four football fields, which would be capable of infinite adaptation far into the future.

AN INSIDE-OUT BUILDING

Physically the Pompidou Center is a building turned inside out; on its dramatic steel skeleton are hung all the things normally concealed inside a building—heating and cooling ducts, the means of transport, water pipes, and electrical wiring. Apart from freeing up the interiors, the grouping of the service elements in this way is another flexible strategy: Each element is independent and can be added to or taken away without affecting the others. Even the long diagonal escalator that climbs the face of the building can be shortened or lengthened as required.

These external means of circulation extend the piazza vertically. The western façade of the building is a moving mass of people, up escalators or elevators, across the face of the building in transparent glass galleries clipped on to each level. Piano and Rogers wanted the façade to be a giant bulletin board as well, and planned to fill it with movie and television

Escalators, air ducts, and other service features are all on the outside of the building, creating more space within (above and inset). Renzo Piano (below).

screens broadcasting information 24 hours a day. But this idea was quashed by the authorities, who were still mindful of the student uprising in Paris in 1968: What if students took control of such a building and its power to communicate?

The Pompidou Center harks back to the Crystal Palace in its factory esthetic—its innovative use of the new materials of the industrial age. In theory, like its famous predecessor, it could be dismantled and moved to another site once its original purpose was served. But its popularity has not dimmed, and the controversy over its design has long abated. Parisians who once derided the building as resembling an oil refinery or a crashed spaceship have accepted it as a new landmark—a machine-made house of art reflecting today's fascination with technology and industry.

177

Globe Theater

London, England

The idea of rebuilding the London theater in which William Shakespeare had staged his greatest plays to popular acclaim had been the dream of historians and actors for more than a century before it finally became a reality in the 1990s.

A remarkable expatriate American actor and director, Sam Wanamaker (1919–93), inspired by a touring production of Shakespeare that he had seen as a child, made it his ambition to rebuild the Globe Theater on its original site. Doing so consumed the last 20 years of his life and, even though he and the original architect for the project, Theo Crosby, died before it was completed, Wanamaker lived long enough to know that it was going to happen.

Wanamaker never deviated from his basic desire to recreate the experience of seeing the plays performed in their original setting, but achieving this seemed almost impossible. Money was the first and biggest problem. Despite the support of the Royal Family, the

Ticket prices in the original Globe ranged from one penny (for spectators who stood) to sixpence for the best seats.

FAST FACTS
- DATE *1989–97*
- STYLE *Elizabethan re-creation*
- MATERIALS *Timber and plaster*
- ARCHITECT *Theo Crosby*
- *The reference in Shakespeare's Henry V to "this Wooden 'O'" relates to the original Globe Theater*

British government would not contribute any money to the project, and Wanamaker had to raise the necessary funds entirely from private donations and tireless campaigning.

There were other problems as well: What had the original Globe looked like before it burned down in 1613? Where exactly was it? Somewhere in Southwark, near the River Thames, but where? The evidence was scanty and there was considerable professional disagreement as to how to resolve these questions and many more.

A site was eventually established to everyone's satisfaction (it was under a municipal swimming pool) following archaeological work in 1989. Though the first hurdle had been cleared, many technical questions remained, and Wanamaker brought together a team of architects, literary scholars, historians, and theater practitioners to try to resolve them.

Exactly how many sides had the Globe originally possessed? The answer, after much debate, was 20. How many people could the theater hold? About 2,000: 600–700 in the pit and about 1,300 in the three tiers of galleries around

it. How was the theater painted? How did the backstage areas work? Would audiences come if there was no roof and it rained? The structure, of hand-carved oak beams carefully fitted together and lined with plaster, had to be as authentic as possible—but how could a thatched roof be made to comply with the strict fire safety requirements?

The team painstakingly found answers to every question, and there were some compromises to make the scheme work. The thatched roof was eventually approved by the authorities, but only if it was equipped with a modern sprinkler system; the necessary visitor facilities, absent in the original theater, were provided in an adjoining building; and there was supplementary lighting to permit evening performances. Beyond that, the building as constructed was as authentic a recreation of an Elizabethan playhouse, and the Globe in particular, as human skill could make it.

After prolog seasons in 1995 and 1996, the building was completed and its first full season of plays held in 1997. Actors are re-learning how to play to unruly audiences standing in the rain, and audiences are responding to the freshness and vigor of seeing the great plays presented in something like their original setting of 400 years ago.

Performances in outdoor playhouses such as the Globe always took place in daylight, at about 3 p.m., and lasted roughly two hours (below). A 1783 engraving of Shakespeare (left), based upon an earlier painting. Shakespeare was a shareholder in the original Globe, as well as acting in and writing many of the plays performed in the theater.

Guggenheim Museum

Bilbao, Spain

When an architect is zany enough to ask, "How wiggly can you get and still make a building?" and daring enough to then put his theories to the test, the answer he arrives at may well be Frank Gehry's masterwork, the Guggenheim Museum in Bilbao.

"I used to be a symmetrical freak and a grid freak," says Gehry (born 1929). "[Then] I realized that those were chains, that Frank Lloyd Wright was chained…You don't need that if you can create spaces and forms and shapes. That is what artists do."

Gehry and Frank Lloyd Wright are a fascinating study in convergence and contrast. Both received a similar mandate from the Guggenheim, nearly half a

The museum contains 19 galleries on three levels. Conventional spaces house modernist classics; irregular-shaped rooms house the often non-traditional works of living artists.

> ### FAST FACTS
> ■ DATE Completed 1998
> ■ STYLE Expressionist Modern
> ■ MATERIALS Steel, stone, glass, and titanium sheathing
> ■ ARCHITECT Frank O. Gehry
> ■ Symbolizes museums as the new cathedrals

century apart: to reconceive the notion of the art museum. Both set out to create a space that would blur the lines between architect and artist, building and sculpture, and natural and human forms. Wright designed an elegantly contained expression of the circular form; Gehry, who was goaded by Guggenheim director Thomas Krens to "make it better than Wright," created a postmodern explosion of circular and curvilinear forms.

Gehry's penchant for free-form assemblages has become his architectural signature. He favors shapes that curl like chips, unfurl like petals, and flow like fishes. Taking his initial inspiration from the environment, Gehry is also known for creating unique interplays between the structure and the site. In Bilbao, the Nervión River and the suspension bridge that traverses it became an integral part of his design.

Other influences on this project included Brancusi's sculptures, Matisse's paper cut-outs, and Fritz Lang's *Metropolis*. Combining these diverse inspirations with his innovative design methods would result in a far-reaching achievement: the transformation of a run-down industrial city into a major cultural destination.

Technical challenges were present at every stage. Gehry's team used a sophisticated 3-D computer modeling system to convert Gehry's swirling, free-hand renderings into calculable forms. Gehry chose titanium for the façade because he liked its warmth and character, and worked with the fabricator to develop a product that was suitably reflective and thinly gauged. The titanium shingles that resulted are barely thicker than a few sheets of paper stacked together: They are thin enough to billow and flutter in the wind, yet are, remarkably, more durable than stone.

AN ARCHITECTURAL SCULPTURE
The museum's centerpiece, a soaring 165-foot (50-m) skylighted atrium, has been described by one critic as a hollowed-out tree trunk and by another as an "undulating, erotic form" that seems to "suck the visitor up into some wonderful dream." Three wings jut off this central space, while the fourth is cut off to reveal the river beyond. Stairways, glass elevators, and walkways suspended from the roof move people through the structure. One only has to see the Oldenburg and Serra

The building's shiplike profile (above) pays tribute to Bilbao's former days as a thriving port. From above (left and below), the museum resembles a metal flower.

sculptures inside the immense "boat gallery" to realize how effectively this innovative space complements the bold contemporary art it contains.

The museum opened in October 1997 with the "Art of the Century" exhibition, which premiered to record-breaking crowds. In the first year, the Guggenheim had nearly 1.4 million visitors, more than doubling even the most optimistic estimates.

"If you can translate the beauty of sculpture into the building," says Gehry, "whatever it does to give movement and feeling, that's where the innovation in architecture is." Gehry's architectural sculpture has brought new movement and feeling to this old shipping town. It is an irresistible ride.

TRANSPORT AND COMMUNICATIONS

*From earliest times, transport and communications
have tested the skills of architects and engineers
and constantly pushed the boundaries of technology.*

Bridges are among humanity's most important inventions. The first long-span structures were developed about 2,000 years ago, when the ancient Romans invented the masonry arch and its derivatives, the masonry vault and the masonry dome. At that time the longest bridge spans were roughly the same as the longest interior spans, about 140 feet (42 m). These spans were not exceeded until the 19th century, when iron, steel, and reinforced concrete came into use as structural materials and the potential for long spans increased rapidly.

The CNIT Hall in Paris was built in 1958 with a span of 718 feet (219 m) and there have been no significant increases in interior span since then. There is a limit to which sporting events can be watched

DUAL PURPOSE *Many structures built for transport or communication combine beauty with utility, such as the Rialto Bridge (above), Macquarie Lighthouse (right), and Grand Central Station (below).*

with the naked eye and, since the invention of television, there is a more effective means of reaching a very large public. Political and other orators,

in particular, have in recent years tended to prefer television to addressing a large audience in person.

Technological progress has had the opposite effect on the building of bridges—there are obvious economic advantages in being able to transport trains and automobiles across a wide stretch of water on a bridge instead of having to use a ferry, so bridges—and bridge spans—are growing longer and longer. At the start of the 21st century the Akashi Taikyo bridge in Japan was among the longest bridges in the world—a total of 12,830 feet (almost 4 km)

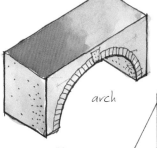

beam

arch

suspension

cable-stay

and incorporating a span of 6,000 feet (1,800 m). But further increases are almost certain to happen as structural techniques improve and the technology of using strong materials progresses.

A functional design, when well conceived, generally produces a work of art, and long-span structures for both interior and exterior spans have therefore always fascinated people, not merely because of their technical achievement. During the 18th century, when young men of quality went on the Grand Tour, they would often go to considerable trouble to look at long-span structures, and this is still true for modern tourists, although to a lesser extent. The enduring popularity of bridges is the reason for their dominance in this chapter.

Other building types covered in this chapter are of great historical interest. Lighthouses were of great importance for thousands of years but have now been largely replaced by radar. The Pharos Lighthouse, built in Alexandria in the 3rd century BC, was considered one of the wonders of the ancient world. It is unlikely, however, that any modern lighthouse will achieve a similar distinction. It may be that no communication tower will ever be erected to exceed the height of the CN

Tower in Toronto, because of the development of satellite technology.

Many more transport terminals will, of course, be built but it is a matter of opinion whether recent ones, like the new Chek Lap Kok Airport in Hong Kong and the International Rail Terminal at Waterloo in London, create more impressive interior spaces than those built a century earlier, such as the present Grand Central Station in New York City.

MOVING WITH THE TIMES *Modern terminals like the Waterloo Eurostar station combine efficiency with elegance of structure.*

Pons Fabricius

Rome, Italy

For the ancient Romans, good communications throughout their domain were of great importance—their huge empire depended upon communications—and that meant that bridges over rivers and ravines were essential. Perhaps as a result, the architect–engineers of Rome developed the first real expertise in the design and construction of bridges. They pioneered the building of secure midstream foundations by developing a reliable waterproof cement called *pozzolana* and a technique of constructing foundations within a temporary enclosure. Perhaps most importantly, they realized the possibilities of what was to become their signature—the curved semi-circular arch. Such an arch could span greater distances than the post-and-beam structures that it replaced, and, though it needed no mortar to keep the blocks together, it was stronger and more secure than anything else that could be built from the materials

FAST FACTS

- DATE 62 BC
- STYLE Arched bridge
- MATERIAL Stone masonry
- BUILDER L. Fabricius
- The Rôman art of making waterproof cement was lost for many centuries after the fall of the empire

available then. The resulting bridges were so durable that some are still in use today.

DESIGNED TO LAST

The Pons Fabricius, the oldest existing Roman bridge, is an excellent example of the Romans' engineering skills. It has survived essentially unchanged from when it was built in 62 BC to connect the Isola Tiberina, the only island in the fast-flowing River Tiber, with the east bank of the burgeoning city of Rome. The west bank was connected by the Pons Cestius, which has been reconstructed many times, most recently in 1892, when the western channel of the Tiber was widened.

Built mainly from tufa, a limestone deposited by spring water, and faced with stone, the Pons Fabricius has two arched spans of 79 feet (24.2 m) and 80 feet (24.5 m) and a wide central pier surmounted by a large floodway to allow

The Quattro Capi, a four-headed pilaster at the eastern end of the Pons Fabricius.

The oldest existing Roman bridge, the Pons Fabricius spans the River Tiber and has been in continuous use for over 2,000 years.

floodwater to escape. Carved on both sides of one of the arches is an inscription in Latin: *L.FABRICIVS.C.F.CVR.VIAR.FACIVNDVM.COERAVIT*, together with the date of construction. This means that L. Fabricius, the *curator viarum* (commissioner for highways) at that time, built and approved the bridge. Also carved into the stonework are the names of M. Lollius and Q. Lepidus, the two consuls who were responsible for carrying out repairs to the bridge after a flood in 21 BC. The only other change occurred in 1679, when Pope Innocent XI built a new balustrade.

Apart from these very minor modifications, the bridge remains in its original form and continues to function just as it did more than 2,000 years ago—as a working bridge carrying traffic over the River Tiber—although these days the traffic is limited to pedestrians only. With its remarkable spans and its longevity, the bridge is a testimony to the soundness of Roman bridge building.

HOW DID THEY DO IT?

A flexible cable slung between two supporting structures sags until it is perfectly in tension. Turn this shape upside down and you have an arch—a compression structure that is free, or almost free, from tension.

The Romans used this principle to build the Pons Fabricius and many other bridges. Using stones that were cut identically, the arches were built over temporary wooden supports, called formwork, that held up the sides. When both sides of the arch were completed, the keystone (a truncated triangle) was fitted in the center.

The arch's forces of compression locked with the perfect cut and fit of the surrounding blocks of stone to ensure a completely stable structure—without the need for mortar.

So vital was the keystone to any arched bridge—and so important were bridges to the Roman Empire—that a special ceremony was held to mark their positioning. The head of the supreme college of priests, known as *Pontifex Maximus*, or chief bridge builder, officiated.

Pont du Gard

Nîmes, France

The Pont du Gard spans the River Gard in southern France, three tiers of stone arches rising 135 feet (47.5 m) above its elegant reflection in the water below. The most famous surviving section of a Roman masonry aqueduct—and the highest bridge the Romans ever built—it is an extraordinary piece of engineering, one that combines functionality and mathematical precision with great beauty.

The bridge was a small but conspicuous part of an aqueduct 30 miles (48 km) long, built by

FAST FACTS

- DATE c. 18 BC
- STYLE Arched aqueduct
- MATERIAL Stone masonry
- BUILDER Marcus Agrippa
- The Romans did not have faucets, so their water supply depended on gravity

Marcus Vespasianus Agrippa around 18 BC to carry fresh water from the rivers Airon and Eure at Uzés to the Roman city of Nemausus (now Nîmes). The aqueduct ran across the valleys between hills, through trenches and a tunnel, along the top of a wall, and over a river.

The water was transferred by the force of gravity. The aqueduct was built on a gradual downward incline, so there would be an even flow of water from the source to its destination. Thus the water that traveled from Uzès to Nîmes flowed down a very gentle slope of just 55 feet (17 m) over its entire journey of 30 miles (48 km). This technical perfection was the secret to all of the many Roman aqueducts, which were an integral part of the extensive system of water supply and sewage disposal that the Romans developed for most of their empire.

AN ARRANGEMENT OF ARCHES

For the watercourse to cross the River Gard, which flowed so far below the required height, a stone bridge of three tiers of arches was

Detail of the middle and upper tiers of stone arches.

Aqueducts such as the Pont du Gard (above) ensured a ready supply of clean water. In the reign of the Emperor Hadrian, 11 aqueducts supplied the water needs of the city of Rome. A builder's inscription on the stonework of Pont du Gard (left).

needed. The lowest level of the Pont du Gard consists of six arches, 67 feet (20.5 m) high, the longest spanning 80 feet (24.4 m). The middle level has six arches, 64 feet (19.5 m) high. The upper level has 35 arches, 24 feet (7.4 m) high; the covered water conduit on top was a deep cement–lined channel. Blocks of stone project from the piers at various heights, probably to support scaffolding or the result of repairs in the masonry, and stones in the arches still bear markings made by the original builders, such as FR S III— *frons sinistra*, meaning "front side left, number 3."

The Pont du Gard was damaged in the 5th century AD, but by then it may have already ceased functioning as an aqueduct because of the barbarian invasions from central Asia, which were slowly destroying the Roman Empire. In 1747 the width of the lowest tier was doubled by the addition of a roadway, with arches to match the Roman originals.

Today, the Pont du Gard is open only to pedestrian traffic; however, the 1.5 million tourists who visit the remains of this magnificent aqueduct each year can cross the bridge on the lowest or the highest levels. Thanks to restorations in the 17th and 18th centuries, and again in the late 20th century, its soaring arches still stand, well preserved— and all without the benefit of mortar.

THE CHADWICK REPORT

The standard of water supply and sewage disposal in Europe deteriorated after the fall of the Roman Empire. Hygiene became a matter of concern with the increasing industrialization of Britain in the 19th century, and the British government appointed Edwin Chadwick (below), a lawyer in its civil service, to study the problem. Chadwick inspected the surviving remains of many ancient Roman water supply and sewage disposal installations and, in his *Report on the Sanitary Conditions of the Labouring Population of Great Britain*, published in 1842, he argued that if Britain could achieve the standards of hygiene and sanitation that had prevailed in ancient Rome, the problem would be largely solved.

Leaning Tower

Pisa, Italy

The world-famous lean is no deliberate engineering feat but a technical failing due to inadequate foundations in soft, wet clay that is still settling after more than 800 years. Yet the tower remains a magnificent example of a medieval campanile (bell tower), part of an outstanding complex of Romanesque religious buildings. Presenting a surreal note of discord within the stately harmony of its companion buildings, the tower has long been an international tourist destination, attractive perhaps because of its strange blending of imperfection, beauty, and persistence.

The religious complex of buildings gracing the Piazza dei Miracoli in Pisa includes the cathedral (1063–92), its baptistery (1153–1278), and a cemetery, as well as the tower (1173–1350). All were built at the height of Pisa's marine power in the late middle ages. Their existence was just as dependent upon the founding and expansion of Catholic monasteries across Europe

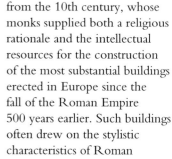

FAST FACTS

■ DATE 1173–1350

■ STYLE Romanesque

■ MATERIAL Limestone

■ ARCHITECT Unknown

■ Despite many attempts to rectify it, the tower has retained its trademark tilt for over 800 years

from the 10th century, whose monks supplied both a religious rationale and the intellectual resources for the construction of the most substantial buildings erected in Europe since the fall of the Roman Empire 500 years earlier. Such buildings often drew on the stylistic characteristics of Roman architecture, most notably the use of orders, columns, massive volutes (scrolls), and rounded arches. The complex of buildings in Pisa is considered an outstanding example of Tuscan Romanesque architecture, where a unity of style is achieved across the different buildings by the repeated use of tiered arcades and decorative marble surfaces.

KEEPING TIME AND KEEPING ORDER

While other religions had called for regular meetings of the devoted, it was the Christian monasteries which were the first to specify prayer times, called offices, at frequent set hours. This required more skill than the simple observation of dawn, noon, and dusk. In response to this religious need, increasingly sophisticated mechanisms for keeping time were developed throughout the middle ages. The times for prayer were signaled by bells, which were rung from a high tower to increase their range. The offices were said or sung at Lauds (around daybreak), Prime (around 6 a.m.), Terce (9 a.m.), Sext (noon), None (3 p.m.), Vespers (6 p.m.), and Compline (9 p.m.), with two more at night—Vigils (midnight) and Matins (3 a.m.). The highly disciplined lifestyle made possible by this time-keeping appealed to the ethic of Christian piety. People in surrounding towns also came to rely on the rhythm of regular pealing bells as a means of ordering the increasingly complex and coordinated activities of developing European urbanism.

The tower's lean contrasts conspicuously with the regularity of the other buildings in the complex (left). The base of the tower is girdled by columns, arches, and carved decorations (inset).

In 1998 the giant steel braces were removed from around the tower and excavations were begun to steady the building. Lead ingots, laid to halt the lean, can be seen at the base.

THE FAMOUS LEAN

The tilt on the tower was already apparent by the time it was 35 feet (10 m) high, within 10 years of the start of construction in 1173. For nearly two centuries, building progress was slow and interrupted while solutions were sought (and, incidentally, wars fought). It is remarkable that its builders persevered at all, let alone attained the considerable height of 185 feet (56 m). Later stories were added leaning slightly to the north, so that the tower is actually banana-shaped. However, no attempts at "balancing" the building have succeeded in stabilizing it. Indeed, some earlier efforts, such as the injection of cement into the ground near the foundations in 1934, actually hastened the lean. In the 1990s, the lean was estimated to be 5.5 degrees from the vertical, a deviation of 16 feet (5 m) at the top of the tower, and increasing at the rate of one-fifteenth of an inch (1 mm) a year. The ever-increasing strain on the masonry walls near the base could at any time result in the tower toppling over, ripping out its foundations, or the south side masonry exploding under compression.

The threat was made real after a tower at Pavia collapsed in 1989, killing four people, and the Leaning Tower of Pisa was closed to the public in 1990. Since then, two intermediate measures have been instituted: In 1992 a ring of steel girders encircling the tower was fitted at the level of the lowest colonnade to reduce stress at its most vulnerable point; and in 1993, 600 tons (610 t) of lead ingots were laid on the base of the tower, apparently resulting in a slight arrest of the lean. Meanwhile scientists and engineers continue the 800-year search for a lasting cure.

Rialto Bridge

Venice, Italy

Once an independent, powerful maritime city-state, Venice is a latticework of canals, and visitors soon discover that the best way to see it is on foot, using the many bridges. Most of the canals are so narrow that bridging them presented no problems even before the technological age. But the Grand Canal, the city's main waterway, is much wider. Even today it is crossed by only three bridges, but until the 19th century, there was only one—the Rialto Bridge, which spans

FAST FACTS

- DATE 1591
- STYLE Arched bridge
- MATERIALS Timber and masonry
- DESIGNER Antonio Conte
- To honor his achievement in building the bridge, Conte became officially known as Da Ponte

the canal at its narrowest point. The first Rialto Bridge was built in the 12th century. It was a wooden structure supported on pontoons, by which it could be raised to let shipping through. It was replaced in the following century by a single-spanned timber toll bridge with a timber roof, which required constant renovation: Repairs were carried out in 1400 and 1431, and in 1450 it collapsed under the weight of a crowd that had gathered on it to witness the Emperor Frederick VII's state entry into Venice. In 1512 a fire destroyed much of the commercial district that had developed around the bridge. Although the bridge survived the fire, the Venetian Senate at last decided to replace it with a stone bridge.

A Daring and Durable Structure

Some of the most famous architects and engineers of the Renaissance put forward proposals, including Michelangelo and Andrea Palladio. The Senate Commission chose a daring design by Antonio Conte—a single masonry span comparable in size to the longer bridges of ancient Rome. The bridge has a span of 89 feet (27 m) and a rise of 21 feet (6.5 m). Most

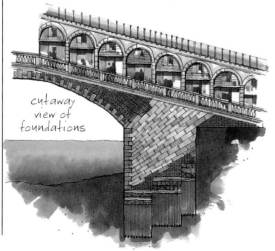

cutaway view of foundations

Roman bridges used semi-circular arches, but Conte employed a shallower arch with a radius of 126 feet (38 m). Despite this, a number of steps were still necessary to climb to the top of the bridge from the relatively low embankment. The span of the bridge left almost the whole width of the Grand Canal free for navigation, and it provided ample clearance for shipping. In particular, it allowed enough space for the ceremonial marine parades that played such an important part in Venetian life.

An aerial view shows the central passage and two flanking rows of shops (above). The second bridge features in Vittore Carpaccio's 15th century painting The Miracle of the Relic of the Holy Cross (left).

The bridge is 75 feet (23 m) wide, with a central passage of 21 feet (6.5 m), two rows of shops, all originally occupied by jewelers, and two passages of 11 feet (3.5 m) between the shops and the bridge parapets on each side.

The ground of Venice is soft and the bridge is a heavy, narrow structure, so Conte took great care with the foundations. He excavated the ground to a depth of 16–18 feet (5 m) on the canal sides of the foundation, but somewhat less on the embankment sides to avoid disturbing the foundations of the existing buildings. He then drove 6,000 piles of birch-alder to refusal, using a Roman-style pile driver. The piles were cut off at the top and covered with a timber grillage of larch. Atop that was solid masonry, which supported the arch abutments and had inclined bed joints to absorb the arch thrust of the bridge.

So innovative was the technique that envious rivals agitated to stop construction, claiming that the bridge was not safe. Work proceeded only after an official inquiry, whose findings were vindicated when an earthquake shook Venice shortly after the bridge was finished. The bridge survived without a trace of damage, thus proving the safety of the construction.

The Rialto Bridge was opened in July 1591, and Conte was given the appellation Da Ponte, a name by which he is generally known today. In the 19th century, during their occupation of Venice, the Austrians built a second and a third bridge across the Grand Canal, both of them of iron, but Da Ponte's 16th century masonry bridge is still substantially as he built it.

Iron Bridge

Coalbrookdale, England

On New Year's Day 1781, the first large structure to use iron as its main structural material was opened; it was the famous Iron Bridge that spans the Upper Severn Gorge at Coalbrookdale in the county of Shropshire.

FAST FACTS

■ DATE 1781

■ STYLE Arched bridge

· ■ MATERIAL Cast iron

■ DESIGNER Thomas Farnolls Pritchard

■ On 23 October 1779, Darby spent 9 guineas on beer for the workmen to celebrate finishing the main structure

INNOVATIVE IRON

Early in the 18th century, the English iron master Abraham Darby had discovered a method of firing cast iron with coke—a hot fuel made from bituminous coal by driving off the tar and oil, leaving only the carbon. Before this, charcoal had been used to produce small

amounts of iron, but attempts to smelt iron using bituminous coal had failed because of its tar and oil content. Darby's discovery was cost-effective and efficient, and it revolutionized structural engineering methods.

East Shropshire, Darby's home county, has been called the cradle of the Industrial Revolution. Ironworks, potteries, and tile-works developed there, based on the area's rich deposits of coal, iron ore, clay, and limestone. River barges carried the finished products to distant markets, but within the area road transport was essential to move raw materials between industrial sites. The advantages of a bridge linking the banks of the River Severn and leaving clearance for shipping were obvious, and in 1775 a group of influential industrialists met to plan its construction.

Prominent among them was a grandson of Darby, Abraham Darby III. He had inherited his grandfather's discovery and was on the lookout for new markets for cast iron. He was certain that it could become an economical

The iron span bears an inscription recording the completion of the main structure.

structural material: Like timber, but unlike masonry, it had tensile strength; and like masonry, but unlike timber, it was fire-resistant. The Severn is subject to sudden and severe flooding, so Darby argued for a single-arch cast iron bridge that would not require piers anchored in the riverbed. It took much persuasion to convince the local authorities that iron was a suitable material for building what was then a long-span bridge, but in 1776 Parliament passed a bill ratifying the construction of a cast iron bridge.

AN IMPORTANT FORERUNNER

Darby commissioned a local architect, Thomas Farnolls Pritchard, to design the bridge. After two rejected proposals, the selected design was based on three concentric ribs forming a semi-circle. This resembled a Roman stone bridge, with the joints replaced by cast iron and the stone blocks by air.

Abraham Darby III was deeply involved in constructing the bridge. The 70-foot (21-m) ribs were cast in his Coalbrookdale ironworks, which were enlarged for the purpose, and he supervised the construction of the stone abutments on each side of the river. The detailed design of the iron members was supervised by

Reflections on the Severn (above left) and details of the intricate ironwork (above and left). There is now a small museum and shop for tourists at one end of the bridge.

Thomas Gregory, the foreman pattern maker. Gregory was a master carpenter—hence the detailing, which includes the mortise-and-tenon joints and dovetail joints that were characteristic of timber construction.

The bridge took 18 months to build and has a span of 100 feet (30.5 m) and a river clearance of 40 feet (14 m). It carried vehicles until 1931, and it is still used for pedestrian traffic. Its only structural problems were due to the inadequacy of the masonry foundations, which caused the sides of the gorge to move toward the river. In 1973 a reinforced concrete invert was constructed in the bed of the river between the two abutments.

The design of the bridge has been criticized as conservative, but it did demonstrate—as Abraham Darby had intended—the structural potential of iron. Thirty years later, iron was first used for relatively light and fire-resistant structures in buildings, and this innovation transformed the structural design of multistory buildings and made skyscrapers possible.

Macquarie Lighthouse

Sydney, Australia

After America's Declaration of Independence in 1776, Britain could no longer transport its prisoners to the "New World" and had to find a new destination for the convicts that were crowding its prisons and overflowing into prison hulks moored in the Thames.

In 1770, the English navigator James Cook had surveyed the east coast of Australia, spending seven days ashore in what is now Botany Bay, an inlet just south of the center of present-day Sydney. *Terra Australis Incognita*—"The Unknown Land of the South"—thus became the new destination for transported convicts, and the penal colony of New South Wales came into being.

In the nature of things, the new settlers were not selected for their skills in establishing a colony. Nevertheless, some of the offenders were destined to play an illustrious part in the development of Australia, and in particular the city of Sydney. One such was Francis Howard Greenway, a competent and talented master builder from Gloucestershire. In 1812 he went bankrupt and was sentenced to death for forgery. His sentence was eventually commuted to transportation and in 1814 he landed in the new colony.

Today's Macquarie Lighthouse is a replica of the original lighthouse of 1818 but was built from stronger materials.

He was appointed Government Architect by Lachlan Macquarie, Governor of New South Wales, and he designed and built some of Sydney's best loved buildings, making effective use of local materials. One of the first was a lighthouse on the southern of the two heads of land that embrace Sydney Harbor. This building was to replace a wood- and coal-fired beacon that had been set up in 1793.

BUILDING BLOCKS

Sydney has a good supply of golden-colored sandstone, laid down in the Triassic period. It is easily cut and carved, but its durability varies in different parts of the Sydney region. Before Greenway came along, it had been used for little but foundations because of a lack of supervisory skill.

The second lighthouse, on the right, was built as the original deteriorated (below). Today, the area around the lighthouse is public open space. Architect Francis Greenway (left).

THE EDDYSTONE LIGHT

The first lighthouse to be built on a foundation that was submerged at high tide was the lighthouse on the Eddystone, near Plymouth on the south coast of England—all earlier lighthouses had been built on dry land. The first Eddystone Light was built in 1698, but the lime mortar was washed out by the high tide and the masonry structure collapsed. Two subsequent wooden structures could not withstand the stormy weather. It was known that the ancient Romans had a waterproof cement, but the secret of making it had been lost. Then John Smeaton, a civil engineer, discovered how to make a waterproof cement using lime with an admixture of clay, and in 1757 he constructed a stone tower on the rock, which remained in use for over a century.

The Eddystone Lighthouse, as depicted in a 19th century engraving.

The Macquarie Lighthouse—started in 1816 and completed in 1818—was one of the first stone buildings in Australia. It stood on a sandstone cliff and the stone was cut from around the site. There was no record of the sandstone's weathering quality, but Greenway, as an experienced builder, had doubts about it. He therefore made a basement under the tower with four massive piers, each with 90 square feet (0.09 sq m) of solid stone, using very big blocks. On each side of the tower he built a small house with a domed roof. One was the lighthouse keeper's quarters and the other a residence for Governor Macquarie, who took a liking to the building and occasionally spent a night there.

This was the first lighthouse in the entire south Pacific. It was, moreover, a building with an architectural quality that had hitherto been lacking in the colony. When it was completed, Governor Macquarie presented Greenway with his emancipation. The first lighthouse keeper, Robert Watson, had served in the First Fleet —the first convict ships to arrive in Sydney in 1778. He was already elderly when appointed, and died within a year.

SIMILAR BUT DIFFERENT

Greenway's solid stone foundation had made the building structurally safe, but the surface of the stone deteriorated even more rapidly than he had anticipated. Iron bands were placed around the tower to help stabilize the building. However, the lighthouse had become an icon of the city, and when it had to be replaced, the Government Architect of the day, James Barnet, built a very similar lighthouse immediately behind it, using stronger sandstone from an established quarry. Greenway's lighthouse was not demolished until the new one was complete, and Barnet's replica is still standing and in use.

The original lighthouse had used oil lamps set in parabolic reflectors, but the new building became one of the first in Australia to use electricity. When it was commissioned in 1883, the lighting mechanism was considered the most efficient in the world. The generator for the electric arc lights was driven by a gas engine, using coal gas piped from the Sydney gas works. The lighthouse was connected to the city power supply in 1933.

Brooklyn Bridge

New York, United States of America

Opened in 1883, the Brooklyn Bridge was the first long-span suspension bridge to carry motor traffic, and it quickly became the model for the great suspension bridges of the following century. Spanning New York's East River, it provided the first traffic artery between Manhattan Island and Brooklyn. Before that, the only transportation was by ferries, which were slow and could be dangerous in winter.

FAST FACTS

■ DATE 1869–83

■ STYLE Suspension bridge

■ MATERIAL Galvanized steel wire

■ DESIGNER John Augustus Roebling

■ Emily, wife of Roebling's son, supervised construction when her husband became incapacitated

The construction of a bridge had been discussed since the early 19th century, but the outbreak of the Civil War in 1861 deflected all consideration of the project. When the war ended in 1865, the bridge became an important issue once more, and in 1867 the New York State legislature passed an act incorporating the New York Bridge Company for the purpose of constructing and maintaining a bridge between Manhattan Island and Brooklyn.

John Augustus Roebling was chosen to design the bridge. Born in Germany in 1806, he held radical views as a student and was listed by the German police as a dangerous liberal. He emigrated to America in 1830 to escape political discrimination.

Roebling proposed a bridge with a span of 1,500 feet (465 m), with two masonry towers in the East River serving as the main piers. The bridge actually built is longer—1,597 feet (486 m), the longest suspension bridge up to that time. It was the first bridge to make use of galvanized steel wire; earlier suspension bridges

The bridge majestically spans the East River.

had used either wrought iron cables or suspension chains.

The cables were spun on site from a previously constructed footbridge. Massive anchorages for the cables had to be built, as there were no natural rock formations to support them. The bridge carried two elevated railroad tracks, two trolley car tracks, single-lane roadways flanking the trolley tracks, and a central walkway. Stiffening trusses were added to insure against sway—a characteristic of suspension structures.

The Brooklyn Bridge, before the 2001 destruction of the World Trade Center by terrorists (above). Pedestrians stroll across the bridge in the 1920s (left).

sickness in May 1872. He was partially paralyzed and was able to supervise construction only through binoculars from his balcony. But his wife, Emily, threw herself into the study of engineering, and was soon able to inspect the site each day and report progress to her husband.

AN UNFORTUNATE HISTORY

Disaster struck early in the history of the bridge. In 1869, even before construction commenced, Roebling was standing on a Brooklyn wharf to carry out a survey for the main piers when a boat collided with the bulkhead of the wharf. His foot was crushed and he died of tetanus three weeks later. His successor was his son, Washington Roebling, who continued to work on the bridge for the following 14 years.

Washington Roebling's health was also doomed to suffer from the bridge. After working for long hours at high atmospheric pressure, he collapsed with decompression

In 1882 the Mayor of Brooklyn resolved to replace Washington Roebling on the grounds of physical incapacity. Emily Roebling requested permission to address the American Society of Civil Engineers, the first time that a woman had done so— and as a result Washington remained the Chief Engineer. After the opening ceremony in 1883, many citizens and officials marched to his home to honor him.

John Augustus Roebling, engineer and designer of the Brooklyn Bridge.

Forth Bridge

Firth of Forth, Scotland

The east coast of Scotland has two major ocean inlets, the Firth of Forth and the Firth of Tay. Edinburgh is only 46 miles (74 km) from Dundee, but before the firths were bridged, rail travel between the two cities took more than three hours using a ferry to cross each waterway, and even longer traveling by railroad around the two firths. In the mid-1860s Thomas Bouch, engineer of the Edinburgh and Northern Railway, was commissioned to design a bridge across each firth.

The first of the two bridges to be built was the wrought iron Tay Bridge. Completed in 1877, it was 2 miles (3.2 km) long, with a clear shipping passage of 88 feet (27 m). The Tay Bridge was universally hailed as an engineering triumph, but in December 1879, while the evening mail train from Edinburgh to Dundee was crossing during a violent storm, the bridge collapsed.

FAST FACTS

■ DATE 1884–89

■ STYLE Cantilevered bridge

■ MATERIAL Steel

■ ENGINEERS John Fowler and Benjamin Baker

■ First major structure in the world to be built entirely of steel

The Court of Enquiry found that the bridge had collapsed because insufficient allowance had been made for lateral wind pressure. Bouch had consulted many authorities about the wind pressure to be expected on the bridge, and had used the highest estimates he had found; the bridge structure had been capable of resisting the pressure of wind on the open girders—but the extra pressure exerted by the wind on the surface of the train had caused the collapse. The Court of Enquiry blamed Bouch, who died shortly after the publication of the official report.

A LESSON LEARNED

The Tay Bridge disaster is important because it had a far-reaching influence on the design of the Forth Bridge. The new engineers, John Fowler and Benjamin

This photograph taken in 1903 illustrates the symmetry and strength of the Forth Bridge.

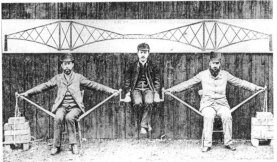

Baker, took no chances. They abandoned Bouch's original design and immediately set up a series of wind pressure gauges, which were read daily for six years to provide accurate information about the maximum wind pressure to be expected.

A panorama of the Forth Bridge at sunset (above). Engineer Benjamin Baker used this photograph to demonstrate the principle of cantilevers (left).

A STRUCTURE IN STEEL

The Forth Bridge was the first large structure to be constructed entirely of steel, instead of the traditional materials—wrought iron and cast iron—that were used in the Tay Bridge. Baker designed a bridge consisting of three huge cantilevers with two short inset spans. This is a flexible structure that allows for unexpected deformations. It uses a little more material than a more rigid structure, but after the Tay Bridge disaster, safety was a prime consideration.

The total length of the bridge, including the viaducts, is 1.6 miles (2.5 km); the two main spans are 1,710 feet (521 m), and the bridge carries two rail tracks. The foundations of the main structure are close to the water so that the wind action is minimized.

Construction started in 1884, and the bridge was completed in 1889. There have been no major alterations to it. When it was opened in 1890, William Morris, the English craftsman, poet and socialist, described it as "the supremest specimen of all ugliness." Today, however, most agree that it is a masterpiece of both engineering and architecture.

THE TAY BRIDGE DISASTER

Thomas Bouch's Tay Bridge carried a single railroad track. A signalman at one end handed a baton to the driver, who passed it to a signalman at the other end, to be given to the driver of the train in the opposite direction, so that he would know it was safe to proceed.

On the night of December 28, 1879, the weather was so bad that the signalman had to crawl to hand the baton to the driver of the approaching mail train. The train's lights vanished, there was a violent gust of wind and a brilliant flash of light, and the telegraph connection between the signal cabins at each end of the bridge failed. The train had plummeted into the water. All 75 passengers died in the disaster.

Tower Bridge

London, England

If only because of its spectacular location next to the medieval Tower of London and the superb workmanship of the masonry cladding of its steel towers, London's Tower Bridge is one of the best known bridges in the world. It was designed by London's City Architect, Horace Jones, in collaboration with the engineer John Wolf Barry. Construction started in 1886 and the bridge was opened in 1894. Jones was knighted by the Prince of Wales for his design.

The Tower Bridge is greatly admired by some, but many find the fake medievalism of the towers ludicrously inappropriate. J. A. L.

FAST FACTS

■ DATE 1886–94

■ STYLE Lifting bridge

■ MATERIALS Steel and stone

■ DESIGNERS Horace Jones and John Wolf Barry

■ Renowned—and by some reviled—for its fake medievalism

Waddell, an eminent American bridge designer of the late 19th century, described it as "the most monumental example of extravagance in bridge construction in the world."

THAMES TRAFFIC

Tower Bridge was originally designed as a lifting bridge to allow the passage of river traffic, which by Act of Parliament took precedence over road traffic. The central span can be opened to allow river traffic to pass through because the roadway consists of two bascules, which rotate about their supports to move from their normal horizontal to an almost vertical position. They are counterweighted so that only a relatively small force, provided by hydraulic power supplied by the mains water system of London, is needed to lift them.

The Tower Bridge's hydraulic lifting principle, though rarely used these days, is probably the most famous engineering feature of the bridge. Skippers of vessels could cause the bridge to be raised in less than four minutes

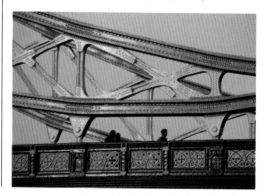

Detail of London's Tower Bridge showing the roadway balustrades and the impressive steel girders.

An aerial perspective of Tower Bridge (left) and a view of the bridge as the hydraulically operated lifting sections rise to allow the passage of shipping (above).

by sounding one long and three short siren blasts. This relatively short lifting time had its drawbacks: In 1952, a London bus was stranded across the opening, fortunately without serious consequences for the passengers.

These days, ships too tall to pass under the roadway of the Tower Bridge rarely go as far upstream as the bridge, so the raising of the bridge has become an uncommon event. Motor traffic is held up while the bridge is open, but pedestrians can continue to use it by walking across the high-level footway that permanently links the towers. It was one of the first bridges to be fitted with elevators to carry pedestrians to the top of the towers.

The central lifting span of the bridge is 230 feet (71 m) and the outer spans are each 270 feet (83 m), supported by suspension cables anchored to the river towers and the abutment piers. Each of the river towers is constructed of four octagonal riveted steel stanchions, connected by diagonal bracing, and clad with granite facings and dressings of Portland stone—the oolitic limestone from which many of the most famous buildings in London are built.

HYDRAULIC POWER

Technically, the most interesting aspect of the Tower Bridge is the hydraulic machinery that is used to open the bascules. Hydraulic power became a practical possibility with the development of a piped water supply. If a water tank were placed high above ground, the "head" (the gravitational drag) of the water provided the necessary pressure.

In 1851, the English inventor and industrialist William Armstrong invented the hydraulic accumulator, in which water was put under pressure by a piston loaded with about a hundred tons of rock. This avoided the cost of building a tall tower to create the necessary high water pressure, and it made hydraulic power an economical proposition. It was the first form of power that could be transmitted through pipes, and Armstrong's discovery made it possible to provide power without installing an engine at each point where power was needed.

Hydraulic power was gradually superseded by electrical power, but in the late 19th and early 20th centuries Armstrong's invention was an important innovation.

William George Armstrong (1810–1900), inventor of the hydraulic accumulator.

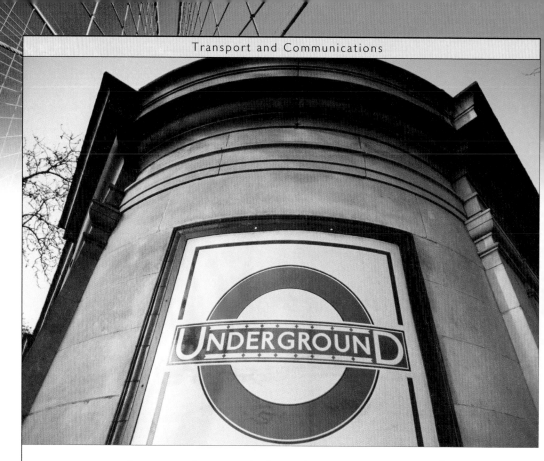

London Underground

London, England

In the late 18th and early 19th centuries, the English Industrial Revolution gave rise to the railroad. Before that, the most efficient means of large-scale transport was by water—first by sea, and from the early 18th century by canal. Trains made land transport more convenient, but rail tracks were an obstruction in built-up areas—a problem vividly reflected in the expression "from the wrong side of the tracks." The London rail terminals were therefore built on what were

then the outskirts of the city's metropolitan area, and it was proposed at an early stage that, as far as possible, railroad lines within it should be underground.

In 1863, London's Metropolitan Railway became the first passenger-carrying underground railway. It was constructed by the cut-and-cover method. This method involved

FAST FACTS

■ DATE Commenced in 1868
■ STYLE Modernist
■ CONSTRUCTION METHOD Tunneling
■ DESIGNERS Frank Pick and Charles Holden
■ In World War II, Londoners used the tube stations as air raid shelters

excavating an enormous trench, generally along the side of a road to avoid the demolition of buildings. The roof of the trench was constructed strongly enough to carry the restored road and any buildings that might be erected above it.

This cut-and-cover construction method necessarily caused temporary but highly inconvenient dislocation. A better method—where it was possible—was to build a tube railroad, in which the space for operating the trains was created by tunneling. But this was possible only where the ground was both strong enough not to collapse after excavation and not so hard as to make excavation an economically infeasible proposition. As it happened, the stiff clay underlying London was ideal for the purpose.

The first tube railroad was the now disused London Tower subway. Built in 1868, it was a single-line tunnel lined with cast iron segments, running from Tower Hill on the north side of the Thames to Southwark on the south. Part of the tunnel ran under

Commuters come to grips with the new automatic ticketing machines at London's Piccadilly station, 1928 (left).

The instantly recognizable logo of the London Underground, and now the whole London public transport system (above left). An early view of a new London tube station (above).

the Thames. Other underground systems quickly developed, the earliest still in use being the present Central Line. At first each railway was privately owned, but in 1933 a unified publicly owned system—London Transport—was formed.

DESIGN DISTINCTION

Between the two World Wars, the London Underground achieved worldwide distinction for its comfortable trains with their clearly marked destinations and routes, and for its well-designed stations, with finishes that were easy to keep clean and—before the invention of spray-paint— almost vandal-proof. The credit belonged largely to two men: Frank Pick, the assistant managing director of the Underground and later Vice Chairman of London Transport, and the architect Charles Holden.

One of Pick's most notable achievements was the development of London Transport's distinctive

graphics. Pick's judgment was not infallible, however; he once rejected a concept devised by a junior draftsman, Harry Beck, for a linear map of the Underground. In 1932 he reluctantly agreed to try the idea—and today the London Underground linear map is one of the icons of a great city.

THE PARIS METRO

The Paris Metro had been noted for the elegance of some of its stations when it opened in 1900, but like all metropolitan railways it suffered from vandalism and poor maintenance. When Charles de Gaulle became President of France in 1958, he determined that Paris would be a better, more attractive city if money were spent on refurbishing the Metro.

Noise was one problem, and this was solved by fitting the trains with rubber wheels. The derelict appearance of the stations was another problem. It was practicable to deal with only a few stations in the city center, but those that received attention have become a pleasure to look at, and some of the decorations are of great interest.

Grand Central Station

New York, United States of America

Cornelius Vanderbilt (1797–1877) belonged to a great American tradition of self-made financiers and philanthropists. He built a major shipping line from small beginnings and then, at age 63, decided that the future of transportation lay with railroads. He sold his steamships and bought first the New York and Harlem Railroad, and then its competitors, the Hudson River and New York Central railroads.

Vanderbilt's decision to build a single terminal for the three lines was questioned at the time—and he was criticized for placing his station too far north—but both decisions proved far-sighted. Construction of the L-shaped structure began in 1869 and was completed in 1871. The designer was John B. Snook, co-architect of America's first great department store, a dry goods emporium on Broadway faced with white marble and nicknamed "Stewart's Marble Palace." The roof

FAST FACTS

- DATE 1903–13
- STYLE Beaux-Arts
- DESIGNER Whitney Warren
- FEATURES Steel-framed structure supporting vaulted plaster ceiling
- Vanderbilt's first northward siting of the station has vindicated all criticism

of the new station was a cylindrical vault of corrugated iron and glass spanning 200 feet (60 m) and covering 12 rail tracks and five platforms. It was modeled on London's slightly earlier St. Pancras Station—the first to use this type of structure.

The increasing population of Manhattan expanded northward, and the rail traffic handled by the station tripled within 20 years, so it was deemed impracticable to further increase the existing terminal's capacity. In 1902 it was decided to demolish and replace it.

THE SECOND STATION

The second Grand Central was built between 1903 and 1913 to a design by Reed and Stem in association with Warren and Wetmore as joint architects. The chief engineer, William J. Wilgus, electrified the railway and covered the rail track down

The light-filled concourse (above). Cornelius Vanderbilt, builder of the first Grand Central (left).

The tiled, vaulted ceiling of Grand Central's famous Oyster Bar (above). Cutaway diagram (c. 1920) of the station's concourse and the various platform levels (right).

Park Avenue, which allowed hotels, stores, and fashionable apartments to extend from Madison Avenue to Lexington Avenue and from 44th Street to 59th Street. An insulation system was developed to absorb the vibrations generated by the rail traffic beneath. To eliminate the bottleneck caused by the station superstructure, Wilgus built an elevated road that wrapped around the terminal and passed over 42nd Street, allowing unimpeded movement from east to west.

The Grand Concourse is 470 feet (143 m) long, 160 feet (49 m) wide, and 150 feet (46 m) high—larger than the nave of the Cathedral of Notre Dame in Paris. It was modeled on the Roman baths, but it has a steel-framed structure from which the vaulted plaster ceiling is suspended. There is, however, genuine structural vaulting over some of the smaller rooms, using tiles set in quick-drying mortar, a form of construction used in Spain and copied in America in the late 19th and 20th centuries.

Ramps lead from the main concourse to the upper level of tracks, and stairs to the lower level. From the entrance to the station, passengers can survey the concourse from a gallery and descend to it by a wide staircase. The concourse was designed to be a welcoming space flooded with natural light.

ADORNING URBAN SPACES

The decorative elements of the terminal were largely the work of Whitney Warren. He had studied at the École des Beaux-Arts in Paris and was a founder of the Beaux-Arts Institute of Design, whose purpose was to encourage the teaching of architecture in American schools through the French *atelier* (studio) system.

A triumphal arch designed in the classical mode dominates the main façade, to the south. Paired Corinthian columns flank three colossal arched windows and support a massive entablature, surmounted at the center by a sculptured group 60 feet wide by 50 feet high (18 x 15 m) depicting figures of classical mythology. An American eagle supports Mercury, the Roman god of merchandizing, flanked by Hercules, the stongest of the gods, and Pallas Athene, the goddess of arts and crafts—and industries.

207

Golden Gate Bridge

San Francisco, United States of America

The Golden Gate Bridge is almost certainly the best known and best loved bridge in America, and possibly in the world. It is an elegant structure with a light-looking bridge deck and exceptionally tall towers, thanks to the need of the United States Navy for plenty of clearance between the bridge deck and high-water level. To witness the bridge emerging

Designer of the bridge, Joseph Strauss (left). San Francisco's famous fogs often shroud the Golden Gate Bridge (below).

FAST FACTS

■ DATE 1933–37
■ STYLE Suspension bridge
■ MATERIAL Steel
■ ENGINEER Joseph Strauss
■ Eighteen iron workers and 40 painters work full-time to maintain the bridge in top condition

from a thick fog over San Francisco Bay is an unforgettable experience—first the towers materialize, and then the whole bridge gradually appears through the drifting mist.

BRIDGING THE GATE

The proposal to build a bridge across the Golden Gate—the entrance to San Francisco Bay—was first made in 1919. One of the engineers who was invited to examine the proposal was Joseph Strauss, who had established a company in Chicago for building relatively short-span opening bridges. Strauss had never designed a long-span bridge, but his was adjudged the best proposal. Strauss was appointed Chief Engineer for the bridge in 1919, and in 1930 a poll was held to authorize the raising of bridge bonds to fund the bridge. Construction started in 1933.

Because of the length of the span and the likelihood of high winds, Strauss originally proposed two cantilevers supported on piers, with a suspension bridge spanning them. By 1929, he had accepted the concept of a conventional suspension bridge, with cables supported by two piers and anchored on land at each end. A barge took the first wire rope

A panoramic view of the bridge and the city of San Francisco (above). One of the bridge's two soaring towers (right).

across the San Francisco Bay, and 25 more ropes were then slung across as supports for catwalks and footbridges. The cables of the bridge were estimated to weigh about 24,500 tons (24,990 t), and they had to be spun in midair—a technique that had been pioneered by Washington Roebling in the construction of the Brooklyn Bridge in New York City. The work was subcontracted to the Roebling Company.

Strauss attached great importance to workplace safety at a time when such concerns were uncommon. All his workers were provided with sunglasses to protect them from glare, and they were examined regularly by a medical team. A safety net under the bridge is estimated to have saved at least 19 lives.

The bridge was opened on May 27, 1937. It is 8,981 feet (2,737 m) long and the span between the towers is 4,200 feet (1,280 m). The towers—the world's tallest at the time—soar 746 feet (227 m) into the air. Each of the two cables consists of 61 strands comprising 25,572 wires.

Since the building of the Brooklyn Bridge 54 years earlier, bridge decks had been built lighter and more flexible. In fact, the Golden Gate Bridge was first made a little too flexible: Although strong enough to resist normal wind forces, under some conditions it had to be closed because of the movement of the deck. In 1940 the deck was stiffened, and in 1989 the bridge survived an earthquake of 7.1 on the Richter scale. The bridge has since been strengthened to resist forces of up to 8.3.

OPPOSITION PROVED WRONG

Like many other famous and remarkable structures, the Golden Gate Bridge met with fierce opposition when it was first proposed, partly because of the perceived damage it would cause to the natural beauty of the area, but mainly because of its cost: At the time only a small population lived to the north of the Golden Gate, and many thought that the expense was not warranted.

They were wrong: By the end of the 20th century, 41 million cars a year, or an average of 118,000 commuters a day, were traveling across the bridge.

Communications Network Tower

Toronto, Canada

Many structures have been built tall for prestige. In medieval times temporal and spiritual princes sometimes built cathedral spires a little taller than any previously constructed, often to our present delight. Today, tall buildings are frequently named for their owners—the Petronas Towers in Malaysia, for example—but there were, and are, practical reasons for building tall. Masonry towers served as defenses against an attacking force—until the invention of artillery rendered them useless. And walled cities could be besieged by rolling movable wooden towers up to the fortified walls.

In late medieval Italy tall masonry towers were built for aristocratic families and their followers as bulwarks during family feuds. The clan with the tallest tower had the advantage—but if the tower was used unreasonably, the prince or the commune could command that the height of the tower be reduced as a penalty. Towers of this kind are still standing in the hill towns of Tuscany.

The main purpose of tall towers, however, has always been communication. Lighthouses depended on the light being high above

FAST FACTS

- DATE 1976
- MATERIALS Concrete and steel
- BUILDER CN Tower Ltd
- The 7-story steel skeleton that houses the restaurant and observation decks was built on the ground and hoisted 700 feet (215 m) up

The tower dominates the Toronto skyline (above), just as the medieval tower of the Palazzo Publicco dominates Siena (below).

ground so that it could be seen from a great distance. Church towers with bells mounted high, and mosques with minarets that enabled the muezzin's voice to carry, called the faithful to prayer, and were also used to warn the people of an impending enemy attack, or of fire, flood, or any other civic emergency.

TELLING THE WORLD

The tallest towers of all time were built after World War II primarily for telecommunication, made necessary by its increasing use and made possible by advances in structural theory and technology. But commercial considerations also came into play. Most had observation decks and many had revolving restaurants. There was also an element of prestige in having the tallest telecommunications tower, particularly at the height of the "Cold War" between the USSR (as Russia was then known) and the Western powers after World War II.

The Communications Network (CN) Tower in Toronto was built by a private company, CN Tower Ltd, an affiliate of Canadian National Railways. The spire of its antennae mast is 1,816 feet (553 m) high, and there is an "eagle's nest" for observation at 1,509 feet (460 m) and a restaurant seating 450 people, part of it revolving, at 1,148 feet (350 m). Below that are two spacious observation platforms and rooms for radio, television, and cable TV receiving 10 channels.

Construction of the CN Tower began in February 1973 and was completed in June 1976. The tower has a triangular cross-section and thus differs from most other super-tall towers that are essentially circular. This has the disadvantage of offering a greater surface to the wind, which increases the lateral force on the tower, but it makes the tower more visually attractive.

The tower stands on a prestressed concrete foundation plate 17 feet (5.5 m) thick, with a diameter of 229 feet (70 m). Its core is a hexagonal concrete tube 36 feet (11 m) in diameter. The upper covering, which was placed in position with the aid of a helicopter, is of high-tensile alloy steel.

Toronto's CN Tower is widely acclaimed as not merely the tallest but also artistically the most significant telecommunications tower in the world. Such towers are still being built but they no longer need to be so tall—technical advances have made satellite technology more competitive.

A glass floor in one of the observation decks provides a dizzying view for those brave enough to look (below).

Chek Lap Kok Airport

Hong Kong, China

After World War II Hong Kong became one of the world's major centers for financial transactions—and for transportation. When the original airport, Kai Tak, was built, it was on the outskirts of the urban area, but the rapid growth of the city and the increase in the height of its buildings eventually meant that planes had to descend at an alarming and dangerous angle onto a runway projecting into the South China Sea. In October 1989 the British Governor of Hong Kong, Christopher Patten, announced the proposal to build a new international airport.

FAST FACTS

■ *DATE* 1998

■ *STYLE High-tech Modern*

■ *MATERIALS Steel and concrete*

■ *ARCHITECT Sir Norman Foster*

■ *The airport occupies an area of 136 acres (55 ha)—nine times that of the old airport*

Nine years later, in July 1998, the new airport was opened by the President of China.

To accommodate the new airport, Chek Lap Kok—a hilly island as big as the entire Kowloon peninsula—was leveled and connected to Hong Kong by new road and rail links that cross several wide stretches of water. Travel to Hong Kong's central business district takes a mere 23 minutes by the Airport Express Railway. The airport's vast design includes 17 bays for commuter buses, 18 for tourist coaches, multitudinous taxi ranks, and parking for 3,000 cars. An airport hotel with 1,100 rooms caters for transit passengers.

The airport terminal was designed by the English architect Norman Foster (born 1935), who received a knighthood in 1990 for his services to architecture. The structural engineers were Ove Arup and Partners of Hong Kong. Foster has been described as one of the leading proponents of the technological approach to architecture. His previous commissions had included London's third airport

Cleaning the ceilings in the passenger terminal requires a head for heights and some dexterity, as this worker (left) shows.

The Chek Lap Kok terminal is built upon a prefabricated steel frame (above) that is anchored to a concrete substructure to prevent it lifting off during a typhoon.

at Stansted and the acclaimed Sainsbury Center at the University of East Anglia.

The roof of the Chek Lap Kok terminal is formed by steel shells 118 feet (36 m) wide, curving longitudinally to give a rise of 20 feet (6 m) at the center. Each shell was assembled on the ground and hoisted into place in one piece onto a concrete substructure, to which it is anchored to ensure that there is no lift-off during one of the typhoons that are a regular feature of the Hong Kong climate. Continuous central skylights bring daylight to the middle of the roof, supplemented by electric lighting as necessary. An interesting feature of the terminal—and an essential adjunct to a large modern airport—is the Meeters and Greeters Hall, which runs through three stories along the entire length of the building.

Passengers proceed from the terminal building along a Y-shaped concourse (covered by a single vault), assisted by moving footways. Those arriving at the airport use the same concourse, but at a different level. Underground shuttle trains run between the East Hall and the West Hall.

One of the triumphs of the airport is its air conditioning:

Hong Kong is prone to intense heat and humidity during the summer months, and its new airport inc-orporates an elaborate air conditioning system, reticulated below floor level, with strategically located outlets.

A FLIGHT OF FANCY

It has been said that all airports are the same airport, and it is true that, above all, an airport needs to be a practical structure that is capable of trafficking large numbers of planes, passengers, luggage, freight, and the associated motor traffic with maximum efficiency and speed. But practical considerations aside, Foster gave his imagination free rein when he designed the complex of hangars and terminals in the shape of a modern aircraft, rather like the Concorde.

layout of the terminal

Chunnel and Eurostar Terminus

Linking London, England, and Paris, France

The Channel Tunnel—the Chunnel—is a joint project of the British, French, and Belgian rail systems. "Eurostar" trains carry passengers and "Le Shuttle" motor vehicles, to avoid the extensive ventilation that would be needed were they to travel through the tunnel using their own engines.

FAST FACTS

■ DATE 1990–93
■ ARCHITECT Nicholas Grimshaw
■ ENGINEERS YRM Anthony Hunt and Associates
■ The tunnel is 31 miles (50 km) long, of which 23 miles (37 km) are underwater

Britain is the only European country that is completely surrounded by water, and it is thanks to this natural fortification (which Shakespeare called "the national moat") that it has not been invaded by a foreign army for centuries. Bridging or tunneling the English Channel became technically possible during the late 18th century, but of all the problems

such a project entailed, the most difficult was that of politics.

The first serious tunnel proposal, involving ventilation chimneys reaching above the water level, came in 1802 from the French Government Engineer Albert Methieu during a brief interval of peace between France and Britain. But in 1803 the two countries were again at war and the proposal lapsed, to be revived in 1880 when Britain and France had once more established cordial relations. A 1922 proposal was defeated by only six votes in the House of Commons. The project received British government support after World War II but the cost was considered too high. In the 1980s, the scheme was finally accepted but only on the understanding that the British contribution would be funded entirely by private enterprise.

LONDON'S NEWEST STATION

The Waterloo Eurostar terminus in London was commissioned in 1988 and built between 1990 and 1993, next to the existing 19th century Waterloo station. It is a fine demonstration of advances in architectural design and technology in the interim. The roof covers only five rail

The new Waterloo Eurostar station (pictured from the air) is the first rail terminus to be built in London for several decades.

Each Eurostar train (above) can carry 766 passengers—twice as many as a 747 jet. The French entrance to the tunnel is at Coquelles (pictured during construction, c. 1992) (below).

tracks, so its span is modest by comparison with the major railroad stations of the 19th century. Their prototype, St. Pancras station in London, has a clear span of 240 feet (73 m). The steel structure of the Eurostar terminus spans only 160 feet (48.5 m), using conventional three–pin arched trusses. But the Eurostar terminus scores for its interesting multi-level design and the quality of its finishes. Older stations were built with iron or steel that required rust protection, usually covered with dark paint, and the size of the glass sheets was limited by the existing manufacturing process. The Eurostar terminus has a much more cheerful aspect, with its large glass panes and bright metal finishes.

It Beats Flying

Eurostar competes with flying rather than with the traditional rail-and-ferry service. This is reflected in the design of the station, with its elegant counters in place of the traditional ticket windows. Access to platforms is by escalator or elevator. As in an airport, the arrival and departure halls are at different levels.

The trains travel through the tunnel at 80 miles per hour (128 km/h), but on the high-speed French tracks they can reach 188 miles per hour (300 km/h). Traveling time from the center of London to the center of Paris is three hours—more than competitive with the time it would take to fly.

A TECHNOLOGICAL TRIUMPH

What made the building of the Chunnel practicable was the TBMs—the tunnel boring machines, giant drills that bored through the soft chalk seabed, simultaneously disposing of the detritus and lining the tunnel with segments of concrete or cast iron. Six were used under sea and five under land; the English team identified them by numbers, the French by women's names. They were connected to computer-linked lasers that guided the two construction teams toward each other. When the two sides of the tunnel met, on December 1, 1990, they were aligned to within a few centimeters of each other, and the construction crews of both countries reached through the small breach and shook hands. The Chunnel was opened for business four years later.

MONUMENTS AND MEMORIALS

Built to honor gods, mythological figures, war heroes,

or ancestors, commemorative buildings are some of the

world's most potent and emotive structures.

MYSTERIOUS SYMBOLS *Although some monuments, such as the Sphinx (left) and the Easter Island statues (below), are instantly recognizable, their purpose remains a mystery.*

Monuments and memorials are not designed as private shelters or as public buildings for worship, administration, or entertainment, but to enshrine communal memories. They are art rather than architecture, and their value lies in the strength of their historical and national resonances.

About 7,000 years ago the Irish Celts built Newgrange and the ancient Egyptians built the pyramids at Giza. Both were burial sites constructed of immense blocks of stone oriented toward the heavens. While we know little about why or for whom they were built, they continue to attract a rich array of stories and legends. By contrast, we know the history of the 20th century Vietnam Veterans' Memorial in Washington DC, but the memorial retains its mystery and evokes complex reactions in those who visit it.

HONORING THE DEAD

Some monuments commemorate individual deaths: The Terracotta Warriors provide a vast underground guard of honor protecting an emperor, and the Taj Mahal was erected in memory of an emperor's wife. Like the pyramids, these structures represent a concentration of the wealth and social organization of the people

who built them, expanding the significance of the monument from the loss of an individual to the expression of a culture. Hiroshima's Atomic Bomb Dome has an opposite meaning: A potent reminder of our potential for barbarism, it also pleads for peace and stands in hope that such an event will never be repeated.

Triumphal arches also commemorate war, but in a more heroic and less critical framework. Rome's Arch of Titus celebrates the conquest of Judea and the Parisian Arc de Triomphe commemorates the victories of Napoleon at the

turn of the 19th century. At first unrepentant about the damage inflicted during war, the message of the Arc de Triomphe was balanced after World War I by the addition of the Tomb of the Unknown Soldier, where a memorial flame burns in memory of the lives lost in battle.

The ancient temple of Ramesses II at Abu Simbel in Egypt, built centuries before the rise of Greece or Rome, is not a tomb or a memorial so much as a mysterious shrine from a long-forgotten religion. Japan's Great Buddha at Nara, also a shrine to god-like man,

REVERED AND REVILED *The Taj Mahal (left) publicly honors the memory of an Indian empress. Once the object of criticism and ridicule, the Eiffel Tower (below) has become a symbol of Paris.*

is by contrast still tended by the Buddhist sect for whom it was built in the 8th century. In later years the Great Buddha also came to represent the institution of a national religion interrelated with the unification of Japan.

This tendency to personify cultural well-being through monuments is even more central to our understanding of the rise and fall of the Rapa Nui on Easter Island in the south Pacific. It is believed that the Rapa Nui lived on their small island in complete isolation for well over 1,000 years, and built the hundreds of megalithic statues dotting their coastline during their heyday between the 10th and 16th centuries. However, during the 18th century they pulled down all their statues as part of an apparently self-inflicted but devastating process of ecological and social breakdown. It was only in the late 20th century that the statues were restored.

A CHALLENGING MONUMENT *War memorials such as the Vietnam Veterans' Memorial honor those who died in battle while also provoking reflections about the nature and morality of war.*

MODERN ICONS

Two significant 19th century structures were both designed in part by the French civil engineer Gustave Eiffel. The Statue of Liberty was a gift from the French people as a sign of friendship with the people of the United States of America, who reciprocated by paying for the statue's massive pedestal on its site in New York's harbor. Neither side could have foreseen the potent role the statue would assume as an international symbol of refuge and freedom. The Eiffel Tower was originally thought by some critics to be an insultingly large and ugly industrial object in the heart of France's elegant capital, and was under threat of demolition when first erected for an international fair in 1889; a century later, Paris would be almost inconceivable without it.

Both these modern structures are excellent illustrations of the characteristic that is common to all monuments and memorials—that their meanings and values are not static, but change over time and with cultural perceptions.

Newgrange

Ireland

The ancient burial monument of Newgrange is one of the oldest and finest megalithic structures in Europe. Also known as Brú na Bóinne (mansion on the Boyne River), it was an important place in early Irish mythology, considered a magical site of transformation between this and other worlds, and thought to be variously inhabited by supernatural beings and kings. Built around 3310 BC (several centuries before Stonehenge or the pyramids), it was effectively lost beneath a rural hillock for millennia, until a farmer

FAST FACTS

■ DATE c. 3310 BC

■ PERIOD Neolithic

■ MATERIALS Granite and earth

■ An estimated 200,000 tons (203,000 t) of rock were excavated over 40 years to construct the cairn

accidentally discovered it in 1699. However, this "cave," as it was at first described, was not recognized to be the mythical place of legend until 1845, and a fully fledged archaeological excavation, conservation, and interpretation project was not commenced until 1961.

Newgrange is one of many prehistoric monuments set within a 3-square-mile (8-sq-km) site bounded by a loop of the Boyne River, 35 miles (56 km) north of Dublin. It is a circular mound, or cairn, 45 feet (14 m) high and 280 feet (85 m) in diameter. Its circumference wall is constructed of 97 massive granite boulders laid horizontally in a circle, crowned by a white quartz wall of rocks and a flat dome of grass-covered earth. From its single entrance, a passage 62 feet (19 m) long leads to a cruciform chamber 17 by 21 feet (5 x 6.5 m) with a corbeled roof of stone slabs reaching a height of 20 feet (6 m). The roof stones were marked with grooves to channel rainwater away from the inner chamber, keeping it safe and dry.

A massive carved threshold stone, 10 feet (3 m) long and 4 feet (1.2 m) high, guards the only entrance to the tomb.

The passage follows the curve of the hill and is lined with upright stones, many of which are richly decorated (right).

Each of the three recesses off the central chamber holds a massive stone basin, thought to have held cremated remains, while two burials were also found underground. The passage is oriented precisely so that a rectangular niche, or "roof box," near the entrance allows the first rays of dawn light on the winter solstice to penetrate the inner chamber. The mound is encircled by a ring of megaliths, 340 feet (104 m) in circumference, although just 12 of the estimated 38 original stones remain, thought to have been placed about 1,000 years after the cairn was built. Of great interest are the ancient and mysterious carvings on most of the stone slabs, inside and out, both displayed to visitors and hidden from view, consisting of abstract forms such as spirals, lozenges, and geometric shapes.

A DOORWAY TO THE AFTERLIFE

The archaeological evidence suggests that the Neolithic ritual functions of the monument were concerned with both death and cosmological observation or sun worship. In early Irish literature, Brú na Bóinne was the home of supernatural people who could travel between the mortal world and that of the gods via earthen cairns such as Newgrange. One scholar has suggested that the triple spiral found carved at various significant points in the monument represents three aspects of existence: life, death, and regeneration or passage into the other-world. Similarly the solstice shaft of light has been seen as an entranceway for the soul to begin its journey to the other world. Newgrange was also claimed to be the burial place of the kings of Tara, real historical figures who ruled before Christianity came to Ireland in the 5th century. It is likely that they wished to entrench their power by identifying themselves with the legendary site. Newgrange has also been thought of as a ritual place for the sun to penetrate the earth in order to render it fertile for the following year's harvest. It has been mooted as a kind of astronomical observatory, with the carvings representing the stars as they appeared thousands of years ago. The engraved drawings have also been associated with an ancient language of music based on five notes, and with the extraordinary array of energies thought by some people to underlie the site.

Sphinx and Pyramids

Giza, Egypt

Thought to be the work of ancient Egyptians from around 2500 BC, during the 4th dynasty of the Old Kingdom, the pyramids at Giza and the nearby Sphinx are the most massive constructions ever built. The three pyramids, named for three pharaohs—Khufu (Cheops in Greek), Khafre (Chefren), and Menkaure (Mycerinos)—are marvels of surveying precision, masonry craftsmanship, engineering ingenuity, and social organization. While scientists still wonder at the technical achievement, alternative thinkers find endless inspiration in these structures, associating them with a religious integration of geometry and

FAST FACTS

- DATE c. 25th century BC
- STYLE Egyptian Old Kingdom
- MATERIALS Limestone and granite
- COMMISSIONED BY The 4th dynasty pharaohs
- The stone was floated across the floodwaters of the Nile

astronomy, pyramid power, deadly curses, and even alien encounters. Most recently, links are being made to the legendary civilization of Atlantis.

A description of some of the features of the largest pyramid, Khufu's "Great Pyramid," may explain its continuing fascination. The Great Pyramid was the world's tallest building for over 4,000 years. Its plan is a perfect square, covering a massive 13 acres (5.3 ha) but leveled so precisely that there is a difference of only 1 inch (2.5 cm) in height across the entire base, while its four sides are almost exactly the same base length—755 feet (241 m). The sides, oriented due north, south, east, and west, are inclined at an angle of 51.5 degrees and originally met 481 feet (147 m) above the ground. The relation of the length of each side to the height (755 ÷ 481 = 1.57) was also the same as the relation of a circle's circumference to its radius—or half of π (3.14…). The presence of this classical Greek mathematical proportion, supposedly not yet invented at the time of construction, may be

The Pyramid of Khafre retains a cap of the white limestone with which all three pyramids were originally faced.

coincidental, but it increases the reputation of the Great Pyramid for geometric perfection.

The Great Pyramid is solid rock, with several internal rooms designed to house the pharaoh's mummified body and possessions. When they were entered by a Baghdad prince around 1200, however, the rooms, superbly crafted in huge blocks of red granite, were bare of both artifacts and ornamentation; grave-robbers had found their way in, despite the sealed and concealed entrance. Yellowish local limestone was used to build the core, and a heavy layer of fine, white limestone provided a dazzling external finish. The casing stone was removed sometime after 1222 in order to repair earthquake damage to nearby Cairo, so the Great Pyramid is now 451 feet (138 m) high—20 feet (6 m) shorter than the middle pyramid, that of Khafre.

An estimated 2,300,000 blocks of stone, averaging 2.5 tons (2.55 t) each, with some weighing up to 20 tons (20.4 t), were used to build the Great Pyramid. Yet the craftsmanship is so exact that a playing card cannot be inserted between adjoining blocks of masonry. How such precisely cut blocks were placed exactly, so high above the ground, by workers with poor access to metal for stonecutting or to weight-lifting technologies, still exercises the imagination. No one architect is associated with the Giza complex, but pyramid design is generally attributed to Imhotep, the high priest of the 3rd dynasty pharaoh Zozer.

THE INSCRUTABLE SPHINX

The Giza Sphinx similarly has been a source of fascination for centuries. This creature, with a lion's body and human head, often featured in ancient art and was associated with wisdom. The face of the Sphinx is thought to be a portrait of Khafre, whose "cartouche" (an oval tablet bearing his hieroglyph) was found buried between the paws. The Sphinx itself spent millennia buried up to its neck in sand. Colin Wilson's *From Atlantis to the Sphinx* describes a theory that geological evidence indicates that the weathering of the Sphinx is a result of the effects of water, not wind and sand. If true, this would increase the age of the Sphinx (and possibly the pyramids) by thousands of years, suggesting that it may have been constructed by a prehistoric but highly sophisticated civilization—possibly Plato's lost city of Atlantis?

The Sphinx, 240 feet (72 m) long and 66 feet (20 m) high, was carved into a huge outcrop of rock near the pyramids.

Temples of Ramesses and Nefertari

Abu Simbel, Egypt

ar up the River Nile, where Egypt confronts the Sudan in East Africa, the warrior-pharaoh Ramesses II, who ruled for 67 years during the 19th dynasty of the New Kingdom, carved from the cliffs his Great Temple at Abu Simbel (c. 1250 BC). Four colossal statues of the powerful ruler gazed out unfalteringly at those entering the southern limits of his empire in Nubia, over 600 miles (1,000 km) from the Mediterranean. They projected a striking warning of the pharaoh's—and Egypt's—power and glory.

The New Kingdom was the period of Egypt's great expansion, from Nubia as far

FAST FACTS

- DATE 13th century BC
- STYLE Egyptian New Kingdom
- MATERIAL Stone
- BUILDER Ramesses II
- Moved bodily to high ground nearby when the Aswan High Dam inundated the original site in the 1960s

as the Euphrates in the Near East. Gold and gems, slaves to man armies and make buildings, and increased trading opportunities all added up to immense wealth. While the Old Kingdom had its pyramids, the New Kingdom showed off with magnificent and monumental temples like Abu Simbel. A new capital, crammed with grandiose architecture, was built at Thebes: Ramesses II built the famous mortuary temple (or Ramesseum) here, as well as structures at Abydos, Karnak, Memphis, Luxor, and the Valley of the Kings.

A Fertile Pharaoh

Ramesses II (c. 1290–1224 BC) was famous not only for his battles and his buildings but also for his fertility. Known to have had at least five wives, he sired 100 children during his long reign, and his familial relationships are proudly presented at Abu Simbel. In the façade of the Great Temple (or Sun Temple), the four great colossi—65 feet (20 m) high, except for one that lost its upper half during an earthquake—

Two of the four immense statues of Ramesses II gaze outward from the façade of the Great Temple at Abu Simbel.

The Great Temple with the four massive statues of Ramesses II, and the temple of Nefertari (above). A block from the Great Temple being moved to higher ground in the 1960s (right).

are interspersed with tiny figures of his mother, wives, and children, who seem to be seeking protection between giants' legs. The deified pharaoh also overshadows the patron gods of the Great Temple—Ptah (the great craftsman), Amun-Re (the supreme creator), and Re-Harakhte (the sun god). The latter's diminutive figure stands in a recess above the central entrance. The smaller temple is dedicated to Ramesses' foremost wife, Nefertari, who likewise eclipses the image of Hathor, the cow-goddess.

LOST AND REDISCOVERED

Inside the Great Temple, a series of interior passageways and chambers extends 180 feet (55 m) inside the cliff. The design was executed with such precision that twice a year, on the pharaoh's birthday and on the anniversary of his coronation, the light of the rising sun penetrates the innermost sanctum of the temple to illuminate the statues of the gods seated alongside Ramesses II.

But for all the pharaoh's self-aggrandisement, 3,000 years after they were built, the temples of Abu Simbel, buried deep in vast sand drifts, were largely forgotten. Rediscovered by the Swiss explorer J. L. Burckhardt in 1813, they became a site of pilgrimage for countless tourists in the 19th and 20th centuries.

Then, in the 1960s, these ancient marvels of engineering were paralleled by a modern, scarcely less impressive one: the Aswan High Dam. The dam threatened to drown the two temples. In an international rescue effort led by UNESCO, the temples were cut out in blocks and transported 200 feet (60 m) up the cliff face. There they were reassembled in exactly their original relationship to each other and to the sun, and were encased in a minor artificial mountain overlooking the waters of Lake Nasser.

richly adorned columns in the Great Temple

Arch of Titus

Rome, Italy

The Arch of Titus (*Arcus Titi*) in the Forum in Rome spans the highest point of the *Via Sacra*, or Sacred Way, the processional route taken by triumphant armies returning to Rome's Capitol. Through the ornamental arch—which itself commemorates a bloody war, the conquest of Jerusalem—the soldiers marched into the Forum, the political, mercantile, and legal heart of ancient Rome. Measuring 50 feet (15.4 m) high and 44 feet (13.5 m) wide and made of Pentellic marble, this monument to the Emperor Titus was finished soon after his death at age 41 cut short a popular and productive reign (AD 79–81).

The triumphal arch was a powerful statement of Roman architecture—a tangible expression of invincibility and strength, and a reminder to future generations of the victories and achievements of the past. There were once three triumphal arches in the Forum—nothing remains of the first, built by Augustus; and the third, the Severus arch, dates from AD 203.

The Arch of Titus, erected in AD 81 by Titus's brother and successor, the Emperor Domitian, is therefore the oldest surviving arch in Rome and a fine example of the genre—a form that greatly

FAST FACTS

- DATE AD 81
- STYLE Imperial Roman
- COMMISSIONED BY The Emperor Domitian
- MATERIAL Pentellic marble
- Commemorates Domitian's brother, Titus, whose rule lasted only two years

influenced the architecture of the Renaissance. Its elegant integration of arch, classical orders, and sculptural reliefs exemplifies the ideals of fitness and simplicity in classical design. However, disregard for such historic Roman relics throughout the middle ages led to the deterioration of the arch when the Frangipani family transformed it into a private military stronghold. Paradoxically, however, this may have helped to preserve the arch, until it was finally freed from service as a fortress in 1822 and then restored by Giuseppe Valadier under instructions from Pope Pius VII. The arch thus honors an emperor and the

A relief on the west side of the arch depicts the triumphal procession with the menorah from the Temple of Solomon (above).

An inscription over the arch reads, "The Roman Senate and People Deified Titus, Vespasian Augustus, Son of Deified Vespasian" (left). A relief shows Titus with allegorical figures (below).

Roman Senate in the original inscription on its east façade and, rather more unexpectedly perhaps, celebrates the contribution of a 19th century Pope on its west façade.

AN EVENTFUL REIGN

The two years during which Titus Flavius Vespasian ruled the Roman Empire were remembered as generally happy and productive ones. Titus himself was perceived as a model Roman citizen, handsome, cultivated, and charming—he was described by the historian Suetonius as "the darling of the human race." Nevertheless, his short reign was far from being an uneventful one. Mount Vesuvius erupted in AD 79, destroying Pompeii and Herculaneum. The following year Rome was ravaged by an outbreak of plague and considerable damage and hardship resulted from a disastrous three-day fire. Titus provided generous relief to those who had suffered from the Roman catastrophes, and he also instituted an extensive program of public works which included the Baths of Titus and the completion of the Colosseum (begun in the time of his father, Vespasian, and celebrated with a festival lasting for 123 days).

COMMEMORATING A MASSACRE

By contrast, the event that is commemorated by the arch is appalling; it is depicted in deeply carved relief panels within the arch. Titus's father, Vespasian, had been given the task of quelling the revolt in Judaea in AD 66; soon afterward Titus was appointed legate, and remained in the east after Vespasian returned to Rome to become emperor. Titus's iron-fisted suppression of the uprising in Judaea in AD 70 led to the capture and destruction of "the City of God"—the revered city of Jerusalem—and to the horrifying slaughter of approximately a million Jews.

The south panel bears a relief, originally multicolored, showing a triumphal procession of soldiers carrying their spoils away from the Temple of Jerusalem—Herod's temple; they are holding high the sacred *menorah*, a golden seven-branched candelabrum looted from the Temple of Solomon. (Because of their sensitivity to the scene, orthodox Jews even today do not walk under the arch.) The massive north panel depicts the toga-clad Titus, surrounded by his legionaries, in his triumphal procession through Rome; he is carried by a two-wheeled chariot, or *quadrigae*, harnessed with four horses, led by a goddess, and accompanied by a winged Victory. The Arch of Titus was once topped by a bronze *quadrigae* carrying the emperor, but this was looted long ago.

On the ceiling of the vault, Titus is depicted as an eagle ascending to heaven, exalting him to the status of a god—the normal fate of dead Roman emperors. In his book *Rome: The Biography of a City*, Christopher Hibbert reports that "Titus had become Emperor in 79 when his father Vespasian, before suffering a fatal stroke, alluded to the customary apotheosis of an emperor in the last of his famous jokes: 'Goodness me! I think I am about to become a god.'"

Moai Statues

Easter Island, South Pacific

Dutch explorer Admiral Jacob Roggeveen came upon a tiny island in the vast south-eastern stretches of the Pacific Ocean on Easter Sunday, 1722. Not realizing perhaps that the indigenous people already knew themselves and their land as Rapa Nui, he named the place Easter Island. Roggeveen stayed only one day but reported some startling observations: That the coast was dotted with massive, somber, stone sculptures, staring inland, which were worshiped by an estimated population of 4,000 islanders; and that the volcanic island was barren and windswept. Later studies confirmed that by the time of this first contact with any outsider in more than 1,000 years, Easter Island was completely deforested. There was no shrub or tree over

The statues have deep-set eyes, originally inlaid with white coral, and dark stone pupils.

FAST FACTS

- DATE c. 900–1700
- STYLE Megalithic statues
- MATERIAL Volcanic rock
- BUILDERS The Rapa Nui
- Among their other achievements, the Rapa Nui developed the only written script in Polynesia

10 feet (3 m) in height and no native animal larger than an insect. The Rapa Nui were in the grip of a devastating breakdown in civilization linked to the ecological disaster they had brought upon their once-fertile island. By the time of the next Westerners' visits in the 1770s, the islanders had begun toppling each other's statues and were engaged in an internecine war. When La Pérouse arrived in 1786, all the statues had been pulled down.

MYSTERIES OF THE RAPA NUI

Finally annexed by Chile in 1888, Easter Island has fascinated scholars ever since. Some wonder what went wrong for this Edenlike culture that had enjoyed a productive land untroubled by enemies and a cooperative social organization that was capable of producing masterly works of art in masonry. It appears that, for once, Western colonization was not the cause of the problem, although over the next two centuries after European contact, slave trading, disease, and economic exploitation accelerated the decline of the Rapa Nui, whose population dropped to just 111 people in 1877. Some see the rise and fall of Rapa Nui civilization as a warning, a microcosm

At the single quarry site where they were fashioned lie dozens of megaliths in various states of completion, suddenly and mysteriously abandoned, along with craftsmen's tools (right).

forecasting the fate of the Earth unless we counter our ecological carelessness. Others are fascinated by the origins of Rapa Nui culture, and how and when the islanders arrived on this most remote of islands, a little triangle of 65 square miles (166 sq km), 1,200 miles (1,930 km) from even the nearest habitable island of Pitcairn.

Norwegian anthropologist Thor Heyerdahl caught the world's imagination in 1947 by taking the leaky raft *Kon-Tiki* on a voyage more than 2,000 miles (3,200 km) from Peru to prove that it was possible for South Americans to have settled on Easter Island. Eric von Daniken captivated others with the theory that the huge statues were the work of aliens. However, re-enactments have demonstrated that a group of islanders were entirely capable of carving and transporting the megaliths, using the materials and technologies available to them.

The most recent consensus, based on archaeological and linguistic data, is that the Rapa Nui were a Polynesian people who arrived from the Marquesas Islands at some point in the 5th century AD. While the grand stone platforms—*ahus*—on which the famous statues, or *moai*, stand have been found in many other prehistoric Polynesian cultures, the *moai* themselves have no counterparts anywhere else in Oceania.

SENTINELS RESTORED

The 800 or so statues have now been restored and returned to their *ahus*. Most are 10–20 feet (3-6 m) tall. Some are over 30 feet (9 m) tall and weigh over 80 tons (82 t), with one uncompleted *moai* shaping up to be 68 feet (21 m) tall. Carved from a soft volcanic rock known as tuff, the statues often sport red tuff *pukao*, or barrel-shaped topknots. They are almost all face, with long, pointed noses and massive chins, their slender, elongated arms and hands almost invisible under their fierce stares. Local legend describes the statues walking across the island to their ceremonial ground. They are thought to have represented ancestral chiefs or important personalities, facing inland to overlook and protect the villages. Indeed, they are now attracting a thriving tourist trade and thus providing a measure of security and stability once again to Easter Island.

229

Great Buddha, Todaiji Temple

Nara, Japan

For well over 1,000 years the Great Buddha of the Todaiji Temple, in the ancient Japanese capital of Nara, has been the largest bronze sculpture in the world, housed in the largest wooden building in the world. One of numerous monastery complexes built throughout Japan during the 8th century by an emperor keen to encourage Buddhism as the national religion, the Todaiji complex was the finest in Japanese history. The Roshana (or Vairocana) Buddha depicted there was considered the "Supreme Monarch," "the great Sun Buddha" or the "Illuminator." It is still tended by the same Kegon Buddhist sect for which it was built between 745 and 752.

The colossal statue's fortunes have fluctuated in the intervening years. Its head fell off in an earthquake in 855 and its upper portion was melted in a fire in 1180, although in both cases restoration was prompt. Worse, after another fire in 1567 during a period of political crisis, the Great Buddha remained damaged and exposed in the open air for

FAST FACTS

■ DATE 745–52

■ MATERIALS Bronze and wood

■ COMMISSIONED BY Emperor Shomu

■ Legend says that by squeezing through a small hole in one pillar of the temple, a person will eventually enter the Buddhist Land of Paradise

more than a century. The 1708 restoration of Todaiji's Great Buddha and its Great Buddha Hall was regarded as a sign of national recovery, although the wooden hall was a third smaller than the original and the bronze sculpting of the statue is considered to be uninspired.

THE SPREAD OF A NEW RELIGION

It took 1,000 years for Buddhism to wend its way from India across China through Korea to Japan. It reached the court of the emperor of Japan in 552 in the form of a statuette of Buddha. This gift from a Korean ambassador was at first housed in a small temple. When a pestilence broke out, those tentatively worshiping the icon were accused of incurring the wrath of the gods of the native Shinto religion. To make amends the temple had to be burned and the little Buddha thrown into a river.

A bronze lantern outside the Hall of the Great Buddha is finely decorated with religious and mythological figures.

Despite this shaky beginning, Japanese aristocrats and intellectuals retained a fascination for the "foreign" religion, and a new status quo that accommodated both traditional and new beliefs developed over the next two centuries.

Emperor Shomu was a particularly enthusiastic advocate of Buddhism and devoted himself during his long reign (715–48) to its institution as the national religion—he was eventually to abdicate so as to devote himself to it more fully. As well as building a number of monastery complexes at Nara, the emperor decreed that every province should build its own Buddhist temple. Moreover, by encouraging all classes of people to contribute in any way that they could to the Todaiji complex, no matter how modest, he turned its construction into a national project, greatly democratizing the appeal of the religion beyond its traditional aristocratic adherents. Shomu also centralized the government administration, following the Kegon Buddhist ideal of seeking the harmonious whole in all things. His court was opulent and prosperous, and 10,000 people joined him in celebrating, with his daughter, the Empress Koken, the ceremonial dedication of the Great Buddha in 752.

The only original part of the much-repaired statue is a few engraved petals of the lotus throne on which the Buddha is seated (above). The present Nandaimon, or Great South Gate (left), dates back to 1199.

CHINESE INFLUENCE

The Todaiji Temple followed the tendency for 8th century Buddhist monasteries in Japan to be based on the Chinese T'ang model. The central focus of the enclosure with its monumental gate was a large Buddha Hall, typically a wooden structure built on a masonry verandah with a tiled roof. There were also pagodas housing other relics, and accommodation for monks, all arranged in a fairly strict symmetrical plan. The notion of a colossal statue was also probably derived from China, since a 35-foot (10.5-m) high Buddha had been built at the Lung-mên caves during the late 7th century.

There was probably an element of national rivalry in creating the somewhat larger Great Buddha of Todaiji—an awe-inspiring 53 feet (16 m) in height. The construction of the colossal statue required 446 tons (454 t) of metal, and so exhausted the country's resources in the necessary materials that no bronze statues were to be cast again in Japan for several centuries.

Taj Mahal

Agra, India

The Taj Mahal ("Crown Palace") was built in the 17th century in northern India by the Mughal emperor Shah Jahan (1592–1666) as a mausoleum for his favorite wife, Mumtaz Mahal, "the Chosen of the Palace," who died after the birth of her fourteenth child. Although it is as high as a modern 20-story building, the Taj Mahal is so superbly proportioned, and so carefully positioned in its formal garden on the banks of the Jumna River near Agra, that it appears delicate, hovering, almost dreamlike. Built of pure white marble from Makrana, encrusted with jewels and exquisitely detailed, the building reflects differing atmospheric nuances throughout the day and season. Similarly, as a monument it invites a variety of different interpretations: "a teardrop on the cheek of time" (Rabindranath Tagore); "the proud passion of an

Delicate inlaid patterns embellish the exterior.

FAST FACTS

- DATE 1631–53
- STYLE Mughal
- MATERIALS Marble and jewels
- COMMISSIONED BY Emperor Shah Jahan
- A moving memorial to the love of a man for a woman

emperor's love wrought in living stones" (Sir Edwin Arnold); a harmonious fusion of Islamic and Indian architectural and craft traditions; a monument to an emperor's might; a drain on an empire's resources; and the site of a contemporary conflict between tourism and the urban expansion of Agra—a city that is encroaching on the Taj Mahal's splendid vistas even as the pollution it generates eats away at the marble façade.

The identity of the Taj Mahal's architect is uncertain. Some say that, to design the monument, Shah Jahan called together a council of the best architects from the subcontinent and beyond, which would surely make this one of the most successful projects ever designed by a committee. Others variously cite the designer as Isa Khan Effendi, a leading Persian architect, or Ustad Ahmad Lahori (or Ustad 'Isa or Istad Usa), an Indian architect of Persian descent. Some European scholars cite Geronimo Veroneo, an Italian goldsmith who lived in Agra, but this seems unlikely because of both his profession and his cultural background. However, Veroneo probably formed part of the formidable team of masons and craftsmen

Strict symmetry governs the entire complex (above). Marble flower friezes are inlaid with colored stone (right).

who flocked from Persia, the Ottoman Empire, and Europe to work on the building. The cost was fabulous; the building took from 1631 to 1653 to complete and employed 20,000 workers.

The Taj Mahal is a complex of buildings within a walled rectangle, oriented north–south and measuring 1,900 feet by 1,000 feet (580 x 305 m). The famous mausoleum, 186 feet (57 m) square and high, stands at the north end on a platform 22 feet (6 m) high and 313 feet (103 m) square. A minaret 137 feet (41 m) high stands at each corner. This platform is flanked on the east by a mosque and on the west by a *jawaab* (described variously as a counter-mosque, prayer-house, guest-house, rest-house, or "building for esthetic balance"), both built of red sandstone. In front of the platform is a formal garden, 1,000 feet (305 m) square, overlooked by a great entrance gate on the south edge of the rectangle. All the buildings are strictly symmetrical, as is the mausoleum itself, with its massive 108-foot (33-m) high entrances on each façade. Under the central dome, 81 feet (25 m) high and 58 feet (18 m) in diameter, is a dim octagonal chamber enclosed by a marble screen. This beautifully proportioned room contains the cenotaphs of both Mumtaz Mahal and Shah Jahan (the actual tombs are on a lower level). Shah Jahan's cenotaph is the only element in the entire composition that is not symmetrically positioned, which suggests that its placement here was a second thought. Legend has it that the Shah planned to build himself an identical mausoleum in black marble close by, but there is no evidence to substantiate this.

RULER OF THE UNIVERSE

The self-styled Shah Jahan, or "ruler of the universe," was the great-great-grandson of the first Mughal emperor, Babur, who had invaded from Afghanistan in 1526. Shah Jahan was the third son of his father, Jahangir, and is said to have executed or imprisoned his brothers and nephews in his battle to become emperor after his father's death in 1627. He is remembered as a great patron of the arts, in which Persian and Indian traditions reached a high level of cultural expression in literature, calligraphy, painting, and architecture. Deposed by his son in 1658, he was imprisoned in Fort Agra, in a room overlooking the Taj Mahal.

233

Terracotta Warriors

Xian, China

When, in 1974, farm workers digging wells in Shaanxi Province near Xian in north-eastern China began unearthing large pottery fragments, eager archaeologists hastened to the site. The tomb of the ancient emperor Shih Huang-ti lay just 1 mile (1.5 km) to the west, and they had high expectations. Their hopes were more than fulfilled—they were exceeded beyond imagining. The site contained an army of extraordinarily lifelike, life-size terracotta figurines of Chinese warriors,

FAST FACTS

- DATE 3rd century BC
- STYLE Qin Dynasty
- MATERIAL Terracotta
- COMMISSIONED BY Shih Huang-ti
- The warriors symbolized the living slaves who would have accompanied the emperor to his tomb

complete with terracotta horses, and the remnants of wooden chariots and weapons.

In the following two decades, nearly 8,000 superbly crafted, individualized figures, arranged in battle formation, were excavated from an area that stretched over 5 acres (2 ha). There was a tradition of pottery figures being interred in the tombs of ancient leaders, but no figures of this size and exhibiting this degree of realism—and certainly nothing on this extraordinary scale—had been discovered before. The terracotta warriors were rapidly incorporated into Chinese national identity as a symbol of the long-standing cultural sophistication of their civilization.

A POWERFUL RULER

The man whose tomb this army guarded was the Emperor Shih Huang-ti (259–210 BC). Son of the king of the relatively isolated state of Qin, he succeeded to the throne at

The warriors prepare to defend their emperor (above). A cavalryman and his horse (left).

the age of 13 and continued Qin's conquest of one "warring state" after another, culminating in China's unification in 221 BC. The dynasty Shih Huang-ti established lasted a mere 15 years (221–206 BC), but in that time he instituted reforms and commissioned works of such significance that his rule is regarded as a watershed in Chinese history. He centralized administrative procedures; introduced standard weights and measures, clothing colors, and chariot gauges; and—most importantly—he developed a standard writing script. He became known as the "First Emperor" of China.

Burial preparations commenced as soon as Shih Huang-ti became king. However, after his imperial conquest, work on both his huge palace at Xianyang and his "subterranean palace"—his tomb—was stepped up, involving an estimated 700,000 workers, including many conscripts and convicts.

PROTECTING THE EMPEROR

The terracotta army was arranged in three groups, between 16 and 23 feet (5–7 m) below the current ground level. Pit 1 was by far the largest, containing some 6,000 figures; Pit 2 had a more varied collection of 1,400 figures; and Pit 3, the smallest, was considered to contain the "command nodule" of the army. While Pits 2 and 3 have been excavated and reburied, awaiting further investigation at a later date, Pit 1 was opened to public inspection in 1979, protected by a huge hangar-type structure.

The figures stand in corridors lined with pottery bricks, facing east, with the emperor's tomb behind them. Each figure is constructed in gray clay, fired to the hardness of earthenware. The legs of both men and horses are solid, whereas the bodies, arms, and heads are hollow, molded in separate parts and then apparently joined before being fired. Traces of pigment reveal that the figures were originally painted in naturalistic colors. While there is consistency in size and style across all the warriors, suggesting the use of common molds, there is also individualized detailing of facial and clothing features. They are the same and yet varied, like human beings.

The convention of burying figurines in the tombs of important men was a humane development on the ancient Chinese practice of interring slaves and attendants alive with their dead masters. Ironically, thousands of Shih Huang-ti's workers were interred with him so that they could not disclose the secrets of the treasures they had helped to create.

With his topknot and mustache, this terracotta warrior has an individuality that has survived the passage of time.

Arc de Triomphe

Paris, France

The largest triumphal arch in the world, L'Arc de Triomphe de l'Étoile, to give it its full and imposing name, was designed by architect Jean-François-Thérèse Chalgrin in 1806. Commissioned by Napoleon I, the arch, which is 164 feet (54 m) high, was part of a substantial urban building program that was initiated during his short rule as consular–emperor (from 1799 to 1814). The Arc de Triomphe commemorates the battles that were fought in defense of the infant

FAST FACTS

- DATE 1806–36
- STYLE Neoclassical
- MATERIAL Stone
- ARCHITECTS Jean-François-Thérèse Chalgrin and others
- The monument has become a tribute to those who have died in war

French Republic, which came into being in 1792 as a result of the French Revolution of 1789.

A NEW REGIME AND A NEW FRANCE

The French Republic offered substantial new rights to its citizens, but it was perceived as a threat by neighboring kingdoms. During a time of great upheaval, the youthful Napoleon provided brilliant military leadership in defending and expanding the republic into surrounding regions. He also exercised a strong-armed—some would say tyrannical—civil rule at home, introducing modern institutions such as a codified rule of law and a state–regulated educational system. He nurtured his own reputation by employing artists, writers, and architects to glorify the new regime's achievements.

When Napoleon lost the battle of Waterloo, he was exiled to the remote island of Saint Helena in 1815, where he died in 1821. His ambitious building program was shelved by the

The Arc de Triomphe occupies a commanding position in central Paris at the crest of the Champs Élysées and in the center of the Place Charles de Gaulle (formerly the Place de l'Étoile), at the convergence of no fewer than 12 avenues.

"restored" monarch Louis XVIII, and the Arc de Triomphe languished incomplete for decades. Work on the Napoleonic monuments recommenced only when the July Revolution of 1830 brought in a new monarch, Louis-Philippe, who found it expedient to encourage the growing legend surrounding Napoleon.

Thus construction of the Arc de Triomphe was resumed with a new generation of architects (Blouet) and sculptors (Cortot, Rude, Elex, Pradier, and Lemaire), and was completed

ALLONS, ENFANTS DE LA PATRIE

François Rude's (1784–1855) *La Marseillaise* (1833–36) draws on classical Greek and Roman forms and contemporary sources. In the massive stone relief, 42 feet high by 26 feet wide (13 x 8 m), Bellona, the Roman goddess of war, leads a charge of volunteers to defend the new Republic. The Bellona figure is drawn from the dominant female figure in Delacroix's 1830 painting *Liberty Leading the People.*

in 1836. When Napoleon's ashes were brought back to Paris in 1840, they were carried through the streets in a procession that passed under the arch.

MILITARY GLORY

A leading example of the ponderous Neoclassicism of the Empire style, the Arc de Triomphe harks back to the great military and cultural achievements of the Roman Empire. The Romans built such monuments in honor of successful battles and great generals. A triumphal procession passing beneath such an arch was the greatest tribute a Roman military leader could receive.

The ceiling and interior walls of the arch are ornately detailed.

The Arc de Triomphe similarly records the names of battles and generals. After World War I, the military aggrandisement of the monument was relieved by the construction of the Tomb of the Unknown Soldier under the arch, where an eternal flame commemorates those who died in war. A landmark in the beautification of Paris, the arch was part of the rationalization of the city plan in the interests of public health and traffic flow. In recent times it has also become a tourist icon signifying the city, second perhaps only to the Eiffel Tower.

237

Statue of Liberty

New York, United States of America

Liberty Enlightening the World—as the Statue of Liberty was originally called—has adorned the entrance to the harbor of New York City since 1886. A gift from France to the United States of America to celebrate the friendship between the two nations, the statue was also intended to commemorate the centenary of American Independence (the Fourth of July 1776) in 1876—unfortunately, technical and fundraising difficulties meant that the present arrived 10 years late.

The copper statue on Bedloe Island—renamed Liberty Island in 1956—is 151 feet (46 m) high. It was executed by the French architect–sculptor Frédéric-Auguste Bartholdi and is one of several Bartholdi sculptures reflecting Franco–American friendship. Also employed on the project were French civil engineer Gustave Eiffel (co-designer of the Eiffel Tower), who designed the internal iron skeleton, and American architect Richard Morris Hunt, who designed the granite pedestal, also 151 feet (46 m) high.

A solemn Neoclassical image, Liberty is depicted as a mighty woman striding forward, the torch upheld in her right hand representing the enlightenment of the world. Under her left arm she holds an inscribed tablet proclaiming the date of American Independence, and the seven rays in her

FAST FACTS

■ DATE 1886
■ STYLE Neoclassical
■ MATERIALS Iron, copper, and granite
■ ARCHITECTS Frédéric-Auguste Bartholdi and Richard Morris Hunt

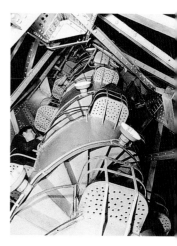

A 12-story spiral staircase leads from the plinth to an observatory in the statue's crown (above).

crown symbolize the seven continents and the seven seas. She is trampling on chains, depicting the breaking away from slavery. The figure evokes the heroic French icon of a woman with arm raised leading men into battle, as in Eugène Delacroix's painting *Liberty Leading the People* (1830) or François Rude's sculpture *La Marseillaise* (1836) on the Arc de Triomphe in Paris.

A MODEL MOM

The idea for the statue originated with a group of Frenchmen, including Bartholdi and historian Eduard de Laboulaye, who were impressed by the victory of the northern states of America over slavery in the American Civil War. Bartholdi began work during the 1870s, at first using his mother as the model for Liberty. But she found the long hours tiring, so Bartholdi searched all over Paris to find a woman who looked like his mother. Eventually he found Jeanne-Emilie Baheux de Puysieux, who was later to become Bartholdi's mistress, muse, and wife.

A cutaway view shows the statue's hollow core, supporting framework, and spiral staircase.

The statue was constructed in Paris from copper sheets ³⁄₃₂ inch (2.3 mm) thick, hammered by hand over an iron framework. The dimensions of one single fingernail—13 by 10 inches (33 x 25 cm)—provide some indication of the enormous scale of the task. When it was completed in 1885, the entire sculpture, weighing 225 tons (228 t), was then dismantled into 350 pieces, packed into 214 cases, and transported by sea to New York, where it was reassembled over four months.

THE NEW COLOSSUS

The money for the statue was raised by the French people, while funding for the pedestal was raised by Americans, led by Joseph Pulitzer, publisher of New York's *The World* newspaper and founder of the prestigious American Pulitzer Prize for literature. Another passionate advocate of the project was Emma Lazarus, whose poem "The New Colossus" is engraved on a plaque at the entrance to the pedestal and celebrates Liberty's sheltering of immigrants. Lazarus's poem was written as part of the fund-raising effort and was attached to the pedestal in 1903 at the behest of a private donor. The closing lines read:

Give me your tired, your poor,
Your huddled masses yearning to breathe free,
The wretched refuse of your teeming shore,
Send these, the homeless, tempest-tost, to me,
I lift my lamp beside the golden door!

The statue and the New York skyline, pictured before the terrorist attacks of September 2001 (above). In 1931, reporters broadcast from inside the statue's head (right).

The statue was dedicated by President Grover Cleveland in 1886, declared a National Monument in 1924, and proclaimed a World Heritage Site in 1984. In the mid-1980s the monument was restored and repaired using $87 million in funds raised by private bene-factors in association with the National Park Service (which now administers the site of Liberty Island and the nearby Ellis Island, with its National Museum of Immigration).

With her pedestal refurbished and an ob-servatory made available to anyone capable of climbing 12 stories to her crown, the Statue of Liberty remains a very popular international tourist attraction that draws more than four million visitors annually.

Liberty's size is stupendous, but perhaps of equal significance is her siting near Ellis Island, the first point of entry for a large majority of immigrants to the United States throughout the first half of the 20th century. In effectively welcoming millions to "The Land of the Free," the Statue of Liberty has acquired considerable emotional resonance as an international symbol of refuge and democracy.

Eiffel Tower

Paris, France

Built amid a chorus of controversy as a "temporary" exhibit for the Centennial Exposition in Paris in 1889, the Eiffel Tower is now considered one of the culminating achievements of 19th century civil engineering in both structural innovation and beauty. At 984 feet (300 m), it was the tallest building in the world for 40 years, until it was overtaken by the Chrysler Building in New York City.

The tower was composed of mass-produced, prefabricated iron parts. It was constructed quickly—in just over two years; cheaply—the cost of 8 million francs was recouped in the first year; and relatively safely by a small labor force—300 workers (there was one fatality). It used the new technology of the elevator, invented only a few years earlier, to offer visitors a ride in a glass cage up a gentle curve to the equivalent of 100 stories above ground, to view an urban panorama at that time extending 40 miles (64 km) on a clear day. Symbolic of the romance of 19th century Paris, the tower has become one of the world's icons, signifying modernity, technological progress, and tourism.

The tower is named for the French civil engineer Gustave Eiffel, although the design was conceived in 1884 by two of

Gustave Eiffel and his chief engineer pictured at the summit of the Eiffel Tower in 1889 (top). The tower (right) contains about 6,300 tons (6,400 t) of prefabricated iron parts riveted together.

his employees, Emile Nouguier and Maurice Koechlin. They designed an iron tower consisting of four massive pylons, airily constructed from girders riveted together and joined at the summit. Eiffel was not at first impressed, but he exhibited the design and patented it under all three names. Later that year he bought out his two employees and enlisted the design help of an architect, Stephen Sauvestre, to improve its visual form. Eiffel and Sauvestre entered their design in the 1886 competition for a tower to be a central monument for the forthcoming World's Fair. Of 107 entries, the Eiffel–Sauvestre design was one of

View from beneath the Eiffel Tower, looking up (above). An early engraving showing the tower's lift and spiral stairs (below).

FAST FACTS

■ DATE 1887–89

■ STYLE Observation tower

■ MATERIALS Steel and wrought iron

■ DESIGNERS Gustave Eiffel and Stephen Sauvestre

■ Survived the storms that devastated parts of Europe in December 1999

three winners. The other winners were given commissions for other major buildings for the Exposition, but it was Eiffel who was commissioned to build the tower, although he had to give a personal guarantee against any overexpenditure of budget. In return, he had an apartment in the upper reaches of the tower, where he conducted aeronautics experiments and entertained friends.

FROM EYESORE TO ICON

The main attraction in an exposition to commemorate the centenary of the French Revolution, the Eiffel Tower was twice as high as any previous human structure. It immediately provoked a furor of fear about its safety and outrage at its "ugliness." A group of French intellectuals wrote to the exhibition's organizing committee protesting against this "vertiginously ridiculous tower dominating Paris like a black, gigantic factory chimney…" One signatory, writer Guy de Maupassant, often lunched there in later years—not because he had changed his mind, but because "It's the only place in Paris where I don't have to see it!"

Eiffel's record for building fabulous, structurally sound bridges across huge spans stood him in good stead. The Parisian establishment agreed that the structure should go ahead, with the concession that it would be dismantled in 20 years' time. When the concession expired in 1909 controversy erupted again, and the tower was saved only because it could be used for the new technology of radio transmission. Later it served as a television transmitter.

Today, any notion of dismantling the Eiffel Tower has become inconceivable. Indeed, the city of Paris recently spent three times the initial cost of the tower in refurbishing its most prominent international symbol.

Atomic Bomb Dome

Hiroshima, Japan

The Genbaku Dome in Hiroshima's Peace Park marks the world's first use of the nuclear bomb as a weapon of war. At 8:15 a.m. on August 6, 1945, the Allied forces dropped a single atomic bomb that exploded directly above the Japanese city of Hiroshima. It annihilated a prosperous city of 400,000 people: 70,000 died instantly, and by the end of that year 70,000 more had died of radiation sickness and other injuries. Three days later a larger atomic bomb was dropped on another Japanese city, Nagasaki. Fewer lives were lost this time, but six days later Japan surrendered, bringing the American–Japanese conflict of World War II to a close.

The scale of the devastation in Hiroshima and Nagasaki was far beyond the normal ravages of war. After visiting Hiroshima within days of the blast, French journalist Robert Guillain wrote: "Our feeling was one of stunned consternation, mixed for me with a heavy feeling of shame … I am ashamed for the West, I thought, I am ashamed for science. I am ashamed for mankind."

The dome, that of the Industrial Promotion Hall of the Hiroshima Prefecture, had been built by Czech architect Jan Letzed in 1915, and was prominent in the city because of its

> **FAST FACTS**
> ■ DATE 1915
> ■ STYLE 20th century industrial
> ■ MATERIALS Steel, ferro-concrete, and brick
> ■ ARCHITECT Jan Letzed
> ■ The dome has became a permanent reminder of the horrors of war

modern, Western design. It was almost directly below "ground zero," the hypocenter of the blast. The surrounding buildings were razed, but the three-story 1915 exhibition hall had been solidly built in ferro-concrete and brick. It was incinerated and its dome exploded, but the steel frame survived. This skeleton, mounted on the remnants of the three-story building, is now Hiroshima's Atomic Bomb Dome—a permanent reminder of the terrible damage sustained by the city.

A Monument to War—and Peace

When the rebuilding of Hiroshima began after the war, the dome, as one of the few structures to survive the nuclear attack, focused local debate. Some saw it as an obstacle to healing and called for its demolition; others, supported by the international anti-nuclear movement of the 1960s, believed that it should be preserved as a reminder of the inhumanity of war.

By 1966 the dome was on the verge of collapse, and the City of Hiroshima passed a resolution to preserve it. A national appeal raised $500,000 for restoration, and a further appeal in 1989 raised $3 million. In the 1990s, there were calls for the dome to be included on the World Heritage List. Initially reluctant to nominate such a "negative" site, the Japanese government at last responded to a petition bearing 1.65 million signatures. In 1996 UNESCO included the dome in its World Heritage List.

But the Atomic Bomb Dome is not a simple symbol of peace. As Japanese writer Okamoto Mitsuo has said: "The A-bomb Dome accuses the Japanese [for their militarist aggression during World War II], even as it accuses the Americans [for dropping the bomb]. It accuses science and it accuses mankind. It is inscribed on the ledger of history as a negative heritage of mankind. And just as the cross on which Jesus Christ died became a symbol of human salvation, the A-bomb Dome, as the symbol of a city that rose from the ashes, will become a symbol of world peace."

The Enola Gay lands after bombing Hiroshima (right). Japanese civilians watch American correspondents inspecting the damage from the blast (below).

Vietnam Veterans' Memorial

Washington, DC, United States of America

The Washington memorial to those who died in the Vietnam War, dedicated in 1982, is an extraordinary monument to an extraordinary era in history. The United States agonized over the rights and wrongs of its involvement in the distant Asian war for 16 years, while its servicemen, most of whom were conscripted, fought in an alien jungle under the increasingly hostile gaze of the international media. Even before the United States withdrew from Vietnam in 1975, returning troops met a cool reception. Many suffered physical and psychological trauma from their grim war experiences but, until recently, received little public sympathy or support.

FAST FACTS

- DATE 1982
- STYLE Minimalist
- MATERIAL Black granite
- ARCHITECT Maya Ying Lin
- This war memorial records the lives lost and invites the visitor to reflect upon the futility of war

This monument is the war veterans' own memorial to their fallen comrades. Unlike most war memorials, the Vietnam memorial is not a statue, an obelisk, or any other vertical projection: It is a horizontal meandering—a long wall of black granite simply inscribed with the names of more than 58,000 Americans who died in the war. Nearly 500 feet (150 m) long, the wall gradually increases in height from just above ground level to more than 10 feet (3 m) at its central point, where it turns a 125-degree corner then gradually decreases again. One wing points directly to the Washington Monument, the other to the Lincoln Memorial.

THE FIRST DEATH AND THE LAST

The 70 panels that constitute the wall are each inscribed with between one and 137 lines, five names on each line, engraved in lettering half an inch (1 cm) high. The names are set out

The wall is embedded in the landscape of a public park (above).
Maya Ying Lin with her winning design for the memorial (left).

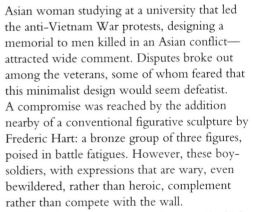

The black granite is polished to a mirror finish (above). Visitors looking at the names of the fallen simultaneously find themselves gazing at their own reflections (right).

chronologically on each wing, starting with the first death in 1959 at the central corner, and concluding there with the last death in 1975. Visitors walk down a path beside the wall, so that the noise of the city gradually abates, to be replaced by a growing recognition of the enormity of lives lost.

Those who come here have different reactions. Some run their fingers lightly over hundreds of engraved names as they walk by; some seem afraid to touch; some rub the name of a loved one onto parchment paper; and others leave offerings such as flowers, photographs, or medals. Visitors describe their experience of the memorial as contemplative, solemn, cathartic, heart-rending, even sublime. John Wheeler, chairman of the veterans' group that raised the seven million dollars to build it, suggests, "It has to do with the felt presence of comrades." The memorial is one of the city's most popular monuments, attracting between three and five million visitors annually.

A SCAR—AND A HEALING

The design of the memorial was chosen in a competition of 1,421 anonymous entries. The winner was Maya Ying Lin, a final-year architecture student at Yale University, just 21 years old. The irony of her identity—an Asian woman studying at a university that led the anti-Vietnam War protests, designing a memorial to men killed in an Asian conflict—attracted wide comment. Disputes broke out among the veterans, some of whom feared that this minimalist design would seem defeatist. A compromise was reached by the addition nearby of a conventional figurative sculpture by Frederic Hart: a bronze group of three figures, poised in battle fatigues. However, these boy-soldiers, with expressions that are wary, even bewildered, rather than heroic, complement rather than compete with the wall.

When her entry was chosen by a panel which imagined the memorial as "a place of healing," Lin explained her inspiration for the design: "I thought about what death is, what loss is. A sharp pain that lessens with time, but can never quite heal over. A scar. The idea occurred to me there on the site. Take a knife and cut open the earth, and with time the grass would heal it."

245

INDEX AND GLOSSARY

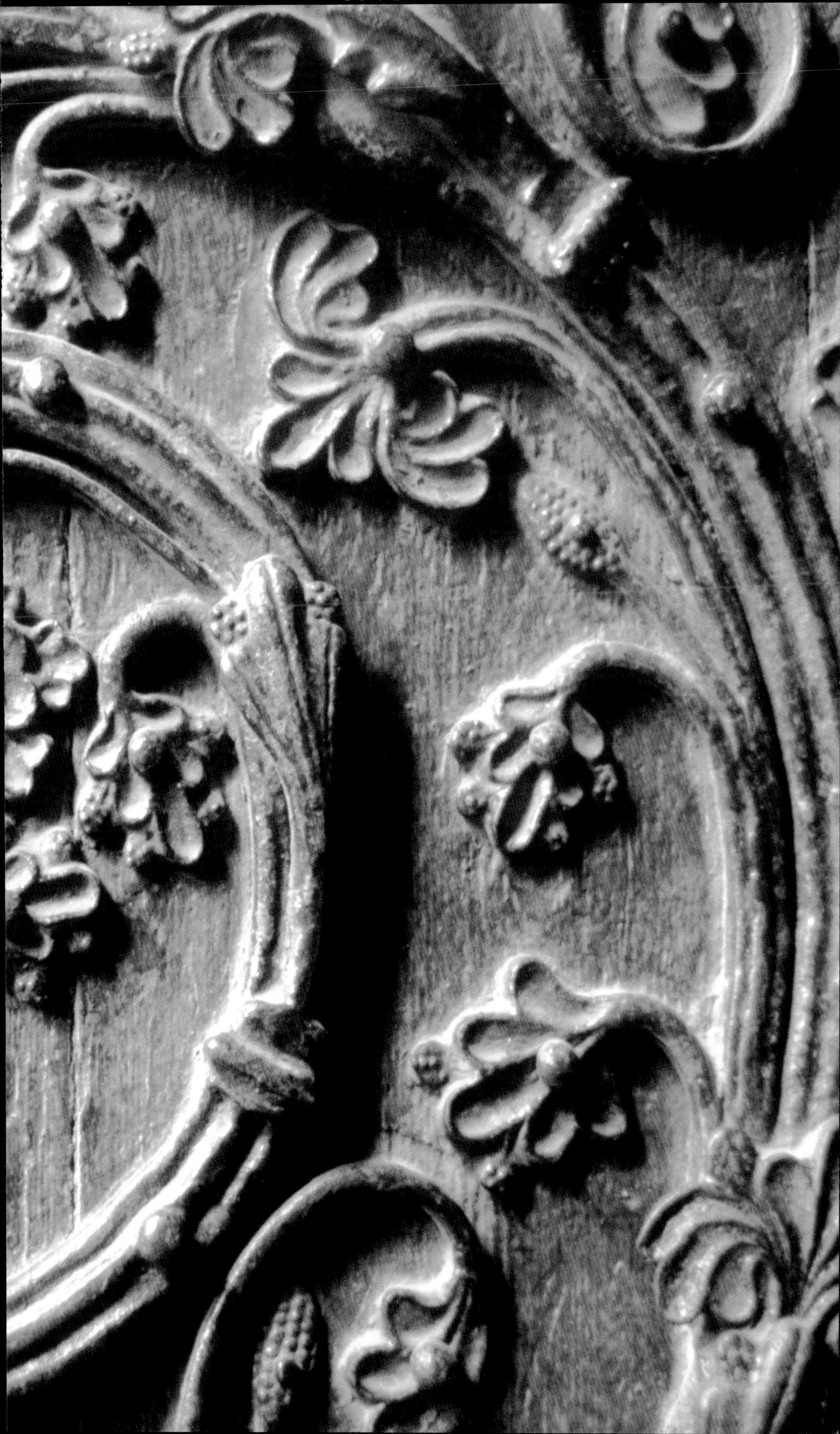

INDEX AND GLOSSARY

In this combined index and glossary, **bold** page numbers indicate the main reference, and *italics* indicate illustrations and photographs.

CONTRIBUTORS

Emeritus Professor Henry J. Cowan is a graduate of civil and mechanical engineering from the University of Manchester, England. He was foundation professor of Architectural Science at the University of Sydney, Australia. Among his many honors he was awarded the Chapman Medal and Monash Medal by the Institution of Engineers, Australia. Professor Cowan is a prolific author who has published 28 books.

Ruth Greenstein has a degree in communications and over 11 years' experience in trade book publishing. She writes and edits in a wide range of subject areas, including art and design, travel, nature, science and technology, religion and spirituality, and psychology. She enjoys the architecture of California and New York, and divides her time between the two.

Bronwyn Hanna completed an arts degree at the University of Sydney, Australia, during the 1980s, focusing on Australian architectural history. She worked there as an associate lecturer, teaching 20th century art history, while completing a research masters degree on public housing in Australia. She has co-written a book on Australian women architects and works as a freelance researcher and teacher in the areas of 20th century architectural history, urbanism, feminism, and multiculturalism.

John Haskell was born and educated in England, where he qualified as an architect and town planner. He was chief architect at the National Capital Development Commission in Canberra, Australia, and in 1975 was appointed Professor of Architecture at the University of New South Wales, retiring in 1993. He has written extensively, has made a special study of urban design in Venice and its territories, and is a frequent guest lecturer on Swan Hellenic Cruises. He lives in Sydney.

Trevor Howells (consultant editor and author) trained as an architect at the University of Sydney and studied architectural conservation at the University of York, England, before working on the conservation of historic buildings in Wiltshire in England. Since 1981 he has taught architectural history and building conservation in the Faculty of Architecture at the University of Sydney. He is also an architectural heritage consultant for the conservation of many historic buildings in and around Sydney and the author of several publications.

Deborah Malor lectures in art history and theory in the School of Visual and Performing Arts, University of Tasmania at Launceston. She has previously taught art, design, and architectural histories at the University of Sydney and at Insearch-University of Technology, Sydney. Her research interests lie in contemporary readings of the built environment, the coalition of art and landscape, and Australian cultural history. She has published and presented papers on these topics in Australia, New Zealand and the USA. She is co-editor of the *Australian and New Zealand Journal of Art*.

John Phillips is a lecturer in architectural history at the University of Technology, Sydney. He holds a B.A. from the University of Sydney and a Ph.D. from the University of London. He has published in the field of medieval Islamic architecture and also in that of early 19th and 20th century Australian architecture. He also maintains a passionate interest in the architectures of Europe and America.

Thomas A. Ranieri holds a B.A. in journalism from Fordham University in the United States of America. He is a senior communications specialist with 20 years' experience as a writer and editor of best-selling reference books, magazines, marketing publications, and Web sites.

Mark Stiles was born in Venezuela. A graduate of architecture from the University of Sydney, he worked as in architect in the New South Wales public service before spending 15 years writing, directing, and producing documentaries, as well as writing scripts for feature films and television dramas. He is now a lecturer in Interior Design at the University of Technology, Sydney.

Bronwyn Sweeney holds a B.A. from the University of Technology, Sydney, and has worked as an editor and writer for more than 10 years in Australia and the United Kingdom. She has traveled widely and visited some of the great buildings of Latin America, Asia, and Europe. She lives in Sydney.

CAPTIONS

Page 1: The 13th century Santo Domingo de Bonaval convent in Santiago de Compostela, Spain, features a dizzying spiral staircase.

Page 2: The distinctive and flamboyant Art Deco arcs of Manhattan's Chrysler Building.

Page 3: The Duomo and adjacent belltower—the famous Leaning Tower—in Pisa, Tuscany, Italy.

Pages 4–5: The Elephant Terrace is a masterpiece of stone carving in Angkor Wat, Cambodia.

Pages 6–7: Grand Central Station, New York, USA

Pages 10–11: I. M. Pei's modern pyramid provides a striking counterpoint to the Baroque buildings of the Louvre Museum in Paris, France.

Pages 18–19: The golden spires of La Sagrada Familia are etched against the clear blue sky of Barcelona, Spain.

Pages 52–3: The decorative walls of the Alhambra in Granada, Spain, are a legacy of its Moorish origin.

Pages 84–5: The partially restored Ziggurat of Ur in Iraq is a remnant from an ancient Mesopotamian civilization.

Pages 118–19: Frieze from the House of the Vettii, Pompeii, Italy.

Pages 150–1: The Pompidou Center in Paris uses modern technology and materials to create a building that elicits a strong response from users and passers-by.

Pages 182–3: The Golden Gate Bridge, which links San Francisco with Marin County, took four years to build and was opened in 1937.

Pages 216–17: The Taj Mahal in Agra, India, is a remarkable synthesis of strict proportion and decorative architecture.

Pages 246–7: Intricate decorative carving on a medieval church door.

ACKNOWLEDGMENTS

The publishers wish to thank the following people for their assistance in the production of this book: Stuart McVicar (banding for each chapter), Puddingburn Publishing Services (index), Patrick Terrett (floorplans).

COVER: Corbis

PHOTOGRAPH AND ILLUSTRATION CREDITS

t=top; b=bottom; l=left; r=right; c=center
APL=Australian Picture Library; MEPL=Mary Evans Picture Library; WFA=Werner Forman Archive; WO=Weldon Owen Pty Ltd; WOSF=Weldon Owen San Francisco.

Photograph Credits

1 Corbis 2 Getty Images 3 photolibrary.com
4–5 photolibrary.com 6–7 photolibrary.com 8–9 APL/Corbis 10–11 Getty Images 12cr D & J Heaton/APL; br David Parker/SPL/photolibrary.com 13tl Rick Strange/photolibrary. com; tr APL/Pacific Stock 14tr photolibrary.com; cr Erich Lessing/AKG London 15t APL/Zefa; br Dallas Heaton/ photolibrary.com 16t APL; b Robert Armstrong/ photolibrary.com 17tl Arcaid; cr Schutze/Rodemann/AKG London; br Robert Armstrong/photolibrary.com 18–19 photolibrary.com 20tl Hilbich/AKG London; tr Photodisc 21tl photolibrary.com; cr Mary Fiennes/Arcaid; br Michael Freeman 22–23t APL/Corbis 24t AKG London; bl APL/Corbis 25t APL/Corbis 26t Louis Dors/ photolibrary. com 27t Hiroshi Higuchi/photolibrary.com; cl WFA; br Warwick Kent/photolibrary.com 28t Roberto Matassa/ photolibrary.com; b www.anthroarcheart.org 29t APL/Corbis; c www.anthroarcheart.org 30c www.anthroarcheart.org; bl APL/Corbis 32 APL/Corbis 33t APL/Corbis; b APL/Archive Photos 34 APL/Corbis 35t APL/Corbis; c photolibrary.com/ Ben Simmons/Diaf 36bl APL/Corbis 37tr APL/Corbis 38t Dallas and John Heaton/photolibrary.com 39t Hiroshi Higuchi/ photolibrary.com; cr Grahame McConnell/photolibrary.com 40 APL/Corbis 41 APL/Corbis 42 APL/Corbis 43t APL/ Corbis; c AKG London 44–45c APL/West Stock 44c AKG London/Hilbich; bl AKG London/Hilbich 46t APL/Corbis 47 APL/Corbis 48–49 APL/Corbis 51t Hiroshi Higuchi/ photolibrary.com; br APL/Corbis 52–53 Getty Images 54tl WFA; c Hiroshi Higuchi/photolibrary.com; bl Larek Camoisson/AKG London 55t Zefa Picture Library (UK)/ photolibrary.com; cr Zefa Picture Library (UK)/photolibrary. com; br APL/Popperfoto—File Collection 56 APL/Corbis 57 APL/Corbis 58cl APL/Corbis 59t AKG London; tr APL/Corbis 60–61t D E Cox/photolibrary.com 60bl WFA 61br WFA 62–63t APL/Corbis 63bl APL/Corbis 63b www.greatbuildings.com/Howard Davis 64t Nigel Hicks/ photolibrary.com; bl APL/Corbis 65t APL/Corbis; c MEPL 66–67t Traynard 66bl MEPL 67c Traynard 68bl APL/Corbis 69tc APL/Corbis; tr www.greatbuildings.com/Howard Davis 70c APL/Corbis 71c Yann Arthus-Bertrand/WO 72–73t APL/Corbis 72bl WFA 73cr WFA 74–75t Osmond/photo library.com 74bc APL/Corbis 75 Clare Forte 76 APL/Corbis 77t APL/Corbis; br APL/Corbis; c Erich Lessing/AKG London 78t photolibrary.com/Tony Stone Images; bc Georg Gerster/ WO 79t Jerome da Cunha/AKG London; c Jerome da Cunha/ AKG London; br Alex Bartel/APL 80–81 APL/Corbis 82t APL/Corbis 83t APL/Corbis; bc APL/Popperfoto—File Collection 84–85photolibrary.com 86t APL/Corbis; bl photolibrary.com/Charlie Oass; br APL/Wes Thompson 87tl APL/Archive Photos; tr photolibrary.com/Doug Armand 88–89t APL/Corbis 88b WFA/British Museum, London 89c APL/Corbis 90–91t Nigel Hicks/photolibrary.com 91c Adam Woolfitt/WO 92bl WFA 93tc Michael Cook/APL; tr Dallas Heaton/photolibrary.com 94 APL/Corbis 95c Rick Strange/ photolibrary.com 96 APL/Corbis 97t Arlene Stickles/www.great buildings.com; bc APL/Corbis 98t Werner Otto/photolibrary. com; bl APL/Archive Photos 99t Jerome da Cunha/AKG London; b MEPL/Cottel 100–101 APL/Corbis 102–103t photolibrary.com/Ed Pritchard 102bl APL/Corbis 103 APL/Corbis 104 APL/Corbis 105r photolibrary.com/ Rafael Macia 106t APL/Archive Photos; b APL/Corbis 107 APL/Corbis 108 APL/Corbis 109 Keith Collie/AKG London 110 APL/Corbis 111t APL/Corbis; bc Rafael Macia/photolibrary.com 112–113b APL/Henryk T. Kaiser 112c APL/Corbis 113 APL/Corbis 114bc Dieter E. Hoppe/ AKG London; br Michael Freeman 115l Nigel Hicks/photo library.com 116l Arcaid/Richard Bryant 117tl APL/Corbis; c APL/Corbis Images New York—Bettman 118–119 photo library.com 120tl APL/Corbis; c APL/Corbis Images New York—Bettmann; br photolibary.com/Paul Thompson 121t Photodisc; b photolibrary.com/Alain Evrard 122bl ÇatalHöyük Research Project 123tl Ian A. Todd reproduced with permission of James Mellaart/ÇatalHöyük Research Project 124t WFA 125t APL/Corbis 126D & J Heaton/APL; bl APL/Corbis 127 APL/Corbis 128t Michael Freeman; bl Robin Smith/photolibrary. com 129t Michael Freeman; cr WFA/N. J. Saunders;

bc APL/Corbis 131 APL/Corbis 132c APL/Corbis 133c Richard Bryant/Arcaid 134–135t APL/Corbis 134bl APL/Corbis 136 APL/Corbis 137 APL/Corbis 138 APL/Corbis 139 APL/Corbis 140bc APL/Corbis 141 C. H. Bastin & J. Evrard 142 APL/Corbis; bl Alain Evrard/ photolibrary.com 143t APL/Corbis; c APL 145c Scott Frances/ Esto/Arcaid 146–147t Paul Rocheleau Photographer 147c Paul Rocheleau Photographer; b APL/Corbis 148–149b Alain Evrard/photolibrary.com 149tr APL/Corbis 150–151 photolibrary.com 152tl APL/Corbis; tr Arcaid/Joe Cornish; br APL/Arthurhustwitt 153tl APL/D & J Heaton; tr AKG London/Robert O'Dea; b photolibrary.com/Rafael Macia 154bc APL/Corbis; t Steve Vidler/APL 155t APL/ Corbis 156–157t APL/Corbis 157br APL/Corbis 158bl APL/ Corbis 159c Steve Vidler/APL 160bl APL/David Ball 161tr APL/Steve Vidler 162t Fretwell Photo/APL; bl APL/ Carnemolla 163t photolibrary.com; c photolibrary.com/ Doug Armand 164 APL/Corbis 165t Michael Freeman; c APL/Corbis 166t Eric Bohr/AKG London; bl APL/Corbis 167 APL/ Corbis 168–169t APL 169cr photolibrary.com/David Messent; bl photolibrary.com/Hulton-Getty 170t APL/Corbis; bl Rafael Macia/photolibrary.com 171t Michael Freeman; c APL/Ben Schnall/Archive Photos 172 PANA Tokyo 173t PANA Tokyo; bc APL/Corbis Images New York—Bettmann 174 APL/ Corbis 175t AKG London/Hilbich 176–177t APL/Alex Bartel 176b APL/Corbis 177c APL/Corbis; br APL/Corbis Images New York – Bettman 178 APL/Corbis 179c E. Scriven/ MEPL 180–181t Rafael Macia/photolibrary.com 180bl Richard Bryant/Arcaid 181 APL/Corbis 182–183 photolibrary.com 184tl APL/Steve Vidler; tr APL/Jose Fuste Raga; cr APL/Jonathan Marks; bl Arcaid/Niall Clutton 185tl Photodisc; b APL/Corbis 186–187t APL/Corbis 186b Prof. Felix Just, S.J./Loyola Marymount University, LA 188–189t Simon Critchley/photolibrary.com 188bl Rick Strange/ photolibrary.com 189 APL/Corbis 190c APL/ Corbis; b WO/Guido Alberto Rossi 191tl APL/Corbis; r photolibrary.com/Tony Craddock 192t APL/Corbis 193t APL/Corbis; c The Bridgeman Art Library 194 APL/ Corbis 195t APL/Corbis; c John Hallett/The Lloyds House 196tr Peter Luck Productions; c Jonathan Marks/APL 197tl Mitchell Library/Peter Luck Productions; c APL/Corbis Images New York—Bettmann 198–199t Alex Bartel/Arcaid 198bl APL/Zefa 199c APL/Archive Photos; br APL/Corbis 200–201t Mark A. Leman/photolibrary.com 200bc AKG London 202t Adam Woolfitt/WOSF; bl APL/Corbis 203 APL/Corbis 204 APL/Corbis 205 APL/Corbis 206b APL/ Corbis; t Dallas Heaton/photolibrary.com 207 APL/Corbis 208–209t Steve Vidler/APL 208bl APL/Corbis; cl San Francisco Museum 209c APL/Corbis 210–211t Doug Armano/photolibrary.com 210cr APL/Corbis 211br APL/ Corbis 211bc Steve Vidler/APL 212 AAP Image 213t APL/ Corbis 214t Arcaid/Richard Bryant; b APL/Corbis 215 APL/ Corbis 216–217 photolibrary.com 218c photolibrary.com/ Sylvain Grandadam; br Photodisc 219t APL; tr APL/D & J Heaton; b Photodisc 220–221t APL/Corbis 220bl APL/ Corbis 221c APL/Corbis 222–223t APL/Orion Press 222bl APL/Corbis 223br David Ball/APL 224–225t APL/ Corbis 224bl APL/Zefa 225cr Hulton-Getty/ photolibrary. com 226–227c Stefan Drechsel/AKG London 226bl Prof. Felix Just, S.J./Loyola Marymount University, LA 227tl Prof. Felix Just, S.J./Loyola Marymount University, LA 227tr WFA 228–229t APL/Orion Press Int 228bl APL/Corbis 229cr APL/Corbis 230t APL/Corbis; bc WFA 231 WFA 232t APL/Corbis; bl WFA 233t APL/Corbis; c Jon Hicks/ APL 234–235t Gonzalo Azumendi/photolibrary.com 234bl AKG London 235t APL/Corbis 236–237t APL/Corbis 236bl Yann Arthus–Bertrand/Altitude/WO 237 APL/Corbis 238tr APL/Archive Photos 239t David Ball/APL; cr APL/Corbis 240tr APL/Popperfoto—File Collection; c AKG London 241t Jean Paul Nacivet/APL; br MEPL 242c APL/Corbis; bl APL/Archive Photos 243c Nigel Hicks/photolibrary.com 244 APL/Corbis 245 APL/Corbis 246–247 Photodisc

Illustration Credits

Andrew Beckett 89; Ray Grinaway 117, 218; Chris Forsey 22, 23, 68–69; Adam Hook 156–157; INKLINK 50, 58, 94, 130, 160, 238; John James 178; Iain McKellar 31; Oliver Rennert 12, 20, 122–123; Ray Sim 61; Marco Sparaciari 117br; Irene Still 13, 14, 17, 25, 26, 46, 82, 90, 124, 135, 144, 146, 155, 175, 185, 192, 213, 225; Rod Westblade 168.